Harvey Pekar
CONVERSATIONS

Conversations with Comic Artists

M. Thomas Inge, General Editor

Harvey Pekar
CONVERSATIONS

Edited by
Michael G. Rhode

University Press of Mississippi
Jackson

www.upress.state.ms.us

The University Press of Mississippi is a member of the
Association of American University Presses.

Illustrations used by permission of Harvey Pekar. All rights reserved.

First printing 2008
♾
Library of Congress Cataloging-in-Publication Data

Pekar, Harvey.
Harvey Pekar : conversations / edited by Michael Rhode.
p. cm. — (Conversations with comic artists)
Collection of interviews originally published in various sources.
Includes index.
ISBN 978-1-60473-085-2 (cloth : alk. paper) — ISBN 978-1-60473-086-9 (pbk. : alk.
paper) 1. Pekar, Harvey—Interviews. I. Rhode, Michael. II. Title.
PN6727.P44Z46 2008
741.5'6973—dc22
2008009424

British Library Cataloging-in-Publication Data available

Contents

Introduction

Harvey Pekar is a quintessential embodiment of the American dream. I'm sure he would disagree with that statement, but he's the son of immigrants who "hauled himself up by his bootstraps" and went from college dropout to jazz critic, from underground comic book writer to National Book Award–winning comic book writer, from file clerk to Academy Award attendee. His comic book, and thus his life, has been fictionalized in the theater multiple times and in an award-winning movie. Pekar appeared on national television via the *Late Night with David Letterman* show until he chose not to do so.

Since 1976, Pekar has lived much of his life in public view. One naturally gravitates towards calling him "Harvey"—we've been reading about him, or a reasonable facsimile of him, for thirty years. Initially through his autobiographical comic book, *American Splendor*, then through more mass media such as television and film, we've followed Harvey's life, or at least the parts he's chosen to tell us about. Pekar's struggles with physical and mental problems, a low-paying job, Hollywood, marriage, adoption, toilets, and finally, success are all laid out in his comics. The result is occasionally distasteful, as Pekar prides himself on depicting his life in all its "splendor."

Pekar read comics as a child, but left the medium behind. He returned to it and was inspired to begin writing comic books by underground comix, and worked with underground cartoonists like Frank Stack, Spain Rodriguez, Paul Mavrides, and of course Robert Crumb. Underground comix, enabled by small publishers and a distribution network outside of traditional newsstands, permitted cartoonists to do stories beyond what the Comics Code Authority would approve.

Most cartoonists took this freedom to what the average American of the 1960s would consider extremes. While Crumb's encouragement of, and artwork for, Harvey's first stories jumpstarted his comics career, Pekar was never really of the underground comix movement. He came to it late, as it was imploding due to crackdowns on the head shops that distributed comix and he had other concerns besides sex and drugs to explore in his comics—a point he returns to frequently in his interviews. Harvey did reflect larger underground comix concerns somewhat as he showed himself masturbating in an early issue, but he soon moved in other directions. Pekar's concerns were those of his own life. A "quotidian" life as he likes to say, and the people he met in it.

After thirty years, it is easy to forget that Pekar was a founder of the genre of autobiographical or memoir comics. His influence is difficult to overstate. Others such as Justin Green or Crumb had done work that included autobiography, but in a more humorous or satirical or scatological sense, and they had not stuck with it. Pekar's work was the first to create a comic book memoir on its own terms. Pekar's collaborators learned from him. A cartoonist like Joe Sacco, who worked with Pekar extensively and whose work at first glance appears very different, in fact inserts himself into all of his journalism much as Harvey had been doing. Alison Bechdel's *Fun Home*, selected as *Time*'s best book of 2006, owes much to Pekar's pioneering approach of showing difficult material in his comix, and she had worked with him on two short strips in 1989's *American Splendor* #14.

Crumb, one of Harvey's oldest friends and collaborators, points out how unlikely Pekar's work really is, in the introduction *Bob & Harv's Comics* (1996). He writes in "A Mercifully Short Preface," handlettered "in the beautiful south of France":

> Hardly anything actually *happens* . . . mostly it's just people *talking*, or Harvey by himself, panel after panel, haranguing the hapless reader. There's not much in the way of heroic struggle, the triumph of good over evil, resolution of conflict, people overcoming great odds, stuff like that. It's kinda sorta more like real life . . . real life in late twentieth century *Cleveland* as it lurches along from one day to the next. If you've never had to live there you can't imagine what a desolate city it is! It is a city that basically has been in a downhill slide since the onset of the 1930s Depression. It is a city that has been ravaged by financiers and industrialists, its population abandoned to their fate, left to freeze their asses off, standing in the dirty winter slush waiting for a bus that is a long time coming. Somehow they go on living

there. And Harvey Pekar is their witness. He is one of them. He reports the truth of life in Cleveland as he sees it, hears it, feels it in his manic-depressive nervous system. There's nobody else to do it. Who would want to? There's no money in it.

Crumb continues by noting, "Harvey is a great story teller. . . . He brings this mundane work-a-day world to life, gives us its *poignant moments*, its humor, absurdity, irony . . . and mostly, it's absolute *truth*. There is no exaggeration in these stories. What you read is what *really* happened." In this short preface, Crumb has captured the essence of Pekar's work.

Local, "cheaper" cartoonists came after Pekar's initial work with Crumb. When self-publishing *American Splendor*, Harvey just made enough money to put out the next issue, so costs, especially how much he could pay his artists, have always constrained his choices and thus *Splendor*'s look. Gerry Shamray, Greg Budgett, Gary Dumm, and Joe Zabel were early regular artists with Pekar. Harvey's earliest collaborators frequently use photographic references and their resulting stiff realism stands in sharp contrast to the looser work of Crumb and Stack. They have continued as part of his stable and remain best known for their work with him. One finds some surprising artists in the first two decades of *Splendor* as well; Alison Bechdel, Val Mayerik (best known for his Marvel Comics superhero work), and Jim Woodring have illustrated his stories.

Pekar's first big breakthrough into the public eye came with his 1986–1988 appearances on the *Late Night with David Letterman* show. Letterman's successful television show commanded an audience literally thousands of times larger than Pekar's self-published comics. His appearances on Letterman made him, and his curmudgeon persona, familiar to millions of people who would never see his comic book. As a result of television, Harvey became a celebrity to a certain degree—known widely for who he is, not for his work. He says in several interviews that appearing on the show never paid off for him in higher sales of his comic book, and eventually financially was not worth doing. One can accept that rationale, but also see that Pekar grew tired of being condescended to. The *American Splendor* movie impetus, however, almost certainly grew out of these appearances.

The reader of *American Splendor*, or of this volume, will soon see what a presence, at times an overwhelming one, Harvey's wife Joyce Brabner is. One wonders about the arc of Pekar's career if Brabner had not made that cross-country trip. Certainly *Our Cancer Year* would be a very different volume if it existed at all; Joyce's contributions to helping

Harvey survive two episodes of cancer probably cannot be overstated. Neither can her work on the book as she co-wrote it. As a character in the comics, Joyce appears frequently as a foil to Harvey—or vice versa— a role that I believe fairly reflects real life after seeing them interact. In the comic book, which one must keep in mind is written solely by Harvey, Joyce is frequently depicted as the dominant person in their relationship, eternally frustrated by Harvey's difficulties. In some ways, one could easily imagine a television sitcom based on the comic book.
In 2008, they will have celebrated twenty-five years of marriage— a marriage marked by cancer, financial difficulties, extreme successes, an adopted daughter—all of which the reader has been permitted to follow though the comic book. As with any of Harvey's stories, it is impossible to know what the "truth" is, but I believe the two have permitted us to see a significant portion of their relationship and their views of it.

Harvey's stable of artists is ever evolving. In the 1990s, new artists such as Joe Sacco and Josh Neufeld began appearing regularly. These artists were frequently drawn from the fledgling small press movement of the 1980s, in which even cheaper reproduction techniques such as photocopying let a new cadre of young cartoonists enter the field, much as the underground movement had two decades earlier. His gradual movement from self-publishing, driven partly by his health and partly by a need for distribution, has led him to several mainstream comic book publishers such as Tundra, Dark Horse, and currently DC Comics' Vertigo imprint. Dean Haspiel, who helped set up the meetings that led to the *American Splendor* movie, also used his ties with DC Comics which led them to publishing Harvey's "origin" story, *The Quitter*. Haspiel illustrated the graphic novel which recounts Pekar's childhood. One interesting outcome of DC's influence has been Harvey's working with artists beyond his usual stable, including Ho Che Anderson, Hilary Barta, Eddie Campbell, Richard Corben, Hunt Emerson, Rick Geary, Gilbert Hernandez, and Ty Templeton.

Pekar himself is not an artist. He provides stick figure layout drawings of his plots to his artists, one of which is reproduced in this volume courtesy of Josh Neufeld. As a result, much of Harvey's writings are in fields other than cartooning. Music and book reviews have been one of his major outlets since the 1960s, and he has done review work for a wide variety of outlets including the *Washington Post* and the *New York Times*. His reviews are frequently of jazz and Eastern European literature. Pekar is self-educated, and his jazz education, influenced by a friend who was a musician and then reinforced through his friendship with Crumb, is discussed in his comic books, especially *The Quitter.* His strips on jazz history were collected in a Dark Horse issue of his comic book. Pekar's reviews share a sensibility with his comics work and may prove of interest to the reader who would like to see another side of Pekar. His comics criticism has appeared in the *Comics Journal* and the *International Journal of Comics Art.*

Pekar by Rick Geary in "You Can't Rush Everything" from *American Splendor: Another Day.*

The *American Splendor* movie is an excellent work and should be viewed by any reader of this volume. Pekar appears as himself, commenting on the movie, while Paul Giamatti does an excellent job transferring Harvey's public persona to a new medium. The movie is a faithful, and creative, adaptation of Pekar's comic books and Pekar himself was happily surprised by its quality. Before it was made, one can follow its progress through the interviews and note that Harvey is mostly interested in the money that selling the rights makes and not the final product itself. The stage versions of *American Splendor* were generally well received and one can see how Harvey's work—generally about two people talking—would lend itself to such adaptations. After seeing his work successfully adapted for larger noncomic readers, Pekar has moved beyond writing just about his life. In the new millennium, nonbiographical work such as *American Splendor: Unsung Hero*, based on Robert McNeill's experiences as a black Marine in Vietnam, *Ego & Hubris: The Michael Malice Story*, and *Macedonia* have all appeared within the past ten years. Pekar's written more of this type of story, and 2008 should see two other books that are biography and history and not traditional *Splendor*.

Pekar as an interview subject always raises some difficulties for the interviewer. Since his work has dealt largely with his own life, fewer questions about his background make sense. Many times the mass-media interviewer, as would be expected, has only a cursory familiarity with Pekar's comic books, or is interviewing him solely on the basis of his *Late Night with David Letterman* appearances or the *American Splendor* movie. Also, like any other person in the public eye, Harvey's told some of his stories so many times that he's overly familiar with them, but he usually works with the interviewer. Of the recorded interviews listened to for this text, two stand out. When Michael Feldman, a local Cleveland radio host, interviews Harvey on *Whad'ya Know?*, Harvey's voice conveys his happiness and playfulness. On the *Spinning on Air* radio show also transcribed in this volume, Harvey is much happier when discussing jazz on the second hour of the show than he was discussing *Our Cancer Year*. When Joyce leaves and he and David Garland settle down to talk about music, his voice lifts up. Although vocal nuances such as these are difficult to capture in transcribed form, the volume nevertheless gives a strong sense of what it's like to be in Pekar's presence.

Credit for this book must go to my wife Cathy Hunter and daughter Claire Rhode, who showed great patience as I worked on it. Of course, the book would not exist without Harvey Pekar who, in spite of the word "curmudgeon" recurring within these pages, was never less than unfailingly helpful, polite, and friendly to me. I have a great deal of admiration for him. Thomas Inge, who suggested the book, and University Press of Mississippi editor Walter Biggins aided me a great deal as did Joseph "Rusty" Witek, who was finishing his *Art Spiegelman: Conversations* as I was beginning this book. Charles Hatfield was fantastically helpful in refining this introduction, and my colleagues Kathleen Stocker and Big Planet Comics store owner Joel Pollack proofread it. Mark Rogers, Rodrigo Baeza, Dean Haspiel, and Pekar artist-turned librarian Scott Gilbert helped find some of the articles I needed. Randy Scott of Michigan State University's Comic Art Collection assisted greatly in finding some of the interviews, and produced the book's index. Jenny Robb of Ohio State University's Cartoon Art Library checked the collections there for me as well. I would like to thank all the authors for their original hard work, and especially those who directly granted me permission to reprint it. Publisher representatives who assisted me include Tom Heintjes of *Hogan's Alley*, Amy Huey and Diana Schutz of Dark Horse Comics, Russell A. James of The Washington Post Writers Group, Trina Higgens of the *Chicago Sun-Times*, Judith Heise Kovalic of *Michael Feldman's Whad'Ya Know?*, Mike McPadden of MrSkin.com, Jennifer Houlihan of WNYC Radio, Meryl Rothstein of *Esquire Magazine*, Debra Weydert and Geysa Rodriguez of The New York Times Syndication Sales Corp., Kristen Cunningham of *USA Today*, and Karon Flage and Warren Bernard of the Small Press Expo.

MR

Chronology

1939	Harvey L. Pekar born to Saul and Dora Pekar in Cleveland, October 8.
1949	Begins working in his parents' small grocery store on Saturdays.
1950s	Lifelong interest in jazz develops.
1957	Graduates from high school, works in his uncle's automobile junkyard and then for the U.S. Railroad Retirement Board as a file clerk. Around this time, professional New York jazz critic Ira Gitler corresponds with Pekar. Joins the Navy, but is soon discharged for psychological reasons. After stints as a file clerk, joins the Post Office as a mail carrier.
1958	Begins going to Western Reserve University.
1959	Briefly moves to New York City and meets Ira Gitler who suggests he write for the *Jazz Review*. His first article on Fats Navarro is published when Pekar is still nineteen. Panicked over a bad grade, Pekar quits school. After an argument with his father, he moves from home and takes a job with Concord Record Distributors.
1960	Marries Karen Delaney, his first wife.
1961	*Jazz Review* folds, but Pekar begins writing for the *Jazz Journal*, *Jazz Monthly*, and *Downbeat*.

1962   Meets Robert Crumb in Cleveland. They become friends due to their mutual interest in jazz.

1965   Begins working for the federal government as a file clerk.

1970   Writes about Crumb for *Journal of Popular Culture*.

1972   Encouraged by Robert Crumb, begins writing comic book stories. His first story is published in *The People's Comics* (Golden Gate Publishing Company). His first marriage ends in divorce.

1973   Writes about Bob and Ray for *Journal of Popular Culture*.

1975   "How'd Ya Get Inta This Bizness Ennyway?" strip with art by Greg Budgett and Gary Dumm appears in *Bizarre Sex* #4.

1976   Self-publishes first issue of *American Splendor* comic book. His stories also appear in the underground comic *Flamed-out Funnies* #1 (Rip Off Press).

1977   Second issue of *American Splendor* comic book published. One issue a year appears through #16 in 1991. Married for second time; divorced in 1981.

1979   Director Jonathan Demme contacts Pekar about abortive *American Splendor* movie.

1983   Pekar and Joyce Brabner meet in person and marry; it is his third marriage.

1985   *American Splendor* first produced as a play in Lancaster, Pennsylvania.

1986   First appears on *Late Night with David Letterman* television show in October. *American Splendor: The Life and Times of Harvey Pekar* with an introduction by R. Crumb is published by Doubleday. Writes book review for *New York Times*. Writes "Maus and Other Topics," a critical review, in the *Comics Journal* #113.

1987   *American Splendor* produced as a play in Washington, DC. Pekar wins an American Book Award for *American Splendor*. *More American Splendor: The Life and Times of Harvey Pekar* collection published by Doubleday. Brabner publishes first issue of *Real War Stories* through Eclipse Comics.

1987–
1989   Writes book reviews for *Washington Post*, including *Bare-foot Gen* manga about Hiroshima.

1988   In August 1988, Pekar argues with David Letterman on *Late Night with David Letterman* following up an argument the previous year over General Electric's ownership of the NBC network. This is his sixth appearance and he does not appear again for years, partly due to his health. "A Notable Among Those Present" story by Pekar, Joe Zabel, and Dumm in *AARGH!* (Northampton, England: Mad Love), appears in a benefit comic for Organisation for Lesbian and Gay Action. Writes introduction for *The Reticent Heart* by Gilbert Hernandez. "A Word to the Wise" text published in *Weirdo* #24. Pekar and Brabner both have pieces in *Strip AIDS U.S.A.* from Last Gasp and *AARGH!* from Mad Love Publishing.

1989   *American Splendor: Bedtime Stories* comic book published by Dark Horse. The first academic study of Pekar is published in *Comic Books as History* by Joseph Witek (Jackson: University Press of Mississippi). Writes foreword to *Ed the Happy Clown* by Chester Brown. "What Superman Means to Me" by Pekar and Dumm appears in *Snarf* #12. Brabner writes and edits *Brought to Light* volume published by Eclipse Books.

1990   Dan Castallaneta appears as Pekar in Hollywood staging of *American Splendor* play. Writes short book reviews for *San Diego Tribune* continuing into 1991. Writes introductions for *Love That Bunch* by Aline Kominsky Crumb and *Dorman's Doggie* by Frank Stack. Pekar diagnosed with cancer in November—non-Hodgkins lymphoma.

1991   Pekar's cancer in remission after a brutal short course of chemotherapy. Pekar attends San Diego Comic-Con, and sees *Splendor* play in Hollywood. Publishes Alley Oop book reviews in the *Comics Journal* #147. *The New Comics Anthology* (Macmillan) reprints his story "Hypothetical Quandary" from *American Splendor* # 9 in 1984. Brabner publishes second and last issue of *Real War Stories* through Eclipse Comics. Tundra publishes *American Splendor* #16 as Pekar recuperates.

1993   *American Splendor* #17, first Dark Horse-published issue, appears in July. Pekar returns to *Late Night with David Letterman* and appears once more in 1994.

1994   *Our Cancer Year*, on Pekar's experiences and co-written with Joyce and illustrated with Frank Stack, is published. *American Splendor Special: One Step Out of the Nest* comic book published by Dark Horse Comics. Pekar has his hip replaced.

1995   *American Splendor: Windfall* #1–2 comic book published by Dark Horse. "Sex, Violence and Theology: Joe Zabel & Harvey Pekar interview Canada's Colin Upton" appears in *Subliminal Tattoos* # 4. Pekar appears in *Dark Horse Presents* anthology comic book #99–104. *Our Cancer Year* wins the Harvey Award for Best Graphic Album of Original Work. Brabner publishes *Activists!* with art by Mark Badger and Wayne Vansant through Stabur Press. Director Bernt Capra is attached to *American Splendor* film option.

1996   *American Splendor: Comic-Con Comics* comic book published by Dark Horse. *American Splendor Presents: Bob & Harv's Comics* collection by Pekar and Crumb published by Four Walls Eight Windows. Writes "Frank Stack: An Appreciation" for *Inks* 3:1. Brabner publishes *Animal Rights Comics* through Stabur.

1997   *American Splendor: On the Job* and *American Splendor: Odds and Ends* comic books published by Dark Horse. *American Splendor: Music Comics* comic book published by Dark Horse and reprints 1992–1996 *Village Voice* comic strips by Pekar and Joe Sacco. Writes introduction for Keith Knight's *Dances with Sheep: A K Chronicles Compendium*. Pekar begins writing book and jazz reviews for the *Austin Chronicle* continuing through 2006.

1998   Pekar and Brabner become legal guardians of ten-year-old girl, Danielle. *American Splendor: Transatlantic Comics* comic book published by Dark Horse. Pekar appears on National Public Radio's *Anthem* speaking with Rick Karr about jazz.

1999   *American Splendor: Terminal* comic book published by Dark Horse. HBO agrees to finance *American Splendor* movie. Pekar writes letter critical of Art Spiegelman to the *Village Voice* during the Rall-Spiegelman feud.

2001   *American Splendor: Portrait of the Artist in His Declining Years* comic book published by Dark Horse. Pekar retires from his file clerk job at the Veterans' Administration. In December, Pekar's cancer returns and he endures a bout of depression while being treated for it.

2002   Has a story in the anthologies *9-11 Emergency Relief* (as does Brabner) and *Dark Horse Maverick: Happy Endings*. Pekar and artist David Collier create *American Splendor: Unsung Hero* (Dark Horse Comics), based on Robert McNeill's experiences as a black Marine in Vietnam. The three issues are collected as a book in 2003. Brabner and Josh Neufeld publish "Typhoid Mary" in *SPX 2002: Biographical Comics Issue.*

2003   *American Splendor* movie opens at film festivals and wins awards at Sundance, Cannes, Edinburgh and Montreal. The Los Angeles Film Critics Association and the National Society of Film Critics both name it Best Picture of 2003, and the Los Angeles critics give it Best Screenplay as well. The American Film Institute includes it on its list of top ten movies of the year. Pekar does thirty-six short radio features on WKSU. Bill Griffith and Pekar collaborate on "No, The River Didn't Catch Fire Again," a strip for the *New York Time*'s August 30 editorial page. Pekar and Dumm's "My Movie Year" comic strip appears in *Entertainment Weekly,* August 15.

2004   The Writers Guild of America gives *American Splendor* movie script the "Best Adapted Screenplay" award. Pekar and Brabner go to the Academy Awards where Pekar says, "It's all bullshit." *Our Movie Year: American Splendor* collection published by Ballantine. Pekar and Gary Dumm do "Ohio— The Heart of It All" a piece of election cartoon journalism for the *Washington Post,* October 31.

2005   Attends the Small Press Expo as the guest of honor. Pekar and artist Dean Haspiel publish *The Quitter*, the story of Pekar's childhood, with DC Comics. Pekar and Haspiel story published in *Michael Chabon Presents the Amazing Adventures of the Escapist* #8 (Dark Horse Comics).

2006   Guest-edits *The Best American Comics 2006*, the first volume in the anthology series from Houghton Mifflin. *Ego & Hubris: The Michael Malice Story* by Pekar and Gary Dumm published by Ballantine Books. He writes the foreword to *Plastic Man Archives* #8. DC Comics' Vertigo imprint publishes a four-issue miniseries, *American Splendor: Another Day*, using artists new to Pekar such as Gilbert Hernandez, Eddie Campbell, and Ty Templeton. It is collected into one volume the following year.

2007   Pekar, co-author Heather Roberson, and artist Ed Piskor release the nonfiction book *Macedonia*. Pekar appears on Anthony Bourdain's television show *No Reservations*. Pekar and Bourdain both write comic strips illustrated by Gary Dumm that appear in the show and on its website. *Students for a Democratic Society: A Graphic History* by Harvey Pekar, Paul Buhle, and Gary Dumm (Hill & Wang, 2008) is projected to appear by the end of the year.

Harvey Pekar
CONVERSATIONS

Wordpekar

MIKE BARSON / 1984

From *Heavy Metal* (December 1984),
pp. 5, 9. Reprinted by permission of
Mike Barson.

Consider the case of Harvey Pekar.

Here's a guy who's *got* to be the crabbiest person east of the Mississippi. (Yeah, he lives in Cleveland—but is that really an excuse?) At the same time, he puts out the best damned comic book you can buy—*if you* can find it. If you can't, you can order it from Harvey: Who, as you might recall, is a real grouch.

Why is Harvey so crabby, you ask? Because of assholes like *you,* asking dumb questions like that all the time. I mean, can't you find anything better to do than bug other people? Especially people who are just trying to get by, working a nine-to-fiver, and then putting together this great mag, *American Splendor,* about the life and times and thoughts and problems of Harvey Pekar—a magazine which never sells worth a damn and is a pain in the ass to get into final form, what with artists always being late with their work, and the printers always fucking up, and the distributors never ordering enough copies. . . .

Well, you'd be cranky, too. And that's just Harvey's point—people can be a real pain in the ass, *life* can be a real pain in the ass, and what the hell is he going to do with 50,000 unsold copies of *American Splendor* stored in attics all over Cleveland?

Worry is what he's doing at the moment. Harvey Pekar has a lot to worry about—he doesn't mind telling you—and all this talk is taking up lots of valuable time. And if you want to know exactly what's worrying Harvey Pekar, pick up a copy of *American Splendor*. It's all in there in black and white: divorce, being broke, dealing with jerks at work, trying to meet girls, trying to figure out what the fuck life is all about. When you get right down to it, what *isn't* there to worry about these days? Not a whole hell of a lot.

And so, Harvey Pekar worries. Now would you *please* just let the guy alone so he can get something done? And for God's sake, buy his goddamn magazine—before attics all over Cleveland collapse.

HM: You've had a wagonload of artists collaborate with you through nine issues of *American Splendor*. How do you determine which artist should do which story?
HP: I try to work with the strengths of each illustrator, and in that way minimize their weaknesses. I'm gradually learning who can do what best, and why. However, keep in mind that for me, getting out an issue is always the art of the possible. Sometimes I find myself down to just one of two dependable artists, so I have to try to recruit others, who often are unknown to me. I can't always have a story drawn by the artists who would have been my first choice.

HM: Where did you discover all the young talent that handles the bulk of the art on *AS*? "Off the streets of Cleveland?"
HP: Some of them came from local art schools; others were introduced to me by people who already were working on *AS*. Considering my limited contracts and the lousy money I pay, I think I've been fortunate to find so many fine illustrators. Gary Dumm and Greg Budgett. Gerry Shamray, Sue Cavey, Kevin Brown—they've each got their own unique style.

HM: I must confess, I first picked up an issue of *American Splendor* strictly because of the Crumb art on the cover and inside. He always seems to get the funniest stories to draw.

HP: Crumb is one of the greatest cartoonists of our time, and I know he is capable of finding the means to handle just about any kind of story. I have been thinking of him primarily for the more humorous pieces, but you'll see a major de-parture in his work in issue number

Pekar by Sue Cavey in "Old Cars and Winter" reprinted in *American Splendor* (Ballantine).

nine. There's a limit to how many pages Crumb has the time to do for *me*, but I'm happy with every piece he's done.

HM: You can see that he really has an understanding of you and what you're trying to accomplish.

HP: Yeah, he does have a real good understanding of my stories; in fact, he's the only artist that I feel comfortable working with over the phone and through the mail. All the other illustrators I use live in the Cleveland area; Crumb gave me a great deal of help early in my career as a comic book writer. The first story I ever published, "Crazy Ed," was illustrated by him and printed in his book *The People's Comics* in 1972. Crumb also turned Willie Murphy on to me, which led to Willie illustrating three of my stories for his *Flamed Out Funnies #1*.

HM: I probably read those stories and never realized who this "Harvey Pekar" dude was. I'd assumed that *AS* was the start.

HP: Yeah, I was in several mags before *AS* got started—*Snarf*, Marvel's *Comix Book*, and an issue of *Bizarre Sex* in which I had the lead story, "How'd You Get into This Bizness, Ennyway?"—it was about a gang bang. So, you could say that my style was established by the time *AS* began.

HM: Writing a story is hard enough, but you took on the additional headaches of the editor and publisher when you decided to put out *American Splendor* by yourself.

HP: It's difficult from beginning to end. I have four different people printing the book—which is what happens when you have to keep your costs down to rock-bottom—one printer for the covers, one to shoot the negatives, one to print the interiors, and a bindery to put the whole thing together. And it's up to me to see that everything gets done, and done right. I actually drive the covers over to the bindery in a station wagon once they're printed—that's 10,000 covers.

HM: Do you ever wish that someone else was handling the publishing end of things, so you could just concentrate on the writing?
HP: I *would* like for someone else to publish *AS*. And I'd like to have it distributed better. It would be especially nice not to lose money on it all the time; then I could afford to pay my illustrators more, which in turn would make it easier to get work from them on time. But I've been aware for a long time that *AS* was never going to be that popular, and that I was letting myself in for a heap of aggravation by publishing it myself. Even so, my life has been greatly enriched since I began the book.

HM: You met your new wife through *AS*, didn't you?
HP: Yeah, she was part-owner of a comic-book store in Delaware that carried my book, and she had to write me to get an extra copy of number six when her own copy accidentally was sold. We began corresponding, and after about a million letters, a zillion hours of long distance phone calls, and several plane trips, we were married; She makes a brief appearance in *AS* number nine, but she's a big star in number ten, so you'll get to meet her then.

HM: It must have been a heck of a correspondence.
HP: The thing that really set it off was when she asked me—I think it was in her second letter—"How can I tell if I'm a member of the working class or not?" That provoked a long answer from me, and the rest just went from there.

HM: And so you whisked her away to Cleveland. Have you lived there all your life? By now, Cleveland has assumed the role of the second most-important character in your stories.
HP: All my life, yeah. I was born in the Mt. Pleasant section of Cleveland's east side at a time when it still had a large Jewish and Italian population, but was in the process of becoming part of the black ghetto. The neighborhood I live in now—the Coventry section of Cleveland Heights—has a great mixture of people from different social classes and ethnic backgrounds. Everyone gets along surprisingly well; it's terrific!

HM: What do you think *AS* offers that mainstream comic books do not?
HP: Most comic book fans prefer fantasy. I'm a realistic writer: I try to push people's faces into their own lives, try to get them to realize how much drama and heroism and even humor there is in the life of the so-called average person. *American Splendor* does not offer escapism, which is what I think most comic book fans are looking for.

Writer Crams Drama into Comics: Pekar Doles out Daily Dialogue

ERNEST TUCKER / 1986

Blowing in from the streets of Cleveland comes this T-shirt clad hipster, a grab-you-by-the-throat talker, true friend and "can-I-borrow-a-quarter?" clerk-hustler. Uh, pause. He's also a neo-realist writer named Harvey Pekar, with a voice like Don Corleone's and eyebrows bristling like flexible antlers.

"I've been called a blue-collar working stiff," said Pekar (pronounced like Pee-car). But there's a twist from this forty-six-year-old guy in blue jeans. He has a vision that makes daily city life—a ride on a bus, a run-in with a boss, or simply buying bread—dramatic. He writes realistic, gritty dialogue, then browbeats comic artists into illustrating his stories in a yearly adult comic book. A selection of this everyman's comic autobiography recently was reprinted in *American Splendor: The Life and Times of Harvey Pekar* (Doubleday).

"Most of the stuff is literal. . . . I try to make it as accurate as possible. I wanna push people's noses in their lives. It's the opposite of escapism, which most comics do," said Pekar, sitting in the morning calm of Billy Goat's Tavern and Grill. His outlet is *American Splendor*, the comic magazine he has published annually since 1975, putting out 10,000 copies of each edition. It typically loses money, though it now sells for three dollars a copy instead of a buck.

"I ain't doing this for money," Pekar snorted, rolling his eyes. He scrapes together extra money hustling "sides" (records), and stability comes from working as file clerk for a Veterans Administration hospital, where he now earns $15,000 annually after twenty years on the job.

"Every day people feel the same depth of emotion. Every day life is real dramatic," he said. "People write about a king losing his kingdom, but if you don't have any money, losing $200 can be just as bad." So can losing your reading glasses, the core of one Pekar story.

If Pekar sounds like a regular guy, it comes from being a regular kid who grew up rooting for the Cleveland Indians and burrowing into comics, later collecting jazz records and writing for *Downbeat* magazine. Clearly, his influences aren't the Saturday morning kid-vids. They are realist novelists, he said, such as Emile Zola or the turn-of-the-century Chicago newspaperman George Ade. There is also a dash of Yiddish gallows humor, inherited from his father, a Polish Jewish immigrant. Then, too, there are comics.

By coincidence, he met Robert Crumb, then an unknown artist, when Crumb moved to Cleveland in 1962. Years later, Crumb became perhaps the best-known underground comic artist (he is creator of the big-footed "Keep on Truckin" figures). Pekar decided to bring his friend's sex-and-drug saturated comics to common life.

Using scenes and dialects jotted on wads of paper, Pekar sketched stick figures to guide his artistic collaborators. Crumb was among the first of a growing army of a dozen or so artists who take Pekar's material and make it graphic. Aside from meager pay, there is the chance for an artist to experiment, Pekar said, adding, "I push guys to do really realistic art."

Though mellowing a little, and married now to publicist-writer Joyce Brabner (his third "crap shoot"), he still finds the daily trivialities of domestic life to have literary possibilities. For example, the tenth issue depicts Pekar at the kitchen sink, thinking, "Poor dishwashing has always been my Achilles heel. If I could upgrade my dishwashing skills, I could really disarm my enemies."

Whoever his enemies, his skeptics also are being disarmed. Last year, a Lancaster, Pennsylvania, theater produced a play based on his works, and newspapers have given his new book positive reviews. Still, fame is not starching his blue collar.

"I'm not an awe-inspiring person," he said. "People just call me Harvey."

The Not-Ready-for-Prime-Time Pekar

Pekar

HENRY ALLEN / 1987

From the *Washington Post* (November 2, 1987), pp. C1–3. Copyright © *The Washington Post*. Reprinted with permission.

God forbid our children should ever see a chicken killed for Sunday dinner, but we like to think we're wired into the way things really are. The raw truth. The back-alley grit. Educated Americans live in protective bubbles of money, media, and prudery that rise from the psychic landscape like those big gray blisters people play tennis in all winter. But there's this nagging appetite for what we think of as "authenticity," be it in figurines from the Franklin Mint, pickup trucks, WASP clothing with little polo-players stitched on it or, for a select few—a cult, even—the comic books that Harvey Pekar has written about himself: "From Off the Streets of Cleveland Comes AMERICAN SPLENDOR-The Life and Times of Harvey Pekar."

Such life. Such times. Harvey Pekar (pronounced PEE-kar) is a balding GS-4 file clerk in a Veterans Administration hospital in Cleveland—a "flunky file clerk," he calls himself, an "alienated schlep" and paranoid sniveler who freeloads doughnuts, whines about loneliness, and screams at women he calls "rotten bitches" until he loses his voice. He has holes in his undershirts. His nose runs. He steals his neighbor's newspaper. He worries about success, because "what right would I have to complain about anything?"

Friday night, the Old Vat Room at Arena Stage began previews of *American Splendor*, a play adapted from the twelve comic books. Doubleday has put out two collections of stories from them. David Letterman has had him on *Late Night* twice. He is forty-eight, a published jazz and book critic, but he knew there had to be more, that his day would come. He's been telling people that Fox Broadcasting even wanted him to audition as a talk show host, and he said no.

He loves telling about how he said no.

"Would you want a talk show? No? Why? I don't want one either, so you and me are on the same wavelength," he says in the frantic tenor of a man whose life involves a lot of fighting his way out of corners or getting other people into them. "I say how can you question me if you don't want a talk show yourself?"

He is in a Maine Avenue seafood restaurant called the Gangplank, sitting next to his third wife.

"He's got no shame, he's got no pride," she says. Her name is Joyce Brabner. She's thirty-three, with thin bangs and huge glasses, and something about her that makes you think of used-book stores and bad arguments.

"I'm certainly not the kind of guy who's . . . "

"He hasn't grabbed the brass ring, which a lot of those guys would've. I mean, he gets offered a talk show on Fox."

"I don't have salable skills, I can't even type," Pekar says, as if he has said it to a hundred employment counselors, a thousand girlfriends.

"I'm teaching him how to type."

"She will never do it, she will never . . . "

"Well, okay."

"I do it to humor her."

"He does it to humor me. He's getting better at it. The truth of the matter is that I think that Harvey has got some kind of learning disability because . . . "

"She has no way of saying that, no way."

"Do I get to say this?"

"I don't know that I have no shame," Pekar says. His upper lip lifts and the corners of his mouth turn down so you see a plaintive trapezoid of teeth. "I just don't think it's any big deal if I stole something when I was a kid and I write about it, or, you know, I was manipulative. Misery loves company. I know the people identify with my work a lot, they say it means a lot to 'em when they write me letters . . . "

Pekar is a hair-in-the-sink realist who shows us a world of iffy morals and petty pleasures amid vistas of meaninglessness bordered by oblivion. The rent is due, the news is bad, the view is phone wires, old cars, and people with their shoulders hunched against the cold.

The stories have titles such as "An Argument at Work," "In the Parking Lot," or "Standing Behind Old Jewish Ladies in Supermarket Lines." He writes the words and gets the pictures drawn by artist friends, including R. Crumb, who was the biggest star of the underground comics scene in the late '60s. The effect is one of cartoon monologues about Harvey Pekar skulking around Cleveland and hating his job; pushing his girlfriend's car out of the snow; eating hot dogs and potato chips for dinner; buying used shoes; bitching at editors, bosses, and coworkers; trying to get to sleep; masturbating; stealing records from a radio station's library; yelling at an ex-wife; and generally coming on like the five o'clock shadow on the face of American life.

"Awaking to the Terror of the Same Old Day" begins on a Sunday night with Pekar walking down the street over a word panel that says: "It's been a bummer weekend. All he's done is hang out on the corner and watch TV." He thinks about how he broke up with his girlfriend a week ago. He thinks about how another woman he knows is a "rotten little flake." He thinks: "The weekends are lousy and the weekdays are lousy. It's just a different kind of lousy."

He goes home to his apartment. He decides not to watch an Abbott and Costello movie on television. He brushes his teeth. He goes to bed. He gets up, shaves, goes to work, schmoozes with the guys on the loading dock about the football game and hangs around the office. By afternoon, he says: "I only feel normally lousy. I hate t'admit it, but workin' sort of helps me keep from goin' nuts. When yer alone alla time, like I am some weekends, y' start concentratin' on yer problems an' thinkin' yer the only person in the world." He concludes: "Sometimes things seem so heavy, other times everything seems like a joke."

That's it, another slice of American life that Harvey Pekar sits on top of, like a fly on a piece of processed cheese.

Why does anyone care?

To begin with, this relentless pursuit of the mundane begins to seem like an enormous gag, like the late Andy Kaufman standing up on stage and lip-syncing to a record of the Mighty Mouse song, or Andy Warhol putting on an endless movie consisting of a single view of the Empire State Building. These stories combine stupendous egotism with Pekar's utter harmlessness in a tour de force of schlemieldom. We're used to people confessing moral monstrosities on the *Donahue* show or in *People* magazine, but who has the guts and ego to go public with confessions of stinginess, chasing women because they're easy to get, and shouting pointless obscenities at coworkers? What a joke! What chutzpah!

Pekar is also a classic American character, one of the last of the hipsters you'd see slouching around city downtowns twenty or thirty years ago, picking through the jazz bins at record stores, their pockets full of bus transfers and library cards and their peripheries blurred by a smog of willful poverty, street wisdom, and egomania. Not hippies, yippies, beatniks, flower children, Weathermen, punks, Panthers, Maoists, Taoists, cosmic cowboys, or sweethearts of the cocaine rodeo. We're talking about a much subtler breed of American human: underground men and saints of self-consciousness with the collective face of a Baltimore Harbor Tunnel guard.

(Where have they all gone? Who still journeys with Céline to the end of the night in bare-lightbulb apartments? Who never watches television, except for *Attack of the Giant Leeches*, which they maintain is the greatest movie ever made, though they only watch it for the carpet warehouse ads? What sexual revolutionaries and sidewalk existentialists lope around in those thick-soled Thom McAn "heavy acid" shoes? Who rants about conspiracies over breakfasts of cigarettes and hot dog rolls? Who steals Allen Ginsberg's syntax? O lost . . .)

Finally, Harvey Pekar and his comic books seem authentic—and in an age when we learn how to raise children by reading books and find out what the weather is by making a phone call, there's an audience for authentic.

The question is: Does authentic mean real?

Pekar puts himself in the realist tradition. "I started writing comic books when I was thirty-two," he says. "Which is kind of old, and by that

time I had a hell of a lot of influences, like novelists and short-story writers and comedians like Lenny Bruce and movies like *The Bicycle Thief*,
stuff like that. But I think probably that Dostoevsky, I remember reading
that *Notes from Underground* and being real impressed with it, but I was
also impressed with, you know, anything like George Orwell's *Down and
Out in Paris and London*, I don't know if you're familiar with it."

Pekar's books certainly seem real. They confirm our worst suspi-
cions about low-rent, near-ghetto, polyester-collar, *lumpen*-treadmill
urban life. Existence is a self-deluding struggle to get through the day.
The characters are trapped in a swamp of typicalities. Pekar is fascinated
with invidious stereotypes: Jews are stingy, bosses are jerks, women are
snooty, everybody hates his job. In a strip called "Pickled Okra," a black
office worker says: "ah ain' nevah ate no pickled okry befo' . . . " Pekar
even shows himself speaking in dialect—most people only notice it in
others, but Pekar is the eternal spectator, especially of himself.

The problem is, Pekar's stories show us not so much the world of
the lower classes, but that world as a lot of people in the upper classes
see it. There's grittiness and poverty, and all of it fits snugly into their
preconceptions. Hence authenticity. To be authentic, all you have to do
is seem real, not be real. Which is to say that authenticity is an idea and
reality is reality. (And before attempting to think about this at home, be
sure to consult a professional esthetician.)

Along with the bleakness, why doesn't Pekar show us the richness in the lives of the lower classes, who have their myths and fervent
legends to protect them from despair just as the upper classes do—the
demigods and popular gospel of honor, Elvis, religion, J. R. Ewing, stock
cars, cancer cures, lotteries, patriotism, television . . . ?

"I'm not into myths, I'm not into legends, I'm anticeremony, I'm
antinationalistic, I mean, you know, I'm sorry that people have to get
through that way," he says.

"Put it this way," Brabner says. "You put him in a beautiful envi-
ronment, he'd see bleak. It's true, Harvey, the knee-jerk pessimist, the
Jewish tragedy, what's the difference?"

"Joyce, I believe the question was directed to me."

"Let's see if he writes down your answer."

"I used to live in a real bleak grim neighborhood where there was a
lot of bitterness around me."

"We don't live in the gritty city," Brabner says. "There's a lot of
things you need to know about Cleveland, including it's nicknamed the

Forest City because they have this terrific urban forestry, so where we live we have more goddam trees than most people have out in the country . . ."

Here in the seafood restaurant, with government employees taking Friday slides to climb onto bar stools with the same hearty finesse that Hell's Angels climb onto motorcycles with, Pekar says: "One of the reasons I write is to push people's face into life rather than to have them try to escape it. If people started to face up to their responsibility as citizens and started to read the goddam paper and find out what the hell was going wrong with the goddam country and worry as much about politics as they know about pro football . . . and I know something about pro football too, you know, I'm a sports fan, I think if they did that they wouldn't, like, elect some guy to be president, some guy who's mediocre, and they choose him, they'll pick people for political office who are, you know, *who are like them*."

Wait a second. Who is he to be condescending—this childless, middle-aged college dropout with twenty-two years in the same job, this shameless flunky whose wife made a doll of him with an "anatomically correct bald spot" and carried it around a booksellers' convention?

"Yeah, I'm kind of a klutzy guy, like a screw-up. I don't feel like I'm a loser but at a lot of things I'm inept, as Joyce has so eloquently testified. I mean, you know, starting with my mother always yelling and screaming at me for screwing up things, you know, I've had that image of myself pounded into myself . . . "

And now he has the right to yell at everybody else?

"Well, first of all . . . "

"Who yells at them otherwise?" Brabner demands.

Such life, such times, such arguments.

Brabner says: "We had a way of solving arguments that maybe we ought to start getting back to—that he could pick me up in the air and I could scream and yell at him as long as I could keep a straight face, and he could yell at me as long as he could hold me up in the air. Then it became insufferably close to Spencer Tracy and Katharine Hepburn cute crap."

"I don't hold her over my head, I just pick her up, I don't know," Pekar says.

"He just holds me up in the air . . . "

"You wouldn't be impressed."

"You'd be impressed," Brabner says.

Interaction between Pekar and Joyce Brabner illustrated by Alex Wald from "Cat Scan," reprinted in *The Best of American Splendor*, p. 146.

"I'm strong for my size, I can do one-handed push-ups, okay? Like, you know, I'll do some out in the parking lot and prove it to you. It's a matter of public record, it's on tape . . . "

"If you don't watch out you're gonna become like Norman Mailer," Brabner says.

"All I can tell you is that on the second David Letterman show I did some one-handed push-ups. I'll do them for you outside."

Outside, in the parking lot, in his lumberjack shirt and corduroy pants, Pekar lies down on his stomach. He puts one hand behind his back. He gets his balance, and he pushes himself up on one hand. He does this four times. It's quite a feat, and you know that when it's being done in a restaurant parking lot, it says something.

Brabner checks to see if anybody's looking, and doesn't say a word.

Voices from the Small Press:

A Conversation with Harvey Pekar

RICHARD RELKIN / 1994

From *Comic Culture* 4 (March 1994), pp. 13–14. Reprinted by permission of Richard Relkin.

Harvey Pekar has been spinning his autobiographical pieces for over fifteen years. His style on *American Splendor* continually pushes the art of storytelling in comics to higher levels. Having beaten cancer, Pekar now resumes his role as comic book creator.

Comic Culture: Your work is primarily autobiographical . . . is there anything that you won't write about from your own life?
HP: I suppose there are a few embarrassing things that happen to me or a few painful things that I haven't written about. A very large percentage of my life I'll write about, more than I think most writers do.

CC: You're writing the story of an ordinary guy trying to get by, with the exception that you have thousands of witnesses. Do you ever do things because you'll write stories about them later?

HP: Well, I know that if I ask certain people leading questions they're gonna give some crazy off the wall answers that are really funny. So once in a while I'll ask a guy something, pretty much knowing what he'll say and I'll hear it fresh and write it down. Even then, though, the person's just re-performing what they did a few days or weeks ago.

CC: How accurate are you?

HP: I try to be as exact as possible, but I don't walk around with a tape recorder. I remember dialogue pretty well, and in a lot of cases I'll write it down right after I speak to somebody so if the story is fairly short it'll practically be verbatim.

CC: How do you find artists for your work?

HP: Over the years, I've worked with a number of different artists, and of course, some have proven to be unreliable and those I just don't work with anymore. Among the ones that I think are reliable, I'll give the stories to the people that I think can do the best jobs on them. All these artists have different strengths. I try to give artists stories that I think they can illustrate very well. Sometimes, my first choice won't be available. Say I have a long story that I want someone to do, but they're working on another large project or something—then I'll have to ask another one to do it.

CC: Most of your artists are local to the Cleveland area—do you let others work for you?

HP: I like to work with local artists, if I can. It's easier. I can watch the work in progress. I can communicate a lot more easily, but I have worked with many artists that don't live in the Cleveland area and I would be crazy not to work with some of these people. Like Frank Stack or Joe Sacco or Robert Crumb for that matter.

CC: *American Splendor* is seventeen issues long and dates back over ten years.

HP: The first *American Splendor* was published in 1976.

CC: Can you talk about the evolution of the book, from distributing it independently to its being picked up by Dark Horse?

HP: Well, it was always distributed nationally, since the first issue. What happened when I was about twenty-two or something like that, I lived in this neighborhood and I was a record collector and a record collecting friend of mine had told me that there was another big record collector that had moved in around the corner from me and I should go meet him. He went over with me and introduced me to him and that was a guy named Marty Pauls, and Marty Pauls' roommate at that time was Robert Crumb, who was a few years younger than me. I saw him working on what I think is one of his best and least appreciated works; a socalled graphic novel, called *The Big Yum Yum Book*.

I'd read comics when I was a kid, but you know, I quickly got tired of them. By the time I was twelve years old, I thought most of them were just junk, kid's stuff, and I still do.

CC: You're doing comics now also.

HP: Yeah, I'm doing comic books, but there's nothing wrong with the comic book form. See, it's just that the kinds of comics I saw were just not very good. The vast majority of comics that are produced today aren't that good. That's not the fault of the form.

To get back to what I was saying, when I saw what Crumb was doing it got me to thinking that comics were as good an art form as any that existed. You could write any kind of story in comics. It was as versatile a medium as film or television. Comics are written words and still pictures, whereas film and television are spoken words and moving pictures. You could just about do anything you wanted to in comics. I kept on thinking about that; developing ideas about comics, watching Crumb go out to California, making it, sending me his work, coming back to visit me. By that time I was sort of familiar with some other underground comics. A lot of them had to do with portraying the hippie subculture. They weren't superhero comics and they did broaden the subject matter of comics, but I thought a lot more could be done with them. I decided that I'd like to try. This was in 1972. At that time Crumb was visiting me, staying in my house. I showed him some stories that I had written and he really liked them. He and a guy named Robert Armstrong, another real good alternative comic illustrator, illustrated the works. That how I got started. That time was the beginning of a long decline in popularity for alternative comix. Nixon and the Vietnam War was over and the draft was abolished and consequently the so-called counterculture of the '60s and '70s just faded away. It was harder and harder to get my stuff published in other comics. I published in other comics before I started *American Splendor*. So I made inquiries about how much it cost to publish a comic. I found that I could save up enough money to publish one

Pekar and Robert Crumb negotiate working together, from "A Fantasy," p. 2, reprinted in *Bob and Harv's Comics*.

and I did. I figured, you know, all these different people have different hobbies that they put a lot of money into. I'm just gonna do it with comics. So that's how I got started.

CC: As the years have gone by it's always been a hobby—you never quit your day job, did you?
HP: Well, it's more than a hobby. It's extremely important to me. I've always had to have a day job, yeah. I couldn't make a living as a book writer and publisher.

CC: How has your circulation fluctuated over the years?
HP: It improved. I sold more and more books, but I'm still not very popular.

CC: What about when you were on Letterman?
HP: Yeah, I was on Letterman seven times.

CC: You we're a favorite of his for a period.
HP: Well, I was on a lot for a period.

CC: There were many more people watching you on TV than had ever read your comics. Did you think about that at all?
HP: It was no big deal to me. When I first started out I wasn't getting very good money. People weren't buying my comics much more as a result of my appearing on the show. I don't like the Letterman show. I think it's a show that features cheap shot humor and I think that most guests are on there to be made fun of. But, I went along; I kept going back for a while because I thought something might come of it. But it didn't really result in anything all that tangible. The last time I was on in the period when I was popular with him, I just decided to go out in a blaze of glory. I got him real mad and had a big argument with him on the show and everything like that. But they called me a few times after August '88, which was the last time I appeared on his show, except for once last April. They called me a few times to come back on, but I never wanted to. The show is a drag. I don't mind being on television and trying to be funny, but I'd like the interviews to have a little substance. There was nothing happening on Letterman's interview. He doesn't read what people write. He doesn't care. Anyway, the segment producer of his show really liked my work a lot. He started calling me again, in February, and he asked me if I would consider coming back on the show. At that time they were paying $600. Money had gotten much better. So I

said yeah, for $600, if you could fly my wife and me in, give us a hotel room like you used to. So I went in and I did it. I think I was pretty successful, by their standards anyway. I wasn't quite as hard on Letterman as I usually am or usually was. The executive producer sent me a real nice letter telling me that I'd been great and that they looked forward to having me back in the Fall when they went to CBS. They did book me to come on the show, but then they canceled and tried to move me to another date that I couldn't make because we were shorthanded at work at that time. I couldn't and didn't really want to get leave; that would have caused a lot of problems. Since then, they haven't called me back, and I think that I probably won't be called back now, because all that I hear about the show is that their object is to get higher ratings than Jay Leno. They don't care how they do it or how dull their show is; they're trying to really avoid controversy like crazy nowadays. So I imagine that they probably think I'm too controversial. They don't want me on for that reason. They don't want to scare anyone anyway. Their audience is much larger now; more of a primetime type viewer watches it.

CC: You have some stories about your cancer. What's your health situation now?

HP: I'm in remission. They operated on me; they gave me exploratory surgery in November of 1990. They found this lymph node that was malignant and they took it out and that's all they found. It's all they ever found. And they gave me chemotherapy, radiation therapy for months after that, which was extremely hard. It would be on anyone. After a few weeks I got too weak to work. On top of this chemotherapy which is extremely painful, I got shingles. I had a really rough chemotherapy regiment. . . . It affected me very seriously from a psychological standpoint. But, I got through it; the only thing is the medicine that I took, particularly, I guess, the steroids that I had to take to keep my resistance up, cut off the circulation to my femur in my hip and some of it died as a result and started to crumble. That's what they call avascular necrosis. That's what happened to Bo Jackson. So now my leg hurts all the time. I walk with a limp, and the only thing I can really do about it is have a hip replacement, and they don't want to do it now unless the pain is unbearable because I'm too young. They figure the hip replacement might not last more than ten or fifteen years and then I'd have to have a hip replacement replacement, so the doctors just tell me to go as long as I can without getting the hip replaced. But I've been back to work since then.

CC: Were the stories dealing with cancer all written afterwards?

HP: I wasn't writing any stories when I was sick. I was delirious a lot of the time. Those are stories after the experience, not while the experience was happening to me. I made references to having cancer in stories, but by that time the stories were about post-cancer experiences.

CC: Will you be writing stories about your experiences during chemotherapy?

HP: In my last comic, I mention that my wife and I are writing, or have written a book, called *Our Cancer Year*, which is about what happened to me when I had cancer. It's also about a lot of my wife's experience during that time. It's a pretty complex book. There are a lot of themes in there besides cancer. There's political stuff in there, stuff about the Gulf War. Some stuff about our involvement with kids who were in an anti-war group. There's a section in there about a visiting nurse that I had. We talk about her and her story. It's not just about cancer. There's cancer but it's in the context of our lives. Also, another major theme in the book is that at a pretty advanced age, fifty, I bought a house. So there's things about the fear I had about buying a house. How we finally got it and stuff. It's been written and it's now being illustrated by Frank Stack. It'll be a two hundred some-odd page book.

CC: Can we expect to see that soon?

HP: Although Frank is almost finished with the illustration, the publication date isn't set until the fall of '94.

CC: What are some of your influences?

HP: I'd say a major influence on my work has been prose fiction writing. Even though my stories are autobiographical, I use a lot of techniques that prose fiction writers use. I guess I've also been influenced by comedians. Timing and pacing is very important to me, like it is to them. That's why comics are a very good medium for me. I can break the work up into panels and it's pretty easy to pace and punctuate with silent panels. Specifically, there have been an awful lot of writers that have probably influenced me, but it's real hard to be specific because I'd read a lot of stuff before I started writing comics. All this stuff was in my head when I started writing comics. It wasn't like I suddenly got acquainted with some guy and tried to write like him or something like that. I was relatively old when I started writing comics. I was thirty-two years old. So, I'd read a lot of outstanding novelists. I'd been influenced by many of them, I imagine.

Pekar expresses his feelings towards David Letterman. Illustration by Joe Zabel and Gary Dumm from "An Almost All-Expense-Paid Vacation," reprinted in *The Best of American Splendor*, p. 43.

CC: You talk about being a big record collector; how much does music influence your writing?

HP: The music of language, spoken language, influences my writing a lot. I like to write in different dialects of English, spoken by different types of people, different classes. I really dig it. I don't think that music as in Jazz or Classical music has influenced my writing.

CC: Are there any points or messages that you're trying to get across?

HP: Well, I'm trying to show that everyday events can be very interesting. So-called "mundane" events can be interesting. Everybody has an interesting life, and the humor in everyday life is way funnier, as far as I'm concerned, than anything you'll see on TV or in the movies. I'm trying to write stories that I think people can identify with. I'm hoping that when they read the stuff that I've gone through, it will give them some comfort. In fact, I've gotten a lot of letters that say that I have comforted people. I really enjoy writing because there's so much that can be done in comics. It's such a wide open field. There's so much you can experiment with because they've been used in such a narrow way for most of their history. I enjoy writing comic stories, using new narrative techniques, using new subject matter. It's really interesting to me.

Stepping Out: ST's Joe Zabel Interviews Harvey Pekar

JOE ZABEL / 1994

From *Subliminal Tattoos* 2, pp. 47–56.
Reprinted by permission of Joe Zabel.

Harvey Pekar is best known for producing the groundbreaking autobio-graphical comic book *American Splendor*, which documents his life as a file clerk in a Cleveland Hospital.

It also deals with Harvey's infamously contentious appearances on David Letterman's show—including the time he was censured on the air by Letterman when he attempted to criticize NBC owner General Electric.

Pekar is a respected jazz critic, has published numerous book reviews and articles, and his comics stories have been dramatized on the stage.

I've worked for Harvey on *American Splendor* for about seven years, most recently completing a thirty-two-page comic titled *American Splendor Presents: A Step out of the Nest* for Dark Horse Comics.

Harvey has a public image of being a grouch, and often in the comics I draw him that way. What is he *really* like? Well, he's never been ill-tempered with me; in fact, he's one of the most reasonable people with whom I've ever worked. He knows exactly what he wants and is very patient in explaining it—plus, he's quite flexible in accepting unorthodox interpretations of his work, so long as they don't obscure what he's trying to say.

Harvey has some interesting eccentricities, however. For example, even though he's a writer, he's never learned to type—not even by the hunt-and-peck method. He gives me handwritten scripts with stick-figure drawings, and sometimes they're so illegible I have to call him on the phone and ask him to translate.

But Harvey is basically an intelligent, serious person who has high standards, and who works very hard to meet them. He had a vision of a realistic comic that broke away completely from the fantasy-oriented comic books of the past, and has pursued that vision with zeal and determination.

That's an achievement we can all admire. I conducted the following as a written interview with the busy Harvey.

Joe Zabel: Tell us about *Our Cancer Year*.
Harvey Pekar: *Our Cancer Year* was written by Joyce Brabner, my wife, and me—and illustrated by Frank Stack. It'll be 224 pages long, and published by Four Walls Eight Windows this fall.

It's about a very difficult period in our lives when I had cancer and had to undergo chemotherapy and radiation-therapy treatments, and Joyce had to take care of me. The chemotherapy regimen was very hard and had severe mental as well as physical effects on me.

There are other themes in the book, however. One is that just prior to my diagnosis, we had bought a house—which was a huge step for us—and we were in the process of fixing it up. The work had to go on while I was being treated.

Also, Joyce got involved in the lives of some teenagers at a peace conference she was writing about—some survivors of the Cambodian Holocaust, some Israeli and Palestinian peace activists, some American kids living in urban war zones.

She tried to maintain contact with the kids after the conference and keep them in contact with each other. This involved buying second-hand computer equipment and sending it to them, and traveling to the Middle East, just as Iraq was invading Kuwait.

All of this occurred while we were buying the house, while I was being treated for cancer, and while the Gulf War was going on.

There are other themes in the book as well; it's quite complex. One of them is my relationship with Joyce—our love story.

JZ: I'm excited to hear Frank Stack is illustrating *Our Cancer Year*. Isn't he great?

HP: Frank is one of the greatest comic book illustrators of the past fifty years. He's very intelligent and superbly equipped technically.

Frank's a professor of art at the University of Missouri and his "fine art" background is perhaps more apparent in *Our Cancer Year* than any other comic work he's done. He did a magnificent job.

JZ: Why do you write so much about your own experiences, your own personal life? Most writers seem to prefer writing about extravagant, dramatic characters and exotic locales.

HP: I write autobiographically because I know more about my own life than anyone else's. I believe almost all of us lead dramatic, interesting lives and have a lot more in common than we realize.

I try to write about various aspects of my life as accurately as possible, hoping people will be able to identify with my work and take comfort from it, realizing that I have some of the same problems they do, that they're not unique in this respect.

I also write about the humorous things I see and experience daily.

JZ: Do you think people spend too much time trying to escape from the important issues of their lives, rather than facing them?

HP: Yes, I think people in general should take more of an interest in societal and political problems and try, in a variety of ways, to solve them. A healthy society helps create healthy individuals.

JZ: What do you think about the current comix scene? Can you recommend some cartoonists to us?

HP: I'm a bit disappointed that more hasn't been happening since the early 1980s, when alternative comics seemed to be on the way back.

Of the younger comic book artists, I particularly like the work of Joe Sacco.

JZ: What do you think the comix art form could be doing that it's not doing now? Are you encouraged by the proliferation of autobiographical comix? And what do you think of the criticism that autobiographical comix are unimaginative?

HP: I'd like to see comics deal with every subject prose and television and movies deal with. I'm encouraged by the proliferation of any kind of comics as long as they're not of the superhero, sci-fi, or fantasy type.

It's stupid to criticize autobiography as a form, because it's such basic and major form. The quality of autobiographical writing, of course, varies; each work must be evaluated on its own merits.

The type of comic that has consistently been the worst, however, is the superhero comic.

JZ: Are there trends in comics that you're critical of, and would like to see less of?

HP: Obviously, I'd like to see less superhero stuff, but that's what sells— and its lousy quality keeps talented writers and illustrators from doing comics.

JZ: You mentioned Joe Sacco, the artist and writer of *Palestine*. Tell us about Sacco. You've worked with him on *American Splendor*; what was that like?

HP: Joe's a very talented writer, a trained journalist and illustrator. His layout work is often brilliant. He's a pleasure to work with—reliable, inventive, and very intelligent.

He understands my work.

JZ: Speaking of *Palestine*, things are changing rapidly in the Middle East. What do you think of the developments?

HP: I'm glad the Palestinians have been granted limited self-rule, but they'll have to get a lot more before the Middle Eastern problems are solved.

JZ: You've just appeared on the David Letterman show. What's your status with them now?

HP: I never know from show to show what my status is, and I don't worry about it.

TV executives don't know what to make of me.

JZ: You got into trouble trying to do political stuff on the show. Have you tried to get back into that?

Life does not get much more quotidian than in this second page of a two-page story, "Peeling and Eating a Tangerine," illustrated by Joe Sacco, *The Best of American Splendor*, p. 38.

HP: Since I got back on I've made a few remarks that have social and political implications. I'll try to work more in, but Letterman's people are really scared of anything controversial.

JZ: Are your conversations with Letterman completely spontaneous, or are they prepared in advance?
HP: I go over some subjects that I can talk about with the segment producer before the show, but both Letterman and I depart from them.

JZ: How much of your "feud" with Letterman was real?
HP: It was real.

JZ: What are the prospects of you appearing on other shows?
HP: I don't know anyone else who wants to use me. Letterman's been the only one, even though I'd rather work in different formats.

So give him credit for that.

JZ: The public is hungry for news about the *American Splendor* movie. Can you tell us anything?
HP: The public's hungry, huh? You coulda fooled me.

I've got a comic published by Dark Horse coming out about September, and the aforementioned *Our Cancer Year* about the same time.

JZ: You're obviously fascinated with Russian literature. Who are some of your favorite authors?
HP: Gogol, Dostoyevsky, Chekhov, Bely, Pilnyak, Zamyatin, Khlebnikov are among my favorite Russian writers. I'm very interested in Russian modernism from 1900 to 1935.

JZ: You're also interested in the literary avant-garde. This may be hard to describe, but can you tell us how one goes about reading a novel in which the sentences aren't intended to make literal sense, and where the author may be working from rules the reader has no way of guessing? Who are some of your favorite avant-garde writers?
HP: I like too many avant-garde writers to list here.

To understand experimental art, you've got to know what it grew from—then it won't seem so far out.

Art evolves step by step, and you've got to keep up with it. If you miss a whole bunch of steps, then current experimentation will puzzle you.

Pekar's view of his work was troubled before the success of the *American Splendor* movie. Artwork by Gary Dumm from "The Terminal Years," reprinted in *The Best of American Splendor*, p. 88.

JZ: Harvey, as a prominent jazz critic, would you recommend some hot new artists to our readers? And why isn't there more about jazz in your comic book writing?

HP: I'm doing a bit more comic book work about jazz since I've been writing more about it lately. From 1976 to about 1991 I wrote virtually no jazz reviews or articles, but I'm doing it again and finding it quite challenging and enjoyable.

I'm particularly interested these days in the work of avant-gardists like John Zorn, Dave Douglas, Mark Ribot, Roy Nathanson, and Anthony Coleman, who—in some ways—have gone beyond synthesizing jazz with other forms and are creating a new music.

JZ: You're a self-described "strident leftist." What do you think about the future of socialism in view of the collapse of the Soviet Empire?

HP: I'm not the first to observe that technology has existed for some years that could lead to the adequate feeding, housing, clothing, and educating of everyone on the planet—yet large-scale human misery persists because currently people are more interested in economic competition than cooperation.

Many individuals would rather have $1.00 and have their neighbor have none than have everyone have $10.00.

If governments all over the world make a commitment to produce enough material to lift people out of poverty and ignorance, ways can be found to distribute the material equitably.

But of course, this requires a different mindset; it requires people to realize that the object is to make a direct assault on poverty, and that by doing so everyone will benefit—including the well-off.

What I'm talking about must happen within the context of a democratic system, of course. The rulers of the USSR and its satellites were primarily interested in increasing the power of the state, i.e. themselves—rather than benefiting the general population, which they exploited for their own benefit.

In the long run I think an economy that stresses economic cooperation and planning will be more beneficial to humanity than one that stresses competition—which is often unfair to begin with, when monopolies and oligopolies exist and there are huge income gaps between the rich and the poor.

JZ: Do you think the Democratic and Republican parties are basically the same, or are the differences between the two important? In other words, do you think it's still important to vote?

HP: Yeah, I think there are significant differences between the Democratic and Republican parties in general, although there are right-wing Democrats and a few moderate Republicans.

And yeah: I think it's important to vote. Think what you want of him, Bill Clinton's pushing for National Health Insurance a lot harder than George Bush would have.

JOE ZABEL and ST: Thanks, Harvey!

Harvey Pekar and

Joyce Brabner

DAVID GARLAND / 1995

Transcribed by Michael Rhode from WYNC's
Radio's *Spinning on Air* (August 22, 2003
rebroadcast of March 1995 radio show).
Reprinted by permission of WNYC.

David Garland: Hello, I'm David Garland. Glad you could turn in for an-
other spin here *on Spinning on Air*. Tonight I'll be joined by Harvey Pekar
and Joyce Brabner. Joyce and Harvey are a couple of interesting people
who have done some interesting things. One of them has just been published. It's a book called *Our Cancer Year* and despite the subject matter that you can hear in the title there, it is in a form of a comic book,
that special combination of words and pictures that we've come to be familiar with from childhood, chances are. But in this case, both the story
and the art are coming from, and going in, a completely different direction from the commonplace fare of comic books. Harvey Pekar has been
writing his autobiography in comic book form, *American Splendor*, since

1976. You may have read some of his jazz criticism as well and he has been an occasional outspoken guest on David Letterman's show. Plus he is still working as a file clerk in that Cleveland hospital you may have come to know through *American Splendor*. Joyce Brabner is a writer, an activist, and a comic book writer in her own individual way too and their recent collaboration, *Our Cancer Year*, is quite a book. That's going to be the topic of our discussion tonight, plus we'll hear a little bit of music and Harvey Pekar is going to be sharing his love of music and his enthusiasm for the musicians John Zorn, Dave Douglas, and others who he thinks are doing important work. I happen to agree with him, and some of their music and music of others will be heard interspersed with the conversation on tonight's program. We'll begin with Harvey reading from the very opening of Harvey and Joyce's book *Our Cancer Year*.

Harvey Pekar: I'm not very good at reading . . .
Joyce Brabner: I know.
HP: You know I don't do it . . .
JB: Just don't rip through it and you'll be ok.
HP: This is a story about a year when someone was sick, about a time when it seemed that the rest of the world was sick too. It's a story about feeling powerless and trying to do too much. Maybe doing more than you thought you could and not knowing what to do next. It's also a story about marriage, work, family, friends and buying a house.

DG: That's Harvey Pekar reading the opening lines from *Our Cancer Year*, a book he wrote with his wife, Joyce Brabner, and they're both here for this edition of *Spinning on Air*. Welcome to WNYC.
HP: Thank you very much.

DG: *Our Cancer Year* is essentially a book with three authors—two who wrote the text and one who drew the pictures. It is a comic book about Harvey Pekar's cancer treatments. It's a comic book over two hundred pages long and Frank Stack is the illustrator. I want to talk about him, but a little bit later. Harvey and Joyce, I know you've both used comics as a form for your work before *Our Cancer Year*, and I believe you both have written and published without any pictures, but what drew each of you to comics as a medium and why'd you approach this project and its subject matter through comics?
HP: Well, I have been doing comic books since 1972, or comic book stories, and I've been writing prose articles that have been published since

1959. I use comics as a story-telling form because I think they're as good an art form as any other art form and they're peculiarly suited to the way I tell stories. Comics are consistently underrated by the public because so much of what's done in the medium is aimed at adolescents or people with an adolescent intellect, for some strange reason. But in fact, they're as versatile a medium as any other medium and they can be as powerful a medium—they are as powerful a medium—as any other medium. You've got access to every word in the dictionary, just like Shakespeare, and you can use a wide variety of illustration styles. When I realized this, I thought I would, you know, try to write comic book stories myself, because I could see where the medium could be expanded and it really excited me.

DG: When was that?

HP: Actually I had been theorizing about this for some time, you know, during the '60s. I guess starting with my knowing Robert Crumb in 1962. Crumb used to live in Cleveland. We were both jazz collectors and at the same time he was already working on his comic book stories. He was then about eighteen, nineteen years old, but he was working on a piece, well, if you want to call it a graphic novel, called his *Big Yum Yum Book*, which unaccountably has not gotten any kind of attention to speak of although it's one of his greatest works.

DG: And it's been published?

HP: Yeah, it's been published. I guess his wife won't allow it to be republished . . .

JB: His ex-wife.

HP: His ex-wife, yeah, his ex-wife Dana. She has the rights to the book. But in any event, I had read comics when I was a kid and when I saw what Crumb was doing, it occurred to me that they were a less limited medium than I thought they were so I started thinking that comics could deal with even a wider variety of topics than even the underground comic book artists of the '60s, who expanded the medium quite a bit, had done. I kept in contact with Crumb, and when he came to visit me in 1972 in Cleveland, I wrote some stories for him, to show him, in stick figure form. He liked them. He volunteered to illustrate some of them and there was another cartoonist by the name of Robert Armstrong— also very good, but who's since quit doing cartoons—who also did some of the stories, and that's how I got started. As I continued to do them, I got more and more ideas about how they could be used, how wider and wider varieties of narrative techniques could be employed and they fascinated me. They appealed to me in particular because of the fact they were a real economical way to tell stories. And they were also peculiarly suited to me because timing was really, really important to me. I like to write dialogue, accurate dialogue, and I could punctuate the dialogue with silent panels that would really help time the dialogue.

DG: Um-hmm. Not everyone listening knows what kind of stories you were writing. Were these autobiographical from the start?
HP: Yeah, they were always autobiographical stories. That's the way I wrote and continue to write. I guess you could look at my work as all being of a piece . . . it's all part of my continuing autobiography, and I hope to write it as long as I can.

DG: Now some people would expect an autobiography to be written by someone with a swashbuckling life and grand adventurous stories to tell. Your stories are often about the conversations at the workplace, about people you meet casually, situations you observe. . . . They're hardly the heroic sort of stories that comic books are often associated with.
HP: Yes, well, I write about what I know about. Most of it has gone into a comic book series called *American Splendor* which I have been publishing since 1976, the first fifteen issues of which I self-published actually. But I think, for example, if a man is in danger of losing his job, and I write about that a lot—the person's in danger of losing their job—it doesn't matter if the job pays like $15,000 a year or $15 million a year. The point is that they're both going to be feeling a great deal of stress. Both situations to me are very dramatic. I use the example of money because people could maybe relate to that. They get really excited when there's a big bank robbery or something that they read about. But I think whether people are involved in mundane events, or whether they're among the few rich and famous, they feel the same kinds of emotions and emotional intensity and they have the same things at stake. So it doesn't really matter if I'm writing about working class life or the kind of stuff that Jackie Collins writes about. People feel the same way about their experiences—about essentially similar experiences. Now I also think that mundane experiences have been ignored for far too long by many authors because mundane events, an accumulation of them, have as much an impact, or more of an impact on people's lives, than traumatic events, life-and-death events. As a matter of fact, it's kind of funny that in a way writing about the mundane adds freshness to my work because it's so seldom dealt with. Robert Crumb wrote that my work was so mundane that it was exotic.

JB: Writing about something like cancer, this is sort of a subject that we're used to seeing on a movie of the week or something like that, written as high drama. The truth of it is that this is something that hits . . . I think we're told one out of three people. So our experience of cancer was just experience with something that was ordinary. That was one of the things we just sort of kept in mind the whole time. There wasn't anything particularly heroic or brave about what we went through when Harvey got sick. It wasn't that unusual really, or that dramatic. It seemed dramatic to us, but there's a lot of other people in the same boat, going through what we were going through now.

DG: Well, it doesn't make it any less dramatic for the individual who goes through the experience, I'm sure. Joyce, what is your background in comics?
JB: Well . . . I read comics when I was a kid and switched over to *Mad* magazine as fast as I could because you had more words per page and I had to buy them myself. And then I realized that I could actually buy a bus ticket and get down to the library, so goodbye *Mad* and there we went. But around the time when I was burning out of doing case work with battered wives, neglected and abused kids, working with people in prisons, I put a little money into a comic book store which sold what I guess you'd call zines now, as well as comics like *American Splendor* which were poorly distributed at the time. I wrote a letter to Harvey trying to get the books from him himself and we began corresponding. We didn't get along very well in the correspondence. I called him up one night and told him, "Shut up, sit down, and listen." I think I've been saying that to him ever since. But we met, we decided to get married the next day. On our second date, we picked out wedding rings; on our third date we were in fact married, and after that. . . . After finding out whether he had any living relatives, a middle name, you know, all these other things I didn't know about this stranger, I found myself as a character in Harvey's comics.

In 1986, at about the time the Department of Defense was trying to pull middle-class kids into the volunteer army to kind of up the quality of recruits, I was contacted by somebody who was doing counter-recruiting propaganda and wanted to put a comic book together in black and white, on newsprint as *American Splendor* was being published. I didn't think that was such a good idea because the appeal to kids had to do with economic necessity. It's kind of tough to be guidance counselor trying to counsel kids about jobs when the Army or the Navy or whatever is landing a helicopter on the roof of the school and doing karate demonstrations and rappelling down the side of the building. So I set about involving mainstream comic book artists and writers—people who do *Batman* and *Superman* for a living—in doing my first comic book, *Real War Stories* which was a series of nonfiction comics done documentary style. That comic book eventually ended up in a federal court in Atlanta, Georgia, because the Department of Defense or the Department of Justice decided it was threat to national security, because it was interfering with recruitment—getting a slightly dumber kid than the one that picked up our comic book and read it. But the bottom line is that we won because our sources were real, real accurate. I had worked in the criminal justice system and knew a lot about evidence and things like that so that's when we were onto something. I was in fact working on another issue of *Real War Stories* when Harvey got sick.

DG: Was there ever any question of approaching the story of Harvey's illness and your participation in any other way, or did you sort of know from the start?

JB: As Harvey said, his series *American Splendor* is about his life and so he would have written about this, or he would have written about a broken toe. The big question is whether or not I'd be involved in writing *Our Cancer Year* with Harvey. That's the worst thing about being married to Harvey; I no longer have an issue of *American Splendor* to look forward to every year.

DG: You mean because you're involved . . .

JB: Because I'm in them. I already know what happens in the arguments about who washed the dishes or things like that. Harvey's particular form of cancer, while quite treatable, the treatment that he chose was very rough, very brutal. He chose it because it would be over faster. He really wanted to get the weekly chemotherapy and then daily radiation treatments behind him.

DG: This is all told in the book?

JB: Yeah, that's all in the book, but what's not in the book . . . in some ways . . . is that he had big gaps in his memory as a result and we also had very different points of view about what happened to us. So it began by [Harvey] asking me to fill in some dialogue and stuff and we realized it probably would work better if we both wrote this book together.

Pekar and Brabner finally meet in person, as drawn by Val Mayerik in "A Marriage Album," reprinted in *American Splendor* (Ballantine).

DG: I see. When a person sees a co-author credit on a book cover, it always makes one wonder who did what? What was the division of labor? In the case of *Our Cancer Year*, clearly it had to be written by two people because there were two parts of the story that had to be fitted together to be the complete story.

JB: There were also things that I didn't know happened to Harvey until I read them. Really sometimes very painful things like . . . One of the things I'm not very proud of is that, towards the end of the time of taking care of Harvey, about the time he kept forgetting how to walk. Every time I'd turn around, he'd collapse and fall down and I'd have to pick him up. I went to move him and I couldn't get him to respond. I guess I was worried that he might have gotten an overdose, because he'd been quite depressed and talking about dying. I think I went to shake him and then to kind of slap his cheeks to wake him up, or pull him together, and I ended up slugging him. I caught myself and heard myself saying, "Why are you doing this to me?" like I'm blaming him, which is what you say when the baby just threw up on your last clean sweater. But in his side of the story, which I didn't see until I saw it in the script, he'd actually been up most of the night. He was really disoriented. He looked at the alarm clock. Somehow or other because he was flashing in and out of consciousness, he thought time was running backwards. He thought he was dying. He got up out of bed and spent the whole night shivering on the bathroom floor waiting to die and then had gone back to bed and was exhausted, and that's why I couldn't wake him up. And I had to see it in his script to know what had happened.

DG: Um-hmm. So putting the book together was putting the whole story together for yourselves as well.

JB: Exactly.

DG: I know there are interesting moments in the course of the book where obviously only Harvey could have known an experience. Other times when you're conferring with a doctor, behind Harvey's back, for Harvey's benefit, that's obviously your part of the story too. Through reading about that sort of experience with Harvey on the floor, and whatever Harvey may have discovered through what you had written, were any of those discoveries profound for you, in sort of revealing something about the other, or about yourselves?

JB: I would have said they were profound if it weren't for the fact that by then we were so burned out, numbed down, and worn out that we literally didn't have much left to feel. I think now as we've dealt with the post-cancer stuff and the shock and the trauma, looking back after a period of time, it's a little bit easier to look at now than it was perhaps when we were writing this. We were working on this book really at a time when our post-cancer life should have started and of course we just turned right around in our tracks and went back to whip the whole thing up again.

DG: Well, perhaps there's no better way to put it behind you either.
JB: It's a lot better to have it in a book on a shelf than to just have it as an ugly memory. That makes it feel better.
HP: Yeah, I'd like to mention that about this "finding out things"—there's some things it's not worth paying the price to get. Yes, I learned some things from having had cancer and more especially from having the chemotherapy treatment which is the most horrible thing I've ever experienced . . .

DG: Excuse me, but ironically in the way you tell the story the cancer itself caused you no discomfort—just the treatment and the removal of the cancer.
HP: Right. Yeah, that is ironic about it; it was the chemotherapy that really almost did me in. Among other things that I learned and found out about was about my own mortality and about having to develop a really stronger sense of it. It became real to me *finally* that I was gonna die. You never think you're gonna die, I mean if not then, then sometime. It's something that I couldn't have understood unless I experienced something like this. But I don't know that I'm a better person for it. It shook me profoundly at the time, and I still haven't gotten over the effect. Now you just wonder what's gonna come up next? What's gonna flatten you next? You start counting . . . you wonder if you're going to make it to seventy-five and things like that. I don't think I'm better off for it. I don't know—maybe if this book sells and makes me a millionaire or something like that—maybe then I could say maybe it was worth it, but at this point I can't say that.
JB: You see, the other thing too is that . . . I feel it's really important to stress two things. One of them is that Harvey's treatment was very, very rough and brutal, but not everybody's treatment is like that. There usually are options, there usually are ways that can be managed. So what happened to us was very particular in terms that this is the way this particular course of treatment affected this person, aggravated by all the

things that make Harvey, Harvey. It was terribly important for him to hold onto his job and his working life. Not for financial reasons because Harvey's been an entry-level file clerk for years and years and years at a government hospital in Cleveland. At least now we don't have to explain to anybody why he didn't quit and strike out to New York to be a writer, because it's the health care insurance that we have there that let us hold onto our lives and our house and everything. He had nine months of sick leave saved up and he could have taken the real long, slow, perhaps easier way out. But he writes about the people he works with and routine is real important to him as well. When he was first diagnosed, we showed his doctor all of his back issues of *American Splendor* so that she would know just how terribly important it was for him to just be out as much as possible. And she read them and she understood him. The treatment that he chose was the one that appeared best for him at the time. A couple of things went wrong during treatment, the most painful being when he contracted shingles which often happens to AIDS patients. It's a real painful kind of blistering that you can't do much about.

DG: This is told vividly in the comic book.

JB: Yeah. Yeah. There's another thing I didn't tell Harvey at the time. When I was taking care of his blisters, one of them burst. This is like *herpes zoroaster*, I think they call it. The fluid squirted up under my glasses into my eyes and I just ran out to the bathroom and started flooding my eyes because I remember thinking, "My god, I'm going to get herpes blisters all over my eyes." I called the doctor and she told me what kind of medicine to take and he didn't hear that until later. But that gave me a lot greater appreciation for the things that health care professionals who work with infectious diseases have to do. These are sometimes high risk jobs when you talk about people getting AIDS from needle sticks and stuff like that. On the other hand, we had it really easy because we knew that with Harvey's cancer—it was lymphoma—he had an 85 percent chance that he would respond well with treatment and go into some form of remission. And then after that, hopefully, be cured, or if not, keep the cancer under control. That was . . . you know . . . I guess what I'm trying to say is that we're living in a time when having lymphoma and having cancer is not the worst thing that can happen to you. There are other things that happen, things people do to each other, that are worse.

DG: This is really, it seems to me, what the book is all about. Of course the focus is the story of Harvey's cancer treatment really, and your caretaking role, but there are many sort of subplots and parallel stories in it, the sum total of which is a look at how people treat one another— exactly as you describe it—also about having a sense of power and powerlessness as well. Joyce, you seem to be a person who's very intent on putting yourself in a position of power in whatever situation you're in— in a healthy way—I mean you want to have information, you want to feel that the people who're building your shelves are doing it properly, you want to be informed about medication, and that sort of thing . . .

JB: Well, that actually comes out of a sense of intense powerlessness. I'm from a large family that had it rough for a bit. We had some very serious medical problems, so I grew up fighting with doctors, or arguing, negotiating, things like that. But the real power that Harvey and I both had was that we're educated people who had the experience of being able to articulate questions. We were used to being listened to, used to being answered; we felt it was all right to challenge doctors' opinions. This has got to deal with education; this has got to deal with self-confidence; this has got to deal with class background, money, whatever. When Harvey was diagnosed, I knew to doublecheck the diagnosis, [I knew] that I could request the slides from the pathology lab be examined by other doctors. That's a kind of a confidence not everybody has. You see a lot of other people are brought up to just listen to what a doctor says, or to not even mention things because they don't want to appear to be any trouble. Our primary doctor, our oncologist, was a wonderful person in that she tried to get to know her patient, she listened. I think in the book I say she'd never take her eyes off Harvey, but she would always hear my questions. We were able to go through this together. I was able to go to all of his chemotherapy sessions. I knew to write down notes, carry a tape recorder if I had to. Not everybody has that as a choice. That's what's really hard. If it was this hard for us, and we were sort of prepared for it, what's it like for other people who aren't used to being listened to?

DG: Well, stories of illness seem to be rarely told except from one family member to another. It's interesting that it really is sort of a field of stories, a world of stories, that exists just within families . . .

JB: Well, see, we use "world of stories' too. Women expect their lives to be interrupted for biological reasons, medical reasons, things like that.

It's the guys that really have trouble getting knocked off track or talking to each other. It's just like there are lots and lots of books out there
about women and breast cancers, but I'm waiting for the guys to start
talking about those scrotums, those groins. You get cancer there too,
guys.

DG: I can't claim to have read a lot of medical literature or how to
books, but it does seem that if cancer is the topic of the book, the purpose is not only to tell a story, but to inform or to guide. For example,
you make reference in *Our Cancer Year* to those books that speak of
positive imaging and that sort of thing and they present sort of a meth-
odology to a reader who's looking for guidance, I guess. But your book
doesn't do that.

HP: No, it doesn't. And it's not supposed to. It was written about events
that happened to me and to Joyce in 1990 and '91. It's sort of a joint
autobiography and I would have written about *whatever* happened to
me in those years. And beyond that, I'm no expert on cancer. Maybe I'm
an expert on my own experience, but that's about all I can claim. I don't
feel like I'm in a position to guide other people because there's so many
different forms of cancer, so many different treatments. Just grouping all
these illnesses under one word, you know "cancer," may even be a mistake. I think that if there's anything that might be of interest to people
who are affected by cancer, either as patients or as caretakers, it's that
you don't have to be a hero to get through. Very often, people who
write about getting over some disease or other, sort of make themselves
look like heroes, maybe inadvertently. But certainly I was no hero. Certainly I acted badly. I panicked. I gave Joyce a great deal of trouble. But I
still got through. I dunno, maybe some people think that I didn't deserve
to get through. But I got through anyway. You can do that. And I think
a lot of people have the same kind of difficulties as me, and maybe can
take comfort from the fact I got through despite the fact that I was no
hero.

JB: You talked about positive thoughts and positive imagery. I was familiar, because a sister gave me a copy, with Bernie Siegel, who talks about
the importance of thinking positively. This is where some of this guided
imagery stuff comes from. I have no problem with anything he writes
in his books; I think he's a pretty insightful and compassionate guy. It's
the people who buy the books and give them to you when you're sick
that I have problem with because it feels like what they're saying is,

"You're depressed and you're afraid. That bothers me. I'm going to give you a book so that you will understand the importance of being cheerful, which is the way *I* want you to be, so *I* don't have to feel affected by what you're going through."

Now, because *Our Cancer Year* is also about everything else that happened to us that year, because the world doesn't stop spinning when you get diagnosed, it's also about the Persian Gulf War. I'd been in the Middle East just when that was getting started working with Israeli and Palestinian teenagers who were working towards reconciliation and staying in a house in Ramat Gan. I was in regular contact with the family I stayed with over there. I guess to give you an idea of what it was like for us, I actually did get so damn desperate one time that I decided I would get all the damn Marx Brothers movies on video for Harvey and play them and stuff like that. You know, do the Norman Cousins thing. But we also had like Stormin' Norman because what happened was we popped the cassette in the TV, there's this little moment while our VCR gets going and the TV heats up and bam, there they were on the news announcing the first Scud missiles had been sent and were hitting in Israel. They mistakenly reported that first time that poison gas was in fact being used. I just went through the ceiling—screaming, crying, doing that stuff and then they're playing "Hooray for Captain Spaulding" in the background and stuff. That stuff didn't really work for us very well.

DG: Well, you show that moment in the book and it's a very effective one. But neither is the book a condemnation of that sort of thing because there's another very dramatic moment in the book. Chapter nine is quite a doozy.
JB: You're gonna have to tell us what's in chapter nine. [laughs]

DG: The art and everything comes together there to be highly dramatic I think.
JB: I'm going to look at it and see . . .

DG: And it may be in that chapter that Harvey seems to be at his most uncomfortable, yet you say you're frustrated that the medicine is nothing better than aspirin.
JB: Yeah, it wasn't working for the pain and so I just started telling him that it was working.

DG: That it was the strong stuff . . .

JB: I lied. I told him I was giving him some super-morphine or something that was gonna work. I dunno . . . Harvey, did it? Did you fall for that line actually? [laughs]

HP: Well, no, I could tell whether the stuff worked or not. The one thing that I think you did that was kind of nice was that I used to panic when my blood count wasn't high enough to get treatment. I wanted to get it over with. And there were some weeks when I couldn't get treated because my blood count wasn't high enough. It wasn't safe for me.

JB: His white [blood cell] count . . .

HP: Yeah, my white count. It wasn't safe for me to get treated . . .

DG: And you thought you were losing time.

HP: Yeah, I just thought this is prolonging the agony, and so what Joyce did was, she got the doctor to give me something intravenously so that I would feel that I was making some progress.

DG: So you felt you were being treated.

HP: Yeah.

JB: It was so physically draining. This is Cleveland, this is a brutal winter to get him up, it's hard for him to walk, he's got sores, he has to give blood and wait for an hour and a half only to be told, "I'm sorry we can't treat you this week because your white count is down and it wouldn't be safe." I asked the doctor—I told you she was a great listener—I said, "What's he usually have in his chemotherapy bag? So I can tell him the truth." And I said, "We're gonna give you some of what's normally in the bag," because there's often something besides just the drugs. I guess that's typical of the reasons why we love that particular doctor because she wasn't afraid to bend the rules for us and do something like that. And the other thing—she wasn't afraid to say when she made a mistake. Where she went wrong on this was to tell Harvey that it was a twelve-week treatment and she didn't tell him that no patient that she'd ever heard of—maybe there was one out there—had it in twelve weeks because it was so harsh. They usually had to be hospitalized at the end and everything else. Harvey just got the idea that since it wasn't on twelve weeks, that he wasn't making any progress and was never going to get better. So she'll never make that mistake again.

DG: In the book you show her realizing it's a twelve-treatment process . . .
JB: Yeah, exactly. She just changed it. She was willing to say she made a mistake. You don't find that in a lot of doctors these days.

DG: Well, there's something for doctors to learn from reading your book as well. Is it available in conventional bookstores as well as comic book stores?
JB: It's supposed to be, but we've got a problem. It's a book about cancer, it's an autobiography, it's also a book about a particular time . . .

DG: So where do they file it?
JB: Next to Garfield the cat anthologies which is really a little bit scary, because remember we were talking about positive energy, so all of those patients who are going and getting *The Simpsons* anthologies and stuff are picking it up expecting it to be jokes—a bit of the "Lighter Side" about cancer. I'm not so sure that cancer patients who are newly diagnosed should be reading this book at that particular point in their treatment. The first thing you really want is you want a book about what kind of drugs to take. Odds, strategy, that information. It's only later I think that you should read a book like we wrote.

DG: Of course it's a book with a lot of meaning and a lot of power for anyone who perhaps, thank god, has nothing to do with cancer.
JB: Yeah, but we all have friends and family and we'll be called on to support them. It's a good book for caretakers, I think.

DG: Yes. Let's talk a little bit about the art, the drawings in *Our Cancer Year*. I think conventionally readers think of the artist in a comic book as being the star of the show. It's what gets the attention. The art is what people become fans of. And yet, Harvey Pekar, you're a writer of comic books, and you are, in a sense, the focus of it. The art here did not grab me right away. The art is by Frank Stack, but I've come to be fascinated by it and really enjoy it. It is sort of casting against type. His work is rather sketchy as compared to conventional comic book art where the reader expects every little detail to be rendered carefully. We're used to a very sort of literal image in comic books. That's not the case with Frank Stack.
HP: Yes, that's true although Frank is capable of, and has done, very detailed drawings. Unfortunately he's kind of an artist's artist who people have to . . . some people at least . . . have to familiarize themselves with a bit to appreciate. But he's, I think, one of the greatest comic book illustrators, and also an outstanding writer, of the past fifty years. He was the first underground cartoonist. He used to go by the pseudonym Fool-

bert Sturgeon and published the first underground comic book in 1961, *The Adventures of Jesus*.

JB: Soon to be followed by my favorite, *Jesus Goes to a Faculty Party*.

HP: Yeah, well, speaking about that, Frank is currently, and has been for years, a professor of art at the University of Missouri, and as I said, he has great technical equipment and can draw very detailed pictures if he wants to, but he chooses not to, sometimes at least, especially in the comic book medium. His work is influenced by Impressionism and to an extent by Degas . . .

JB: Frank is a guy who can really drawing feeling. He's just got that sort of sensitivity. He knows when

BE CAUSE I WORK SO HARD FOR THE VETERANS ··· THAT GIVES ME THE STRENGTH OF TEN.

THE END

Frank Stack's depiction of Pekar as a knight in "Veteran's Rights," reprinted in *The Best of American Splendor*, p. 190.

to bring you close to something and when to pull away from it. He came to stay with us for a period of time . . .

DG: Was he there during the illness?

JB: No, he came afterwards. Our doctor let us take over the chemotherapy lab in the part of the hospital where Harvey was treated and we had to stage all of these different shots again so he would know how these went. And we found that we were getting flashbacks. We're getting shakes and stuff like that.

DG: You were reenacting this horrible experience . . .

JB: You know, strapping Harvey to a chair and stuff. And Frank . . . I think we said in the book, it was kind of like being tailed by *National Geographic* because when he was at home following us around, he'd like move towards us. He was always drawing, drawing us sitting down, arguing—we do a lot of arguing—get all the different angles of us arguing, but also, just posing a few of the shots. He's got this deep accent and I kind of got used to him saying, "Ahhl raaaght, nahhh I need to haaave Haaahvey collapse on the right side. Can you have him fall down again?" I don't think we could have done it with anybody who didn't

have the easy good humor and life experience . . . I'd even say wisdom
that Frank has, because he made it comfortable.

HP: Well, I'd like to go on with what I was saying by mentioning that
the effect of the Impressionistic influence on Frank was to make him
use, in many in instances, texture instead of line and that accounts for
what some people might think of as a lack of detail. In some respects,
his drawing *is* quite spare, but he has a gift of focusing on the essential
things. This is something that not only I think, but has been pointed out
by other people in letters to me, praising Frank's work. Frank is on the
essential, at the same time sort of eschewing detail that doesn't *need* to
be in there. I think if the book has a strong impact on them, I think that
they can pretty much safely say that, whether they realize it or not, that
they like Frank's work.

DG: This, I guess, gets back to the whole concept of why write a story of
this kind, or any story, in the form of a comic book? What, for you, is it
that the combination of words and pictures can do that just words can't?

HP: Well, I mean it can do the same as a combination of words and pictures in film and television. The words and pictures support and supplement each other. It's just that in film, it's moving pictures and spoken
word and in comic books it's still pictures and written words.

JB: People who ask us . . . they keep asking, "Why comics?" and I guess
the implied thing is always, "What good reasons can you come up to
justify doing comics?"

DG: I'm not asking for a justification.

JB: Ok, well, because we've heard a lot of this, well, "How would it
have been if it had been a real book?" This is a real book. This is real. It's
what we do. This is the way we think. This is what we do. Some people
make music. Some people make photographs. At this point we make
comics. My reasons are different in many ways than Harvey's. I'm often
taking stuff that people don't want to hear about. It's the kind of thing
that a small politically active press might be able to sell a book on for
5,000 [copies], but *Real War Stories* #1 was 65,000 copies that got out
and read. It's like making a documentary I suppose, except you don't
have to hire a helicopter to go find a jungle.

DG: And you wouldn't if you could? Or would you?

HP: *I* wouldn't.

JB: See, I would try everything because I'm that kind of a person. Sure,
I'd go for it. Why not? Why not?

HP: I don't see any hierarchy in the arts. I think comics, as I have said, are certainly on a level with film and with television and they can do as much and they can do it as intensely. As a matter of fact, *American Splendor* has been dramatized on more than one occasion. In theaters in Los Angeles, where Dan Castellaneta played me actually; that's the voice of Homer Simpson. He's a very fine actor. Previously he had been with Tracy Ullman on a really outstanding television show. And also it's been done as a play in Lancaster, Pennsylvania, and Washington.

JB: The Arena Stage in Washington . . .

HP: Yeah, right. And I also have signed two film options. One expired and I signed another one. I'm not excited about the idea . . . I mean at least excited from an aesthetics viewpoint . . . about the idea of *American Splendor* being made into a movie or a theatrical production because comics are my medium, and they are more interesting and stimulating to me than other art forms, partly because there's so much left to be done in the form.

DG: And it would seem that perhaps a movie would be the wrong scale for these stories.

HP: Well, I don't know . . .

JB: Ask us again later because the people we're working with now, they're intelligent, they're clued-in, they're creative. They've had some success, but we've had so much to deal with these past couple of years, I don't know what we'll be thinking about in two years. Anything's possible for us now because Harvey's in remission. He's doing really well. He's out of pain. It's like stuff is opening up for us again.

HP: The movie, by the way, is a project that involves Bernt Capra who directed a film called *MindWalk*, that some people might be aware of out there, starring Liv Ullmann.

JB: And Sam Waterston and John Heard. He's Fritjof Capra's brother. He's Austrian . . . and just an all-around nice guy whether it gets made or not. It's just a great experience to sit down and talk ideas with people. You know, we live in Cleveland. We don't have little pockets of intellectuals gathering at every corner.

DG: Like we do here in New York. [laughs]

JB: Oh, I'm sure you do. Yeah, I'm sure you do. I'll tell you the relationship between New York and Cleveland. We are the people that all those anorexic vampires with their little black miniskirts and their black leather jackets come to with their video cameras to document Rust Belt chic. MTV people knocking on our door, asking to get pictures of Harvey emptying the garbage, asking if they can shoot footage of us going bowling. But we don't go bowling, we go to the library, but they don't want to shoot that. So, that's it. We're just basically these little pulsating jugular veins waiting for you guys to leech off some of our nice, homey, backwards Cleveland stuff.

HP: I am, I am, I should mention, a file clerk. That's how I make my living—a file clerk at the VA hospital in Cleveland, so that's why people are attracted to my working class life, I guess.

DG: Well, that's the life that you've chosen to tell us all about.

HP: That's right. It's the only one I know about too.

DG: [laughs] *Our Cancer Year* is now available, and it's a very powerful book. It's a comic book in form; in content, it's not what you're used to from that medium, but it uses the medium well and it's a fascinating read for anyone closely or tangentially or anyway associated with illness which I guess means everyone alive.

JB: Um-hmm. Everybody's got a story, right. We're talking about it as a cancer book, but the bottom line is it's really a book about marriage.

DG: Yes.

JB: There's other things happening. We're buying a house and we're talking about why wouldn't the shelves work properly and stuff like that. Our entire life had been put in boxes and then turned upside down by the cancer and everything else that was going on to us.

DG: Well, I hope a bunch of people out there can get a copy of this book and read it because as Joyce is speaking just now about the sub-story of buying the house and everything, that reminds me about several strata to the story that we haven't even covered and couldn't hope to. They're best covered simply by reading the book and getting the full dimension of that interesting story.

Now Harvey, you're going to help us share some music with the audience, right?

HP: Sure, if I'm asked.

DG: You're asked.

HP: I'll be more than happy to.

DG: Thank you, Joyce.

JB: I'm going.

HP: Yeah, I'll you see you in a bit.

DG: Okay, so Harvey Pekar, in addition to writing *American Splendor* his comic book that has been published annually since the mid-'70s, has been writing jazz criticism longer than that.

HP: Yes, I started in 1959 with the *Jazz Review*, a very fine, maybe the best, magazine that I've ever written for in terms of coverage of jazz.

DG: How long did that last?

HP: It only lasted about three years, but it was a wonderful publication. It was founded by Martin Williams, who went on to make quite a name for himself in the field as the director of the Jazz Studies program at the Smithsonian Institution and Nat Hentoff who's more well known now as a columnist for the *Village Voice*, a civil rights and civil liberties colum-nist. And then I wrote in the '60s for *Downbeat*, and I wrote for *Coda*, and I wrote for a couple of English magazines, the *Jazz Journal* and *Jazz Monthly*. I wrote for . . . *Coda* is in Canada. I had something published in the *Evergreen Review*. I quit writing about jazz for about fifteen years, then I started again recently.

DG: Why did you quit?

HP: I quit because it was . . . to tell you the truth, first of all, I was re-ally burned out. Second of all, I was on reviewing staffs and things like that, and I was assigned to re-view records that I wasn't inter-ested in writing about. Sometimes they were bad, and I don't enjoy putting people down, and a lot of other times, they were just so-so and I didn't really want to talk about them, because there wasn't really that much to say that hadn't been said before. Now, since I've gone back to doing it, I can choose the material I want to write about and I frequently will call up mu-sicians to talk to them about the

Pekar was getting tired of reviewing uninteresting jazz al-bums, as shown by Greg Budgett and Gary Dumm in "The Day Before The Be In," reprinted in *American Splendor* (Ballantine).

cds because I really like to write in specific musical terms rather than im-pressionistically. So if I like something, I'll call up someone and ask him, "What's the structure of this tune, and what meter are you using here?

Is the improvisation here based on chord changes or not?" That's very helpful and I guess it's very, very seldom done because the people I talk to are very often kind of amazed, taken aback, that anyone would take the trouble to do that. I guess one of the reasons is that so much music criticism in general is impressionistic and does not deal with the music in specific terms.

DG: It is odd that the musicians are not often asked to comment about it, because I'm sure rather than reading another review of their work that misunderstands it, they'd really welcome the opportunity to clarify it, if someone's interested.

HP: Yeah, sure, it's a shame that more people aren't interested because it's mutually beneficial. It helps the musician, it helps people understand why their music is significant or unique, and it helps me be a better critic.

DG: So what inspired you to get back into writing about jazz, and maybe you could suggest that we hear something now of that kind?

HP: Well, I actually started out by writing about a band called the Jazz Passengers which is an outstanding experimental band here in New York. It just so happened that coincidentally I knew one of the co-founders of Jazz Passengers and co-leaders, Roy Nathanson, a brilliant saxophonist. He also plays the clarinet. I'd known him through a friend of his actually, and I didn't really realize it until I started to hear the Jazz Passengers re-cords, that Roy was into avant-garde experimentation. But when I heard the stuff, I was just very, very impressed. So I started writing about him, and I had been reviewing books at the time, and I just kept on broad-ening my horizons. I think that meeting John Zorn was a real revelation. I'm very, very impressed with John's music. I think he's one of the major figures to emerge in music, in any field, in the past twenty-five years or so. And then through John, I met a wonderful trumpet player-composer by the name of Dave Douglas who certainly deserves far, far more rec-ognition than he's gotten. And Tim Burns—I got very interested in this so-called New Music. This music that's being created as we speak which involves musicians not only synthesizing various forms of music, but actually going beyond that to create new types of music which have their own characteristics. It's like when you compare a compound to a mixture in chemistry. A mixture can be separated out into its individual parts, but a compound takes on characteristics of its own and that's what I think some of this New Music is. It has its own characteristics. It truly is New Music, just as jazz was new music at one time although drawn from a variety of early sources like various forms of pop music and African American music and ragtime.

DG: And now jazz itself is one of the strands that are being woven together.
HP: That's right, although it may continue to have its own identity. That's fine with me, because it's certainly got a distinguished history and is the form of music I'm most interested in.

[The rest of the interview was not transcribed as it focused on discussing specific musical groups while playing musical selections from them.]

Pekar for Beginners

Joel Greenlee / 1996

From *The Brownstone Letters* #104
(May 23, 1996).

For those of you who are unaware of Harvey Pekar and his ground-breaking comic, *American Splendor* . . . shame on you! Not only is it the best thing to come out of Cleveland since the traffic light, but it serves as inspiration for a whole slew of comic artists like Los Bros. Hernandez, Alan Moore, Aline Kominsky, R. Crumb, and Dennis P. Eichhorn. His slice-of-life autobiographical style of writing paints a vivid picture of a man living in a world that he has no control over. It's modern day Cleveland, folks, and in his comics we see how one man lives through it.

JG: Can we have a brief history of *American Splendor*?
HP: I've known about comics for a real long time. As a kid in the forties, I read them a lot, but I quit reading them about the time I went into ju-

nior high school. I had outgrown them, or at least I thought I did. I did outgrow the mainstream comics of that day, but what I didn't realize is that there's absolutely nothing wrong with the form. The form was as good an art form as any.

In 1962 I met Robert Crumb and saw what he was doing in comics. Crumb was a neighbor of mine in Cleveland. It got me thinking "anything can be done in comics." So I decided to do stuff myself. I theorized about it for a number of years and in 1972 I actually started writing comics when Crumb was over my house. He, along with an artist friend of his named Rob Armstrong, illustrated some things for me. That started a few things that got published.

In a few years, things weren't going really fast. I had written a whole bunch of stories and there wasn't any place to put them. The counterculture that supported alternative comics was fading. So I decided to put out my own book even if I had to take a substantial loss. So that's what I did. I started to publish a book out of my own savings. In 1976, I started publishing *American Splendor* and I've been doing it ever since.

I've been a writer since 1959, getting stuff published about jazz. I've never made a living off of being a writer, though. As far as making a living, I've been a file clerk at the V.A. hospital for thirty years.

JG: Have you always published your own work? Doesn't Dark Horse publish you now?
HP: What happened was I got sick so I quit publishing. I had an issue that was ready to go out, but I was too messed up to publish it. So I checked around and Tundra said that they would do it. Then Dark Horse picked it up and they've been doing it ever since. I've done four issues with them.

JG: How do you feel about the comics industry today?
HP: I don't pay much attention to the industry, there are some good comics out there. A couple of guys that do work for me, Frank Stack and Joe Sacco, put out great comics. They're terrific. There are others out there too. I just don't follow the scene all that closely. Big companies like Marvel and DC have nothing to do with the stuff I'm doing. It's the same form, but the content of their material is much different than what I'm doing. It's like saying that just because I write prose I should keep up with every prose writer out there. People wouldn't ask me that if I was known as a prose writer.

I just hope that alternative comics make it. I kind of got disgusted with all of the politics of the scene. That's why I just don't bother with it anymore. I just do my stuff and that's it.

JG: Would you like to tell us about *Our Cancer Year*?
HP: That's a book that came out of my having cancer. It was written with my wife, Joyce (*Real War Stories, Activists*) Brabner. This is a book, like all of my other comics, that is autobiographical. In a way, I'm writing one big autobiography and these individual issues are just installments of it.

So I wrote about having cancer in *Our Cancer Year*. I would have written about anything that happened to me in 1990–91. So I wrote about what happened to me. My wife added a very valuable section about what it was like to deal with people who have it. As with my other work, I try to make it as realistic as possible. I don't try to idealize myself. I was really scared when I had cancer and I wasn't heroic about it at all. I think that's the way a lot of people react to having it.

It's a novel-size book, about 226 pages, illustrated by Frank Stack. It's a nice book.

JG: You stated earlier that the comics business doesn't influence you. What does?
HP: Prose writers have really influenced me, a whole lot of them. I've been reading prose for a long time before I started writing comics and a lot of them influenced me. It's kind of hard to sort it out. I remember being impressed by certain types of writing like that of Dostoevski, James Joyce, and Daniel Fukes. I think all of these writers are very good. As far as autobiographical work is concerned, Henry Miller is the one who really got me into that. Sometimes he can be a real wind bag, but the general style he used was good.

JG: Is there anything we can expect from Harvey Pekar in the next couple of years?
HP: This project that I've embarked upon, which is the writing of *American Splendor*, is what I'm using to evolve my writing style. I'll try to deal with new subject matter, but there are themes in my life (like everybody's) that are like ongoing stories.

Right now, one of my goals is to retire from work. I'm fifty-six years old and I got over thirty years in at the V.A., working for the federal government. I can qualify for pension, but when you retire at fifty-five, you get 55 percent and that's not enough for me. So I have to build up other sources of income. That will keep me going until I'm sixty-two when I can collect my social security. I'll collect two pensions, one from civil service and one from social security.

I've also been writing a lot about jazz recently. I just did something for *Jazziz* about swing as an element of jazz. There's a controversy whether music that doesn't swing can be called jazz. I also write for a number of other publications like the *Boston Herald*, the *Village Voice*, the *Free Times* here in Cleveland and about ten other publications. I'm just trying to keep busy . . . I guess you can say that's what's shaking with me.

Another Survivor's Tale:

The Harvey Pekar Interview

Jim Ottaviani and Steve Lieber / 1997

From *Hogan's Alley*, vol. 1, no. 4 (1997),
pp. 117–25. Reprinted by permission of
Jim Ottaviani.

David Mazzucchelli, in the winter 1995 issue of *Crash*, captured the
feelings of a lot of erstwhile comics readers: "People who've read comics as kids and gave them up . . . are apt to see something in comic-book
form and just say: 'Oh, I know what comics are,' and not want to spend
time with it. No one I know goes to a movie theatre and says, 'I know
what movies are. I don't want to see this.'"

Harvey Pekar has spent the last twenty years making sure that people who "know what comics are" don't. *American Splendor*, which
made its debut in 1976, is the medium's longest-running autobiographical series. Self-publishing until 1990, when his non-Hodgkins lymphoma
made this impossible, Pekar has written about his experiences as a record

collector, writer, street-corner comedian, and working stiff at a Cleveland VA hospital. *American Splendor* has maintained an underground
feel by sticking to newsprint, featuring artists like R. Crumb, Spain, and
Frank Stack and by suffering from spotty distribution.

Joyce Brabner, who married Pekar on their third date, has even less
name recognition in the comics world than her husband, although she
has worked with many of its highest-profile writers and artists. She edited Eclipse's *Real War Stories*, which brought Mike W. Barr, Steve Bis-
sette, Brian Bolland, Rebecca Huntington, Paul Mavrides, Dean Motter,
Denny O'Neil, and John Totleben (among others) together on behalf
of the Central Committee for Conscientious Objectors. Her work on
Brought to Light with Alan Moore and Bill Sienkiewicz brought everyone
involved critical praise from both the artistic and activist communities.

Pekar and Brabner collaborated on *Our Cancer Year*, the longest
chapter of *American Splendor* yet. It ties Pekar's illness with Brabner's
activist concerns, and as she says, they "argued unsuccessfully with our
publisher about tagging it as 'health/autobiography' but we ended up in
the graphic novels/sci-fi and humor ghetto again." Though not a bleak
and depressing book, *Our Cancer Year* is neither humorous nor (science)
fictional. But like Art Spiegelman (whose *Maus* was initially placed on the
bestselling fiction list) Pekar and Brabner work hard to shake both their
readers and their publishers out of comfortable assumptions. Though it
doesn't benefit from the same superb production values as *Maus*, *Our
Cancer* Year is also a survivor's tale that has stood on its own outside of
comic-book specialty stores. —Jim Ottaviani

Jim Ottaviani: There are some contractual-obligation questions to ask,
but I don't feel like starting with any of them, so . . .
Joyce Brabner: A radio talk-show host asked me our favorite question so
far, "How did it feel, Joyce, in the middle of your ordeal, to know that
someday it would all be just a comic book?" Go ahead and ask that one.

Ottaviani: So, Joyce, how did it feel, in the middle of your ordeal, to
know that it was just going to end up some lousy comic book?
Brabner: Well, it wasn't going to end up a lousy comic book because,
of course, we're committed to graphic art [laughter]. But the new story
line, the post–*Our Cancer Year* story, has me inheriting a cosmetics empire, committing a couple of undetected murders as I claw my way to
the top, and then, with all that money, I get to wear suits with shoulder
pads [laughter].

Ottaviani: That sounds really good, unless you're going to do animal testing. You know, Berke Breathed's "Mary Kay Commandos" . . .
Brabner: Listen, that's what some of my next comics are going to be about. Mark Badger and I are doing a series of animal-rights comics.

Ottaviani: Seriously? You want to say something about that?
Brabner: Yeah, Harv, is that OK with you?
Harvey Pekar: Why not?
Brabner: Will you let me talk about my brilliant career?
Pekar: Can I stop you?
Brabner: I was asked to do some comics by PETA [People for the Ethical Treatment of Animals]. Because I grew up dealing with serious illness, and because Harvey's had cancer, that's a difficult assignment. Opposing the use of animals to test consumer products is easy. We don't need more shampoos or oven cleaners. But, Mark has MS, multiple sclerosis. Someday, he might not be able to draw anymore. And Harvey could get sick again.

So because even the idea of looking at the use of animals for medical research made us uncomfortable, we decided that was a signal that maybe we'd better go forward and look even closer at what's going on.

We're writing about something young activists and med students will have to pull together and resolve—about why we need a far more compassionate, humane way of doing science.

So far, we've looked at incredible waste and cruelty, government contracts for tests that should never have been conducted to begin with—redundant experiments, tests that prove nothing or give people a false sense of security. PETA likes to use the drug thalidomide, which was animal tested, though researchers defend that by saying that not enough animals were tested.

A more objective source, a science writer named Deborah Blum, won a Pulitzer prize in 1992 for a series of newspaper articles that inspired her new book *The Monkey Wars*. She talks a good deal about how primate testing can create new viruses and cause epidemics or other hazards to human health. According to Richard Preston's *The Hot Zone*, the suburbs of Washington, D.C., just experienced a near-miss.

But, that's me just wading into the issue, entering at the point where I feel most comfortable. We would rather hack away at stuff that's in everybody's best interest to let go of first rather than confront our own self-interests.

Pekar: By "we," who do you mean?

Brabner: Mark. Me. But, on the other hand, who's the new vegetarian in the house, ever since I told you I wouldn't let you watch any of those animal-testing videos?

Pekar: Well, I don't want animal testing, and I'm not uncomfortable saying that.

Brabner: But, we've never looked to see if any of the drugs you took during chemo were developed through animal testing. Because we're afraid of what we would find even though we had no choice. Meanwhile, Mark's in line for clinical trials. He wants very much for a new drug to be tested on him.

Ottaviani: Do you see any polarizing issues on the horizon, ones that will clearly divide the pro-testing/anti-testing community? For instance, I would've thought that AIDS might've done it.

Brabner: Remember, this is still stuff I'm learning about. The world is running out of excuses. Animals that think, feel, and communicate still suffer because most people are convinced that's necessary, even when they understand that pain, captivity, and murder are wrong. Who else could we test? Only terrible people? Someone in jail? Well, I worked with people in prison for nine years. I know about coercion. I know who can and can't give informed consent. On the street, I've seen people sell blood.

Years ago, my sister dated this anorexic punk with a blue mohawk and a bad attitude who got paid as a test subject. He would just sit in a chair all day while they shot him up and now he's even more f—ed up than he was before.

Do we use people in comas they're not going to return from, people who are brain dead? Why don't more people list themselves as organ donors? Every day, healthy people die suddenly. Why pursue an entire line of experiments that end with killing a baboon for a heart transplant?

Ottaviani: Did experimental drugs figure into *Our Cancer Year?*

Brabner: Harvey's doctor was interviewed about the book in the *Journal of the National Cancer Institute* where she was "outed" as Dr. Ruth Streeter. We called her "Dr. Rhodes." She told the writer Harvey was treated before they started using a drug that would have done a lot to minimize the suffering he experienced during immunosuppression, when he was blistered all over and trying to sleep on the palms of his hands and on his knees.

He felt so bad, he wanted to die and would have swallowed any-thing on the chance that it might help. But, it's usually the people who face worse odds than Harvey did who go right into clinical trials for cancer.

Getting into clinical trials can be competitive. Mark's still waiting. A lot of times, that has to do with manufacturing costs or legal costs. And then there's how important we think people like AIDS patients are.

In *Our Cancer Year* we have two queer (and nameless) friends who sort of turned their apartment into a shelter for AIDS patients. In the early '80s, they organized a bunch of gay potheads and med students who made trips in and out of the country through Mexico, smuggling in drugs patients couldn't get here until much later, when it became clear AIDS wasn't just a "gay" disease.

I can't sit here and say that Harvey's alive because this rat died, or . . . [laughter] The real reason that Harvey's alive is because we're edu-cated people with access to good health care. We know how to ask questions, when to get help, and how to follow instructions. We had very good health insurance because Harvey is a VA hospital file clerk. Everything, except for the costs of the visiting nurse that were picked up by Harvey's brother, cost us only a couple hundred dollars each year be-cause our benefits made all doctor visits free.

Steve Lieber: So you didn't have a crippling deductible or anything at-tached to all this?

Brabner: No. The crippling deductible is the stub on his paycheck. It's what they take out or underpay him. Harvey's been earning the second-lowest government pay rate for, like, thirty years, Harv?

Pekar: Uh, it'll be thirty years at the end of January.

Brabner: The big thing is that we knew we had to take that lump in his groin seriously. When we talked to doctors, we believed that we were entitled to treatment. And when you think you're entitled to good treat-ment, then you fight for it. You know, a lot of other patients are just paralyzed with fear or not sure what to do. Sometimes it's a class thing. An education thing.

Some people think doctors are better than they are. I mean, to Har-vey doctors are f— -ups who lose the file charts he's paid to find and shelve [laughter].

Lieber: How difficult was it to get past that doctor aura and summon up what it takes to fight with them?

Pekar: I work with them, and, I mean, I don't say I have contempt for them or anything like that. But there are varying levels of competence and varying levels of humanity, obviously.

Brabner: And obviously negotiation was much better than combat. I mean, you can't negotiate with some people, like the nurse who just stepped right over us when Harvey was on the floor, crying and screaming. But his oncologist was always open to any ideas about what might make things better. And she was willing to admit when she made mistakes and learn from us. That's why we trusted her.

She used to tell patients like Harvey that his particular combination of drugs for chemotherapy was "a twelve-week treatment." She now calls it a "twelve-part treatment" because no one gets through it that fast. It's too hard on your body. But when Harvey felt he was behind schedule, he panicked. He thought he would never get well.

Ottaviani: Harvey, you've done *American Splendor* since 1976, to a whole lot of acclaim. But both you and Joyce have written quite a lot of straight prose. Did you have to choose or negotiate the medium, or was it obvious that you wanted to tell this story in the comics format, or did you think about straight text?

Pekar: I never did. I don't think Joyce did either.

Brabner: No, and I wasn't even going to be involved with this until Harvey began working on it.

Pekar: No, I mean I look at comics as my main medium, and I don't look at various art forms as being ranked in a kind of hierarchy. I think comics are as good a medium as any other, and they are particularly interesting to me, and I never considered using any other medium.

Ottaviani: You do write in other media. You write essays, and . . .

Pekar: Yeah, I write essays, and I write a lot of music criticism, and I write a lot of book reviews.

Ottaviani: When did you decide to do the book?

Pekar: Myself, I figured if I got through it I was going to do it. I mean, I'm writing a continuing autobiography.

Ottaviani: How different did the book become once Joyce got involved?

Pekar: I initially thought I would write *Our Cancer Year* by myself, but I wanted to include Joyce's point of view. The result wound up being richer than it would've been if I'd done it alone.

Brabner: He had a lot of memory loss because of the medication and the stress.

Pekar: So I asked her about it and she suggested that she write part of it, and . . .

Brabner: It wasn't quite that polite [laughter]. It was like, "Look, I'm not writing this for you so you can put it in your book."

Pekar: But you have to admit I capitulated in a hurry.

Brabner: Yeah. Yeah . . .

Pekar: Discretion being the better part of valor . . .

Brabner: We only did that once before, and it was again with a story I didn't want him to get away with owning completely, the peculiar story of how we met and got married. We decided to get married the day we met. On our second date, we bought rings, and the third was when we tied the knot.

Ottaviani: I remember that panel! You're just about to meet each other and you've got all these R. Crumb and Gerry Shamray, and . . . [laughter]

Brabner: Yeah, I didn't know if he would turn out to be this hairy, sweating, stinking Crumb thing or Shamray's Marlon Brandoesque guy with a high forehead. Which I later discovered was a receding hairline.

The idea of opening *Our Cancer Year* up to what was going on the rest of the year—the Persian Gulf war, the kids I was working with, the comic book that I didn't do—that was something that I pushed into the mix. Harvey agreed very quickly, but other people attacked that. It started when an artist—not Frank Stack—looked at the script and said, "It's a shame more girls don't read comics, Harvey. This is a girl book." And there were snide comments about "Joyce's third-world politics" tainting Harvey's magnum opus.

Pekar: Well, they're my politics, too, and I wanted the book to be multi-themed. Initially I guess, I wanted to filter Joyce's experiences through me. That's how I thought I'd write it because I've written stuff like that before, you know, where I would interview people or talk to people and say, "How did you feel about this? How did you feel about that?"

Brabner: You've got to remember the nature of what went on with Harvey's illness. A lot of the same stuff kept happening over and over again. Days blurred together. And Harvey's already done these odes to boredom, about just being eroded by dailiness. Whereas I was mobile, I was able to walk, to go places, to react.

I think our publisher expected some kind of to-the-bone survival story, where Harvey rips the scab off cancer to expose the pain beneath.

JIM OTTAVIANI AND STEVE LIEBER / 1997   67

And these days, the honest-to-God truth is that while cancer is a pretty horrible experience, and for most people the worst thing that could happen to you, it's not the worst thing that happens to other people. Like, we never would've for a minute traded places with Dana while she waited for Scuds to fall, with her gas mask on. Or what Khim and Saroeum experienced under the Khmer Rouge.

Pekar: What's the worst thing that could happen to you, though? Cancer can kill you. So, I think most people would think that.

Brabner: Harvey's got one more year to go until he's pronounced "cured." Then his chances of having cancer will be the same as everyone else. Trouble is, one out of three people today will die of cancer.

Ottaviani: It's not very heartening to move it back to one in three.

Brabner: Yeah, he's working his way up to those odds.

Pekar: I don't want to depress you, Jim.

Ottaviani: Since you just mentioned Frank Stack, that leads to one of my next questions. How did it come about that you chose him? I don't think R. Crumb would have been appropriate for this, but he's one of the many artists I've admired who have worked with you. I'm thinking of Sue Cavey, Sean Carroll, and Val Mayerik, for instance. When I first heard you were going to do what became *Our Cancer Year*, the first name that came to mind was Gerry Shamray, for his really realistic style. But Steve has pointed out to me that this probably would have taken a lot of the humanity out of it.

Pekar: Well, I'll tell you, Frank Stack was the best choice I could have made. He was considering a sabbatical and very much wanted to do something like this.

Brabner: Frank is a fantastic artist who doesn't get a lot of credit.

Pekar: As a matter of fact, Robert Crumb told me that Frank was the best possible choice that we could have made. He and Pete Poplaski, I guess, were both talking about how good Frank is at sustaining visual interest. Jim Woodring said the same thing in a letter to us; they both really raved about his work.

Frank brings an intelligence, his own life experience to the book. Writing about sexuality, the loss of sexuality, losing body hair to chemotherapy . . . I used a myth. And Frank could draw that without making it look like some sword-and-sorcerer thing. He's not someone who learned anatomy from Steve Ditko.

Brabner: The guy can do anything, detailed photorealism or something impressionistic. He can use humor.

Frank Stack's cover to *Our Cancer Year.*

Ottaviani: Talking to Frank, we started by discussing the cover, which I really liked for a number of reasons. Though vibrant, it subtly introduces the emphasis on the daily struggles, personalities, and setting—the house, the yellow ribbon—of the book. He said that it's basically a pastel rough of what he intended to do over in, say, acrylics if you liked it. Apparently you liked it so much as is that he merely tightened up the figures a bit and went with it. Did you have something in mind before you saw Frank's cover? Why did this one strike you so?

Pekar: Joyce wrote and sketched out the cover. It was her idea, her concept.

Brabner: And we cheated a bit, because the trees our neighbors tied yellow ribbons around are actually a few feet outside the frame. This is the first we've heard about it being a rough Frank intended to do over but, if it was good enough for him, it's good enough for us.

The only thing I'd change about the cover would be to indicate on the back what *Our Cancer Year* is about. I argued unsuccessfully with our publisher about tagging it as "health/autobiography" but we ended up in the graphic novels/sci-fi and humor ghetto again.

Pekar: I like it fine.

Brabner: He was comfortable for us to work with. He took a lot of pains, listened to ideas, and made really intelligent choices. He paid attention to detail and worked with the reference materials we gave him.

Ottaviani: Did you take a lot of videotape while this was going on?

Pekar: No. Joyce had videos of some of the stuff that went on out of the country. Joe Sacco also helped with pictures from Palestine. Frank came and stayed with us for a while and we took over the hospital's chemo ward (with the assistance of our oncologist) late at night and staged a lot of shots.

Brabner: That wasn't too easy on us. They strapped Harvey into a chemo chair again and "hooked" him up to an IV. He started to get real green. Both our tempers were going. It was post-traumatic stress and Frank understood that. He's got a light touch, and knew when to make us laugh and when to step back.

Pekar: Well, you know he's been an art professor at the University of Missouri for many years. He used to be chairman of the department and has got an awful lot of, not only knowledge and intelligence, but talent and technical skill. When he wants to, he can draw real, real detailed photographically accurate portraits and landscapes.

His etchings, for instance, are great. But, on the other hand, his style's influenced by Impressionism, where you very often substitute texture for line. And so, his drawing in some ways is pretty economical and spare. And I think—you can correct me if I'm wrong—Steve pointed out how good he is at highlighting essential things. That's one of the things he did real well.

Lieber: Frank handled different sequences in very different manners. How much direction did you give him on the really subjective sequences?
Pekar: Not a lot. I've worked with Frank long enough to realize that he's really a consummate artist. I'm sure that we included some instructions to him, about what people looked like and stuff like that, and what settings were like. And he came to Cleveland and we actually showed him the stuff so that he had an idea . . . But as far as what style of drawing . . . You'll notice that he would draw more or less detailed panels. That was up to him.

Ottaviani: In the opening of Chapter 7 he goes from very realistic to very expressionistic from one panel to another, and it's really striking.
Pekar: Yeah. There's an awful lot of meat in that. A lot of stuff he does is real subtle, at least for somebody that's not familiar with that kind of work. And unfortunately an awful lot of comic book fans aren't. Their idea of a really great artist is a guy like Frank Frazetta, drawing people who have big muscles, showing lots of detail.

Ottaviani: You were speaking of memory loss earlier. There are no page numbers in the book, which makes it hard to refer or go back to a certain specific spot. Which is how memory, or at least my memory, works—you can't just go right back and get a specific incident without getting other things close to and associated with it. Did you do this on purpose?
Pekar: No, Frank wrote page numbers on the pages. Our publisher didn't use them. So, the first printing was all screwed up. Frank not only wrote the page numbers down, he said "page such and such facing page such and such." But you know, whatever works I'll take credit for [laughter].

Lieber: I was really impressed at the range of moods he was able to create with light. And also without overloading the reader. I thought if every picture was brought to a full level of rendering, the whole thing would be a visually exhausting experience.

Brabner: When we're interviewed about the book, Harvey gets the most ink because he was the patient. Then me, because I'm the other "real" person and people can identify with us. Frank's often overlooked. Admittedly his research and development on the project wasn't as arduous as ours [laughter], but he deserves more attention.

When we started shaping the script, once we realized we were working with Frank we began to, in some ways, write for Frank. Stuff that we knew he could handle that other artists couldn't. I always tell people that *Our Cancer Year* is more a book about marriage, not cancer. As three married people working together, I'm not going to say quite that it's a "more mature" work, but . . .

Ottaviani: Do you read any of the current crop of writer/artists who do slice-of-life work?

Pekar: Yeah, any comics people send us.

Brabner: I like Mary Fleener's stuff an awful lot. I always have. And another person I consider "current crop" who is getting overlooked is Colin Upton. I think his insomnia story was terrific. He's got a great sense of humor. He knows history, confronts sexism, and I get pretty angry because people like him or Joe Sacco can't really make a living off of what they're doing.

Pekar: Yeah, I get pretty angry when I think I can't make a living off of it too. You know, I like a lot of the stuff I've seen by guys like Joe Matt and Chester [Brown] and a lot of people. I like Ed Brubaker's work . . .

Brabner: Generally speaking, though, we don't buy comics. We only read what people give us. Some of that's because we do so much reading anyway and a lot of books and records come into this house every week. But also, it's just that we don't really think to go into a comic book store for something to read. For me it gets back to a decision I made when I was seven. I realized that with twenty cents I could either buy two comics or get down to our library and back on the bus. And the Oz books were at the library . . .

Pekar: We got an advance copy of *Stuck Rubber Baby* by Howard Cruse. It's real good. I really haven't had time to read the entire thing because we went on a signing tour, you know, so we were out of town and I had a lot of work back up on me. I do a real lot of freelance writing. I'm just starting to get caught up.

Brabner: The person whose work I miss the most would be Dori Seda. I think women pull off autobiographical comics much better than a lot of male writers do. Maybe because they're writing about stuff that's interesting to me. I once half-seriously said I think that because women's comics aren't published as often, they spend a lot more time per panel. Someone like Leslie Sternbergh, all that detail!

It really bothers me when good people are not even acknowledged by the so-called independent-comics press and have to worry, "Can I afford to keep doing this? Can I afford to print my own stuff?" That makes me damn mad.

Ottaviani: This may be an economic artifact, but almost all this biographical/slice-of-life work has been in black and white. Given your druthers, would you rather work in color?
Pekar: No.
Brabner: I've worked in color. It influences storytelling, and I prefer to use color for shorter stories. I would always prefer to publish a longer book in black and white rather than spend the money on color processing.

Ottaviani: Why do you think self-publishing is good in comics, but perceived as bad in the prose, book-publishing industry? I mean, you probably don't give much thought to, or even receive, prose from the vanity presses. Is it perhaps the presence of ads for the rest of the line of books, making your work shill for other books, all in some house style of questionable artistic merit?
Pekar: Self-published comics, especially those viewed as artistically successful, are welcomed by some as striking a blow against the comic-book oligopoly of Marvel and DC. Plus, they're frequently alternative comics and appeal to alternative comic fans who have no use for superhero comics. By contrast there are more viable small-press "prose" publishers who don't really provide an alternative to genre work.
Brabner: Are vanity publishers even still around, now that we have desktop publishing and paperless publishing on the Internet? The lady who paid someone to publish memoirs of her poodle can now do the job herself. Your "prose, book-publishing industry" doesn't include art books, poetry chap books, etc., which are numbered and often prized because of their small print runs and where most self-published comics fit in.

I respect people who put their own money down and self-publish, because it means they respect their own work, they've crossed over past self-doubt, and they're working instead of watching. That matters to me.

Labeling certain comics "alternative" implies some other kind of art and writing sets all standards. It's also apologetic. People who say they read "alternative" comix-with-an-X are ashamed to be caught looking.

Lieber: I have a question about the structure of *Our Cancer Year*—obviously the order in which things happened makes a lot of the decisions for you. But how much went into outlining things and deciding what goes in, what gets left out?

Brabner: Want me to take that one, Harv?

Pekar: Yeah, go ahead and take it.

Brabner: I get to explain this because it's something I sort of invented when we got stuck. OK, Harvey writes all of his scripts as storyboards on photocopy paper that he divides into six squares. He lays the stuff out with little stick figures, but he also includes things like reflective pauses or reaction shots and stuff—he sort of choreographs. I write pretty conventional typed scripts.

Pekar: This wasn't difficult to write because it was painful. It was difficult to write because it was a large project and I had to work with somebody else on it. Just getting the structure of it together, and dealing with Joyce, and her dealing with me. It wasn't easy, and that's what caused the most difficulty for me, not the writing about the painful experience.

Brabner: We had problems writing about events we experienced together but interpreted very differently. Harvey had memory loss because of all the drugs and radiation. We weren't sure how to deal with that. And I think it was really hard to take all this in while still figuring out how to work together.

For instance, I didn't have any idea what happened to him the night he thought he was dying, when he thought the clock was running backwards until I saw what Harvey wrote. He must have been having lots of little blackouts while looking at the dial—it's digital. I thought maybe he took an overdose or something and that's what set me off. I began punching him.

It was also very uncomfortable looking backwards when learning to live post-cancer meant we really should have been putting that stuff behind us, instead of ripping it apart for dramatic content. So, when it got difficult I got a deck of index cards and we began to go in any direction, after any kind of a topic or question that came up. We would prompt each other: "What happened the first day you had radiation?" "What happened when you talked to your cousin?" "Tell me about your dreams."

Each card contained a sort of a beat: "Harvey's buddy came over/ and tried to tell Joyce how to take care of me/so Joyce got angry/she explained everything/she told him to go out and get some dope because she heard that helps with nausea and pain/Harvey couldn't figure out how to use a bong."

It was kind of like film, because a lot of movies are shot out of sequence. You just do all the scenes at one location. Then move to another set. Instead of film, we had cards we could put on the floor, like putting together a puzzle and there you'd see correspondences. Obviously it created a chronology, but there are different times when things are linked by theme. I guess the most obvious one is the baking soda and water—something that Harvey needed in his body at certain times to prepare him for chemotherapy. The same stuff Dana was told would save her if Saddam used poison gas and she was scared because all the kids knew that was bullshit although everyone had boxes of the stuff, just in case.

With the cards, something we could both pick up and move around, we had a way to put together an outline, then fleshed out into scenarios . . .

Ottaviani: Did each card became a panel?
Brabner: No, they were "beats": action or purpose. I'm not even sure people doing theater even say this anymore, I think it's Stanislavski. Or Viola Spolin.

It turned out that my skill was in assembling and stitching things together, collecting and finding commonality. I can link. But Harvey's the one who knows when to economize and he's got a much better ear for dialogue than I have. I may have remembered more things or said, "This belongs with this," but Harvey knows when to stop and when to start. Harvey knows when enough is enough.

Plus, there were things that happened to me that he had nothing to do with and vice versa. That's where we wrote independently. It's pretty clear in most of the book who wrote what, although from time to time I'll pick up a paper and read about some brilliant "Pekaresque" this, that, or the other and say, "Hey, I wrote that!" [laughter]

I'll be able to pawn off all sorts of unpublished Pekar when you're dead, hon.
Pekar: No doubt. You're welcome to it.

Lieber: One of the things I really liked about it was the way things would interweave between the objective stuff—the two of you together at the doctor—to the much more subjective materials. We referred before to your Scottish legends part as an instance of Frank Stack not making it into sword and sorcery. Or the really nightmarish sequence where Harvey's losing his sense of time. I imagined the placement of a lot of that was just trying to figure out where the rhythm of the story wanted it.

Brabner: Yeah. We paid attention to how we found ourselves telling other people about what happened. Which is kind of how Harvey started doing *American Splendor*. He started out as kind of a street-corner comedian and would tell the same story over and over again, like the Harvey Pekar name story.

Most of my work is about making other people's voices heard. So, I pay attention to when I hear them the first time. Then I watch other listeners. Work-in-progress readings of *Our Cancer Year* made most people nervous because of all the different story threads: "Where's this going?" "What's with these kids?" They drop off the page, you know, when we're at our most self-centered. And then they show back up again. But, I think in the end it more or less all worked although it's not all tied in a nice, neat knot.

Ottaviani: Well you do get a sense of closure with the end, because it has brought the two stories together there at the waterfall.

Brabner: Yeah, but there were arguments about where to end this, because Harvey had a whole different ending that he wanted to do.

Pekar: I didn't want a whole different ending in terms of where to cut it off. I always wanted to cut it off, to end it, with the kids. But I'm much more pessimistic than Joyce. So, I forget exactly how, but that ending was like a compromise. I wanted to end it by just, you know, just me going out to door to work while the same old problems hit me.

Brabner: Yeah, and I said, "You've done that." My take was that all of the kids had a really rough year, like us, but we were already friends who could talk to each other. Everyone knew each other except Ju and Harvey. They kind of stuck together, a little bit outside. She would help him with the stairs. They would talk.

One day I came home and all the other kids were at the beach while Harvey and Ju had this look on their faces. I knew they had done something, like two guilty little kids. It turned out that Harvey had taken the car and driven Ju out to Chagrin Falls.

Ju told me all about it. She was radiant while Harvey downplayed it, of course. But, I could tell they both had a great time and that he was finally able to think about someone besides himself. That meant he was getting well.

Our instructions to Frank were that it not be Victoria Falls; it's a little bitty waterfall but big and important to Ju, because she doesn't get out much. It was special because Harvey could be like her older brother or father that day. Both were murdered by the Khmer Rouge. Ju saw that happen. It's real important to Cambodian kids when an adult pays attention to them, anyway, because they honor their elders. Adult friendship is considered a really wonderful thing.

But Chagrin Falls isn't some place where you'd want to sit and meditate. It really is just this dinky waterfall next to a bookstore and a popcorn and ice-cream shop. So we told Frank to make the passersby look ordinary, fat, whatever, let's have a dog and some dog shit and it'll be OK [laughter]. The dog shit was my idea [laughter]. Because we knew Frank did good dog shit.

Anyway, it gets down to what you choose to remember. Harvey, then, was much more depressed and in pain than he is now.

Pekar: Well, yeah, we discussed the ending, this is the conclusion we came to, and I think we're both pretty happy.

Brabner: It's who we are. I still kind of keep pulling up his spirits because cancer really does a number on your emotions. Harvey's been profoundly depressed and sometimes really seriously disoriented—mentally ill, as a result of drugs, stress, trauma and everything else. He really did not know at one point if he was a "real person" or a character in a book.

Pekar's anxieties went beyond surviving cancer as he is seen worrying about a trip to New York City in "A Step . . . . . . Out of the Nest," illustrated by Joe Zabel and Gary Dumm, reprinted in *The Best of American Splendor*, p. 58.

Ottaviani: This brings to mind a quote from Kurt Vonnegut, that ties back into this "are you a person or a character?" question, and also to the autobio comic-book creators. To paraphrase, he said, "Don't be a writer. Be something, then write." And a lot autobio folks seem to write about the "writer/artist of autobio comic books" life. It seems that you've kept it pretty clear that you're somebody who works at the VA. Do you consider yourself a writer who works at the VA, or a VA staffer who writes? This conversation comes up in one of the previous stories.

Pekar: Issue #9, yeah . . . I guess a lot of it has to do with what other people consider you, maybe. You just go out and you do things and you're judged by people. For most of the time that I've been writing comics my work hasn't been very well known, especially by people in Cleveland. I was known to thousands of people, but that was as a file clerk at the VA. We have a real big hospital here—a teaching hospital which is tied in with Case Western Reserve medical school. It has hundreds of beds and everything like that. I spend eight hours a day working there, interacting with all these patients that came in because my job was to get their charts and very often the chart would be lost and I'd have to go and talk to them, and that way I got to know a lot of them. So, you know, I got really well known to a lot of people, like maybe the guy who sells peanuts next to the biggest building in town does or something. Anyway, I was sort of like a landmark figure there. So I guess I did for a really long time, and maybe still do, think of myself as a file clerk.

Brabner: We've been on tour and the further away we are from Cleveland, the bigger the audience is, more or less. In Minneapolis we met more than a hundred people. In Oberlin, Ohio, maybe forty-five. At Bookseller's in Shaker Square, which is next to Cleveland Heights, where we live: twenty. By the time we get up to our own door and inside the house, even we've forgotten that we're writers.

Pekar: Well, you know, I make the majority of my income as a file clerk.

Brabner: At the same time, you know what I thought when I married him. I still say the same the thing. "Why do you tell everybody you don't make your living as a writer? I married a writer."

The other really odd thing about being comic-book characters is that we keep meeting these people who know a lot more about us than most of our relatives and neighbors. People have very definite ideas about what we must be like. But, if they've missed a couple issues . . . [laughter] A reporter from Detroit came to interview us. He looked up and said, "Inky!" when this little black cat runs into the room. But Inky died in an issue he hasn't read yet. That's a new little black cat—and a much nicer one, too!

Or they have the idea that Harvey's going to be a meat-and-potatoes, working-class kinda guy they're going to take down to a bar and drink some beer with. They got "working-class" right, but they forgot he's a middle-age Jew . . . and they don't know he isn't eating meat any more. Or Spaghetti-O's.

Weird things happen when people come here looking for "authentic America." Remember in "A Step Out of the Nest" [published by Dark Horse Comics]? *Good Morning America* wanted Harvey to be a guest host on a show about working-class heroes . . . until they actually read some *American Splendor*.

Pekar: It didn't happen. They said my stuff was "too dark" and "too real."

Brabner: They told us it's their job to get America up and off to work with a smile on their face but, if people read Harvey's stuff, they might not want to get out of bed [laughter] . . .

Pekar: I didn't want to be responsible for bringing the economy to a grinding halt.

Lieber: I'd like to go back a bit further and ask more about the involved peoples' reactions. Essentially, for the past seventeen years we've been getting a look at Harvey's diary. For instance, have the other characters in *Our Cancer Year* seen the work?

Pekar: Sure. We've given them copies. A lot of them already knew they were going to be in it.

Ottaviani: Even "Nurse Ratched"?

Pekar: No. Not her. Not the people we didn't like. The people we liked, which were a lot of people, knew about it and we gave copies of it to them.

Brabner: I went over the script with most of the kids. Dana insisted that we not show her the book until it was published. She said, "It's not my book. It's the way you saw it. Put down anything you want and spell my name right."

"Uri" and "Zamir" are pseudonyms. They've grown up a lot since I first met them, but telling their stories to reporters was not healthy for them four years ago and I'm not so sure they really need to know what's in an obscure little book published in English, seven time zones away.

"Uri" just e-mailed me about visiting us next month. If he makes it over here, we'll talk.

Ottaviani: How is *Our Cancer Year* relevant? How would you like people's behavior to change after having read it? How did it change yours?
Pekar: Well, I write about my life, choosing incidents that I think will be, for one reason or another, significant to people. Often because they may have experienced the same things, and often because few or no people have written about them before. I hope that in reading them people can identify with the character and in some cases take comfort from what I write or know that maybe they're not the only person in the world that's had this experience, so they shouldn't feel so weird about it or something.

As far as *Our Cancer Year* goes, I guess I wanted to show people, among other things, that you don't have to be a hero to get through cancer. You can be a craven coward and get through. You have to stay on your medication and take your treatments, that's all. A lot of cancer stories that people have written have made themselves out to look real heroic and stuff . . .
Brabner: Patients are either role models of courage who die, teaching us "left behinds" the meaning of love, or they're somehow transformed and today make every moment count.

I was nervous about showing the book to cancer patients in the beginning because we had it really easy compared to a lot of people, or so we thought . . .

We sent preview copies of the book out to people we didn't know, cancer patients and cancer professionals. Some survivors found *Our Cancer Year* "too real" and said we brought back bad memories. At the same time, they called us honest. They liked that. We also found out, and this really surprised me, that a lot of cancer patients are angry about always being lectured about positive thinking. They say the world doesn't want to see pain. In cancer movies, your skin doesn't turn orange. You still have a neck, eyebrows, and eyelashes. When your hair falls out, your skull is beautifully smooth and symmetrical. Maybe your cheeks appear a bit hollow but no ribs stick out. You don't have sores all over your body. You never see puke, although you hear a few off-camera coughs.

Lieber: The Ali McGraw syndrome: as you get sicker you get more beautiful.

Brabner: Marshall Kragen, of the National Coalition for Cancer Survivorship, said using comics made it uniquely possible for people to really see what cancer can do to your body. We showed something readers can't infer from text and don't see in movies or on television. You see a healthy Harvey, and then you see him wasting away.

Plus you also see other ugly stuff. You see that I'm not a warm, totally supportive, loving wife all the time. I get really burned-out and abuse him. I assume I can do more than I really can and end up in pretty bad shape. Movies and "inspirational" books don't show that. We don't see the bitching, the moaning, the fighting, the wrong turns, the mistakes that people make during something like this, only noble choices and maybe one long, hot-tempered speech, because that's dramatic, but no day-to-day whining.

Some of *Our Cancer Year* is instructional. If readers didn't know it before, they know now you can pull your files off someone's desk and make doctors explain stuff to you. You can confront doctors. You can take the sides of a hospital bed down and climb in next to each other. You can do that. And people know now that non-Hodgkins lymphoma is treatable, especially if it's caught early. There are people out there, in the middle of treatment, who want to know "If I'm doing so well, how come I don't feel better?" And there are bystanders, friends, or family members who want to know that, too. So, there's a reason we called it *Our Cancer Year*. That lets people know that it's a fixed period of time. There is an ending in sight. We didn't want to tell readers, "Step into this hole and keep falling."

Ottaviani: A while back you mentioned that there had been some major illnesses in both of your families. And your friends talk about AIDS early on in the book. Did you find yourself incorporating some of their experiences into *Our Cancer Year*? I guess I'm asking whether you fictionalized things.

Pekar: The book is factually accurate except for in some cases we disguise people's identities by changing their name and/or occupations or appearance. But, for example, I talked about my cousin Norman who died of lymphoma. That's true.

Brabner: When there are details that can be traced back and hurt somebody, we made changes. We renamed Harvey's oncologist because, when we went to press, the awful nurse was still working for her. The nurse who posed for Frank as her character is actually a wonderful nurse—and a two-time cancer survivor herself, we found out later.

Ottaviani: In "An Every Day Horror Story," Harvey, you worried about dealing with serious illness. Did you handle this the way you expected to? I mean, you wrote about it, and that's one of the ways I would have expected you to handle it, but . . .

Pekar: Yeah, from that throat problem I extrapolated and I figured I was going to really react badly to something more serious, and I did. I didn't disappoint myself: I fell apart [laughter].

Brabner: For almost all kinds of cancer, it's like being parachuted into the middle of a war—bam! You don't have time to get used to the idea. You're forced to make fast decisions because tumors grow: 2 times 2 is 4; 4 times 4 is 16; 16 times 16 is . . .

Pekar: You've got to make a lot of decisions when you're in shock and the next thing you know, they're pumping poison into you that can screw up how you think and feel. And every time it can be different chemicals. And your body is changing.

Brabner: I don't feel like Harvey let me down or anything. But, he made it hard on me when he said he was going to have chemo every week, instead of once a month. Stuff got very bad, fast, and we had no time to get used to that.

What pissed me off were people who said stuff like, "Well, I hear Harvey is sick but he'll be OK because he has such a strong will to live. He's tough." And there's Harvey crawling up our stairs on all fours because he's so weak. And he can't stop crying.

So many people panic when trouble happens. They whisper and disappear real fast. Then there are people you don't even know who suddenly show up and do seemingly simple things that really count. Like the neighbor who drove us to the hospital when our car battery died.

Pekar: Yeah, Marge Petrone. Marge is wonderful.

Ottaviani: Is there another story "Bringing you up to date" [which appeared in *American Splendor* #17, which predated *Our Cancer Year* and gave away the book's ending: that Pekar survives], or is it time to move on?

Pekar: What I have going for me are some new stories—I don't know under what title they're going to be published. Some of 'em deal with the avascular necrosis I developed after I had cancer as a result of the drugs I took during chemotherapy. The prednisone cut off the circulation to my hipbone, part of it died, turned to powder, so I went around limping for two and a half years, and then finally it got so bad that I had a hip replacement. So some of the stories will at least make reference to that. I've written them, actually, and they're in the hands of the artists. I thought that since the cancer-year book has been so well received that Joyce, instead of writing a story with me, should just write one or two stories, whatever she feels is appropriate . . .

Brabner: I'm haggling with him over the page rate [laughter].

Pekar: . . . from her point of view.

Brabner: The story I think I want to write is sort of an "Oh, excuse me, I forgot you're able to take care of yourself now" story. About relinquishing all of this decision making. Maybe that really belonged in Harvey's story "Inky Dies" [from *American Splendor* #17]. Our cat was very old and very sick. I had to make another decision having to do with doctors, living and dying.

People said, "You've been through so much. Even though Inky is not in any pain at this minute, you should have him put to sleep now rather than cause yourself the agony of watching and waiting." But I couldn't do that and kept asking, "Can you give me stuff so I can euthanise him myself the moment he starts to hurt?" That was against the law, I think. So, I just kept watching him, which was too much like watching Harvey. This went on for weeks.

Inky was finally put to sleep at the animal hospital, while I held him. (Harvey was too upset to go in.) Driving home, I told Harvey to put the seat back because I felt sick. I threw up seventeen times that night. I don't know why I counted all the times, just that it was like throwing up the cancer, the anger, the fear, the decision making, all that shit. So I think I have to write something a little more like that, like a delayed-stress syndrome.

Ottaviani: Who do you see showing up at your signings? Comic-book fans? People who've written you in the past, talked to you before?

Pekar: Yeah, people who've written me in the past show up. I don't have a large percentage of comic-book fans. The people who like my work most are readers of novels and short stories. There are also people, in this instance, who've had experience with cancer in one way or another, including doctors and nurses. Also patients and people who've had friends with cancer, or relatives of people who've had cancer.

There aren't too many people who like mainstream comics interested in my work. And that's to be expected. It's just like assuming that just because a person likes one type of prose book that he's going to like all types of prose books. There's a variety of prose that you can write, and there also can be a vast variety of comic books you can write. Any subject you feel like writing about. It's unfortunate that people haven't availed themselves of the opportunities that comics offer.

Ottaviani: Have people approached you for new projects on the basis of this book? Artists, for instance?

Pekar: Do you mean have they been awakened to my work as a result of this book? No, most of the people that I've dealt with were familiar with my work. But that's not to say . . . The most intriguing proposal that came to me going around doing book signings was that a woman who painted murals on walls suggested that maybe I write something for her that she could do a mural of. But even in her case she knew my earlier work.

Lieber: This is more a question that applies to your whole body of work: There's a lot of places, particularly in *Our Cancer Year*, that feel like pure literary moments. The part where you lost your wedding ring, for instance. Reading a novel you'd immediately look at that as an important symbolic moment in the story. Do you find your brain double-tracking at times like that—looking at your life for symbolism or reading your life like the book?

Pekar: I don't know. Yeah, I guess I'm conscious of what I'm doing, but . . . I don't know that you specifically asked this, but the primary influences on me have been fiction writers. I don't know how much fiction is contained in certain novels. Having written what I've written I look at novels that I read and wonder if the novels aren't really just true accounts of things with the names changed. For example, if I'd written all these stories about a character and named him something besides Harvey Pekar, I wonder if maybe there wouldn't be some people that didn't realize that I was a real person. Especially if I didn't give out details of my life and they didn't know anything about me.

In terms of using symbolism, I don't use it a lot. I use it occasionally, but I don't try to use it very much—not consciously anyway. There have been a few occasions when I have done it deliberately, though.

Lieber: I'm thinking of the story with the bat trapped in the room [from *American Splendor* #16].

Pekar: That's right. There was one whole story that was like an allegory that I wrote in my sixth book about junk shopping, about going to a rummage sale in a church and I found a whole lot of objects at the sale that most people would've thought of as garbage, and I found some very useful things there. It's sort of like, you know, look at your own life. You may be underrating the richness of it, the interest that people might have in it. It goes along with my notion that every life is the subject of a potentially great novel.

Ottaviani: Having lived it, then written about it, *Our Cancer Year* is another step removed because you had Frank Stack interpret it. Which part of the book works best for you, now that you've read it?

Pekar: I can't speak for Joyce, but in terms of what I wrote, I guess the part I'm proudest of is probably the sequence where I'm so weakened that I collapse at home and then I'm brought to the hospital, stay in the hospital a couple days, and then have the hallucinatory experience, and then the next day. That would probably be my own favorite part of the book. That's some of the best writing I've ever done.

Brabner: I like tying things together, like the business with the baking soda and water. Or how Harvey's wedding ring was too big for my finger then, later, too big for him and losing it and finding it. The part where the new scar on Harvey's forehead nearly matches the scar his brother has when they see each other again, after so many years. Another part of tying things together was blending voices and deciding whose narration is heard: "Joyce Now?" "Harvey Then?" "Us-in-Agreement Today?" "Third Person Omniscient?" "Fourth Person Confused?" What's best about the book is not having to write "In Memory of" on the first page. Everyone made it.

An Interview with Harvey Pekar: Will the Truth Really Set You Free?—*American Splendor*

MICHAEL EVERLETH / 1998

From *diRt Magazine* (February 24, 1999).
Reprinted by permission of
Michael Everleth.

Most kids grow up reading comic books, but, for me, they became a
lifelong obsession. Originally attracted to the gaudily colored exploits of
superheroes, the garish fantasy of comics seemed more attractive, and
infinitely more entertaining, than reality. But as I matured in my teen
years, so did my reading tastes.

Having read nothing but astounding critical praise for Harvey's annual, self-published autobiographical comic, *American Splendor*, in the
fan press for at least a year or two, I was finally able to locate a copy
of one at a comic book store during a weekend visit to a college I was
thinking of applying to. Along with *American Splendor*, I think I also
bought Frank Miller's sci-fi opus *Ronin*. While I have bought just about

every single *American Splendor* since that day about ten years ago, I
have rarely bought anything else by Mr. Miller.

While I still enjoy a good dose of escapist entertainment, I am more
fascinated with the real life adventures of real people than I am with fictional characters. So, when Dave asked me to contribute to his website,
I thought I would follow the lead set by Harvey and write about myself
rather than simple commentary on the world of popular culture.

Why I particularly wanted to interview Harvey for *diRt* was because
I have come to discover that this autobiographical thing isn't always
easy. It's caused friction in at least two of my relationships, and I get
strange reactions from people—friends, family, and strangers—respond-
ing to my stories since I generally tend to cast myself in a not particularly
flattering light (to put it mildly). I wondered if Harvey had to deal with
issues like this since he has been such a tremendous influence on me.

Harvey: You wanted to interview me?

Mike: It would be real quick. I have like eight questions.
Harvey: You have them now?

Mike: Yeah.
Harvey: Alright.

Mike: You just wanna go for it?
Harvey: Yeah—if there's something I have to stop and think about that
would be one thing, but I mean, they're usually questions I've answered
before. So, what's up?

Mike: First, what made you start writing autobiographical material in the
first place?
Harvey: Did you ever read that thing I wrote called "The Young Crumb
Story?"

Mike: I'm not sure.
Harvey: I write about all that, but what really happened was that I knew
Robert Crumb for a real long time. He used to live in Cleveland. At that
time, when I met him, I was totally uninterested in comics 'cause I had
given up on them as an eleven-year-old. There were a few titles that I
thought were good, like *Mad* and stuff. But I kept on following Crumb's
career as he moved out of Cleveland and became an icon of comic culture and it got me to thinking about comics and theorizing about them
and I realized that comics were a medium like prose or film or theater.

But, for some freakish reason, they were being used in an extremely limited way. I think you know what I'm talking about. So, I thought it would be great to expand their use. It seemed to be something that cried out to be done.

Mike: You wanted to do something that you saw nobody else was doing pretty much?
Harvey: Yeah. And there's still an awful lot of ground to cover.

Mike: But why did you pick specifically to write about yourself?
Harvey: Because I know myself best. Everybody in a way writes about themselves even if they sublimate it through other characters. They deal with these issues that are important to them whatever they may be. And I've always been a guy that was really into direct kind of commentary. There was a time when I was about nineteen years old, which was well before I started writing comics, when I just tried writing short stories and I went back and found a couple of them and it turned out they were autobiographical the same way my comics were. So I guess I was just meant to write autobiography. Also, in terms of comics, for me, they have some peculiar advantages. I like to go about things real directly. Comics offer me that opportunity because it's a pretty economical way to tell a story. The backgrounds and a lot of that stuff, that's drawn in.

Mike: You can just concentrate on the dialogue and stuff, the characters.
Harvey: Yeah. Well, I concentrate on what's in the picture, too. I lay the stories out, tell the illustrators what to do. Also, I like the way you can time stories with panels. For example, you can build tension by using a wordless panel.

Mike: When you first started, did you feel that you were completely honest about all aspects of your personality? Or did you start out hiding stuff and slowly grow into the more revealing stuff?
Harvey: At first, I used to use different names, but I think there's about the same degree of accuracy in my stories. I've always tried to make them real accurate. Sometimes, I've compressed things in time.

Mike: I meant more specifically your personality. Were there things you didn't want to share in a public forum, that you hid?
Harvey: No, I think I was always about the same. I was always pretty frank about that.

Mike: Because a lot of your writing, also, exposes darker aspects of your personality. Do you think writing about that in a public forum acts as a form of self-therapy?

Harvey: It might, but the reasons I do it primarily is because I'm not embarrassed about the stuff I write about. I suppose there are some things I am embarrassed about that I don't write about. I suppose that's true of everybody. But some things I say about myself maybe other people would have more difficulty saying them. If anything, all things being equal, I'd rather portray myself in a bad light, or in a less good light because I don't want to make myself look like a monster either, because I think it's more believable. I'd like people to identify with my stuff and I'm certainly not going to do that if I write out all my faults and just present myself as some wonderful guy. I mean, what's the point.

BUT I KNOW I WANNA LIVE, NOT DIE, THESE DAYS, SO FUCK IT, I KNOW WHAT I GOTTA DO TO ACCOMPLISH WHAT I WANNA ACCOMPLISH. I'M GONNA TRY TO DO IT, WORK AT IT EVERY DAY THROUGH THE PAIN AND HOPE THINGS FALL INTO PLACE, THAT MAYBE SOMETIME IN THE FUTURE I'LL START TO FEEL BETTER AGAIN. THAT'S EASIER SAID THAN DONE, BUT SO FAR I'VE BEEN ABLE TO KEEP GOIN'.

Pekar was frank about his ambitions in spite of the pain from a damaged hip. Illustrated by Gerry Shamray for "Bringing You up to Date," reprinted in The Best of American Splendor, p. 161.

Mike: Are you conscious of creating a Harvey Pekar comic book "character," or do you let each story be what it is with your place in it?

Harvey: Yeah, I write about myself, so I guess I am conscious of creating a Harvey Pekar comic book "character."

Mike: How close do you think the character is to the "real" Harvey Pekar?

Harvey: I think it's real close. But that's just my opinion. Maybe you should ask some people that know me. I think the stories are pretty accurately done, but we all have to make some selections and maybe some people would think I'm leaving out stuff. My wife seems to think I'm a nicer guy than I show myself to be. What can I say? I'm footin' the bill for the call, right?

Mike: Yeah, that's real nice of ya. And you met your wife, Joyce, through your writing pretty much, right?
Harvey: Yeah.

Mike: Has your relationship with her, or anyone else, benefited directly from your writing?
Harvey: Not in any real surprising ways. I mean, it got me a wife. That's one benefit. People tend to respect me more because I'm a published writer. I've written a lot of other stuff besides comics. I write for a lot of weekly papers around the country.

Mike: Like what?
Harvey: The *Austin Chronicle*, *Riverfront Times* in St. Louis, *Isthmus* in Madison, Wisconsin, the *Metro* in San Jose, California. I write for a couple dailies—the *Cleveland Plain Dealer* and the *Boston Herald*. I write for a couple national jazz magazines—*Jazziz* and *Jazz Times*.

Mike: Is that all music and literary criticism?
Harvey: Not all reviews. Sometimes I write articles. I write essays as well.

Mike: I guess my last question is, have you ever had a relationship, either friendship or romantic, that suffered or fell apart because of your writing?
Harvey: No, I don't think so. If I have a favorable impression of a person, I tend to portray them favorably. If I don't like a person, I'm not their friend and I don't give a shit what they think. Maybe I want them to be hurt.

American Splendor is now published by Dark Horse Comics and can be found in any good comic book store. There's a couple of reprint collections of his work also out there, but I highly recommend, to comic and non-comic readers, Harvey's full-length graphic novel *Our Cancer Year*, co-written with his wife, Joyce Brabner, and illustrated by Frank Stack. It's a brutal look at Harvey's year-long bout with cancer and chemotherapy and it's absolutely heart-wrenching.

(And a brief thanks goes out to Dave Estrada of Dark Horse who helped set up this interview.)

Michael Interviews . . .
Author Harvey Pekar

MICHAEL FELDMAN / 1998

From *Michael Feldman's Whad'Ya Know?*
radio show (June 13, 1998). Transcribed by
Michael Rhode and reprinted by permission of
Michael Feldman.

Michael Feldman: I'm here right now with Harvey Pekar, ladies and gentleman, author of *American Splendor*, this wonderful series of illustrated novelettes I think you'd call them, more than comic books, and Harvey, how are you?

Harvey Pekar: I'm fine. Thanks for having me on the show and you've gotten off to a wonderful start.

Feldman: Well, thank you . . .

Pekar: I think your taste in music is even hipper than Garrison Keillor's.

Feldman: Whoa! And that's saying something, ladies and gentleman. To think I'm hipper than Macedonian zither music is really kind of an excit-

ing notion. *American Splendor*—these things are great. You've probably seen Harvey—actually you've been on the Letterman show.
Pekar: Yeah.

Feldman: We have that in common; I had a bad experience on the Letterman show. I was on there once.
Pekar: Yeah. I had eight of 'em, man. [laughs].

Feldman: I was on there once, he didn't know who I was or what to do with me . . .
Pekar: That's par for the course. He's a frat boy, whadya want?

Feldman: A frat boy?
Pekar: That's right.

Feldman: Ok. Enjoying your challah there?
Pekar: I am. It's wonderful.

Feldman: Who donated this challah? Somebody brought it up. Whoever did, thank you very much.
Pekar: We're having a challah-day.

Feldman: Yes, a challah-day—so c-have some . . .
Pekar: . . . all kinds of humor . . .

Feldman: The amazing thing is . . . you do these . . . they're not really comic books, I mean comic books are like kid's books.
Pekar: They are really comic books except that people think that comic books are only, you know, kid's books. But comics are just a medium, like any other medium. You could do anything you want to in comics, just like with prose or with movies, but people just think that all you can do in them is kid's stuff. *I don't know why*. It's kind of unfortunate.

Feldman: It has to do with Superman and all those comics that came out of Cleveland actually.
Pekar: Yeah, that's right. Jerry Siegel and Joe Shuster.

Feldman: Yeah, who got nothing for it.
Pekar: I don't think they got nothing.

Feldman: They sold it for $35 or something.
Pekar: Nah, I don't think that's true, Michael.

Feldman: Oh, you don't?
Pekar: I think they're a little sharper than that. They're Glenville High grads, back in the days . . .

Feldman: . . . Back in the days when it meant something?
Pekar: That's right! Benny Friedman. Benny Friedman was down there, you know. Know who he is?

Feldman: No.
Pekar: You don't know who Benny Friedman is?

Feldman: Who's Benny Friedman?
Pekar: Benny Friedman was the great All-American quarterback at the University of Michigan who went to Glenville High.

Feldman: Oh, I didn't know that.
Pekar: Now you know.

Feldman: Well, I'm from Wisconsin, whad'ya want? Give me a break here. I'm from out of town. So how do you come to this medium? You are not an artist, yourself, but you are . . .
Pekar: Yeah, I'm a writer. The way I came to it was I knew Robert Crumb, and I read comics when I was a kid.

Feldman: So Crumb is from Cleveland too?
Pekar: No, he's not. He's from Philadelphia, but he moved here and he lived around the corner from me. I was watching his progress and I saw that you could do all sorts of things in comics. You know, back in the '60s, in the alternative comics days, it occurred to me that you could do way more than the alternative comic book artists were doing.

Feldman: More than the *Furry Freak Brothers* and that sort of thing?
Pekar: Yeah, you could do anything. You could do real grim, mundane kind of things, you know, stories about everyday life, like I do. *Quotidian!*

Feldman: Quotidian. Who said "the malady of the quotidian?" Was that William Carlos Williams?
Pekar: I dunno, man.

Feldman: One of those guys.
Pekar: I didn't go to college. [laughs]

Feldman: But you're very well read and very erudite.
Pekar: Yeah, I am. I'm a Renaissance man, Michael.

Feldman: You are, I know. The tights prove it, I think.
Pekar: Yeah. [audience laughs]

Feldman: So when you have an idea, the story ideas are from your life . . . your life is an open book, basically.
Pekar: It's an open book, right.

Feldman: Are there things you wouldn't put in a book? I mean, you are very revealing.
Pekar: Yeah, there's things that I [don't] put in there. You'll just have to guess about those. I can't even hint at them. I would face retribution.

Feldman: So Harvey Pekar in these comic books is a character. You could say it's not exactly the same as Harvey Pekar in real life.
Pekar: Nah, it can't be. You have to select, but you know, there's certain people out there that I don't want to rub the wrong way.

Feldman: I can't imagine that for some reason. Why is that? [audience laughs] I mean Letterman, you really let him have it.
Pekar: Yeah, I know, Letterman, but I had nothing to lose, I don't care about him. He wasn't paying me any money . . . you know, a little bit, a pittance, but not enough for me to be nice to him for Chrissake. [audience laughs loudly]

Feldman: So, what're we paying you?
Pekar: Well, you guys, thanks to my wife . . . you know, I'd do this for nothing, Michael.
Feldman: I think you are, aren't you?
Pekar: Yeah, yeah. No, she's forcing you to pay me. I'd do it for nothing.

Feldman: We gave you some challah. I think that's about it.
Pekar: That's a fringe benefit. I appreciate that. It's good, too, whoever made this, and I know my challah, and this is good.

Feldman: When you have an idea, a story idea, how do you sketch it out? Do you sketch it out in stick figures or something and then give it to an artist?
Pekar: Yeah. [wonderingly] How'd you find that out? Yeah, I storyboard it.

Feldman: I'm not as stupid as I look, actually. [audience laughs]
Pekar: I storyboard them. [laughing]

Feldman: You storyboard them . . .
Pekar: Yeah, I write . . . I divide a piece of paper up into panels, and I put in stick figures and balloons and dialogue and captions and stuff like that, and directions to the artist. And then after I send them to them, I speak to them about them and tell them what I want. But I'm not really too heavy on them because they come up with a lot of great ideas themselves, and also they get mad if you tell them what to do in too much detail. Discretion, you know, is the better part of valor.

Feldman: Do you find yourself getting somewhat romanticized by some of them? The figure of Harvey Pekar, does he take on a little different . . .
Pekar: Yeah, of course. You know, like superhero guys . . .

Feldman: How do they treat you differently? If Frank Stack does you as opposed to R. Crumb doing you?
Pekar: Well, I mean, Crumb makes everybody look real crude and stuff like that, so he's got me drooling and looking like a raving maniac. I don't know if it's *that far off*, but . . .

Feldman: Yeah. No, I was scared to meet you from those drawings . . .
Pekar: Yeah, right.

Feldman: . . . but you're a nice looking person. You don't scare me now.
Pekar: Thank you. I look like George McGovern, right?

Feldman: Yeah, I said, "You look like McGovern, what was I scared about? What am I worried about?"
Pekar: Yeah, a very benign type of guy.

Feldman: I saw what you did to Letterman—that's what I'm worried about. [laughs] That poor guy was quaking.
Pekar: Well, he deserves that, you know, or more of that . . .

Feldman: Ok, well, let's get this out of the way—what about him is it that ticked you off to that degree? There's something about him . . .
Pekar: Well, he tries to control everything for one thing. And for another thing, I wouldn't say the guy is stupid, but he's . . .

Feldman: But . . .
Pekar: . . . he's very anti-intellectual and he doesn't want to know anything, he doesn't want to learn anything, except for maybe about

A page of Pekar's script provided to Josh Neufeld for "Reduction."

automobile racing. Consequently, it amounts to the same thing as being stupid! [audience laughs]

Feldman: Yeah. But one is active, one is passive, right?
Pekar: Yeah.

Feldman: If you're being actively anti-intellectual, at least you're doing something. You're not being passively . . . stupid.
Pekar: He also tries to . . . I don't know that he was very daring on his show. Maybe compared to Johnny Carson, "the jaded one" [laughs] he was kinda daring, but . . .

Feldman: Who else do you like? Jackie Gleason? Is he alright by you? Art Carney? Any of those guys?
Pekar: Yeah, they're alright. Steve Allen, how about that?

Feldman: Steve Allen's great.
Pekar: Yeah.

Feldman: I had him on the show a couple of times.
Pekar: I'll tell you who else. I think you're doing a nice job. I think you could lose the quiz show part of it.

Feldman: [Laughs] I'm thinking of losing the interview part of it, to tell you the truth. [audience laughs]. No, I'm actually not saying that because of you. I'm actually enjoying this.
Pekar: I know you are. I would too if I were in your shoes.

Feldman: In one of your stories I was reading, there this character that comes up to you and wants to talk to you in the worst way. I think it's at your job, I'm not sure, when you're working at the Veteran's . . . in the file thing . . .
Pekar: Yeah. That's right. I'm a file clerk at the Veteran's Hospital here in Cleveland.

Feldman: Someone came up to you in that context, or elsewhere, and said, "I have a story I want to tell you. I have to talk to you really bad."
Pekar: Yeah. Yeah, yeah.

Feldman: And he said he had a Harvey Pekar story.
Pekar: Yeah. Right, exactly.

Feldman: What did he think he had and what is a Harvey Pekar story? I mean, what makes it into your magazine?

Pekar: Well, I write about . . . my work's autobiographical because I know myself better than anyone else so I think I can write more accurately about myself. What he had was—this particular guy had a story that was about everyday humor . . . about a funny guy he met. I think the humor I witness, and sometime participate in, on the job and in the street, is a lot better than the stuff that you hear comedians put down. I mean it's a lot fresher. There's no clichés in that kind of stuff. Guys don't plan it, you know, it's spontaneous. So I think the humor of everyday life beats the hell out of the humor of the stage . . . even maybe radio. [audience laughs].

Feldman: I wouldn't argue with you. It's not punch line oriented. It's situational, and the irony is kind of inherent in it, very much so . . .
Pekar: That's right. It's inherently ironic.

Feldman: And also, the stuff you do on the job . . . this one I'm looking at in *American Splendor*, the whole issue is about you're trying to get records for someone who's coming in for an appointment, and the battle you wage working there simply to get this man's file.
Pekar: Right, exactly. Well, you know, I'm writing about the 99 percent of life that gets ignored by most writers. They want some big dramatic thing, but I look at life as—get this—a war of attrition. [laughs] I hear the murmurs out there, huh? I scored.

Feldman: Well, they're dying off one by one . . . [audience laughs]
Pekar: [Laughs] I think that an accumulation of events has a larger effect on a person than one single big event, so that's what I . . . I know no other way of life, so that's what I write about, but fortunately I think there are other people like me out there and a few of them buy the comic book. Not enough for me to make a living at it, but . . . [audience laughs]

Feldman: They say everyone's life has a story, everyone's has a novel in it . . . do you think anyone's life would make material like this if you sat down with . . .
Pekar: Sure. Yeah, that's right.

Feldman: R. Crumb would sketch some things out and say, "Here is my day last week. Something happened that was kind of interesting."
Pekar: Yeah, sometimes I write about other people . . . you know, through my eyes. Some of it's biographical, rather than autobiographical.

I just did a comic book where a guy's featured who I was corresponding with from England. This guy's autistic, but he's a *brilliant* writer and an outstanding illustrator. The guy's right now on welfare, but he's a great talent and it's gonna come out pretty soon. Certainly I think his life is very interesting, and I think your life would be interesting too, Michael. *All* of us.

Feldman: [Laughs] I guess not. I don't think there's much . . . well, it's incorporated in what I do, but I don't think I'm as revealing as you are. For example, about cancer . . . you wrote a book about having cancer.
Pekar: Yeah, that's right. That's something that Letterman wouldn't mention, by the way. He didn't want anyone to know I'd had cancer.

Feldman: Yeah, *My Cancer Year*?
Pekar: *Our Cancer Year*. Right. That's right, I wrote that with my wife, Joyce Brabner.

Feldman: That was rather a courageous thing to do. Was that hard for you to write that? Was it like reliving the pain?
Pekar: A little bit. But it wasn't that bad.

Feldman: Relieving or reliving the pain?
Pekar: Nah, I'm not that . . . the bad part about having cancer . . . it wasn't like I was suffering before they diagnosed it. It was the chemotherapy that really screwed me up. But I was a coward through it all.

Feldman: Yeah? Are you a lousy patient? Is that part of the problem?
Pekar: Yes, I was, and I think a lot of people out there are. I don't go along with these books where this guy makes himself out to be a big hero and stuff like that. It's funny. I heard a show the other day on *This American Life* . . . you know that show?

Feldman: Um-hmm.
Pekar: Yeah, out of Chicago . . . where a woman was talking about her experience with cancer . . . I didn't get her name, but it was somewhat similar to my experience. I think if you have cancer or something like that, don't be upset about being afraid, or even acting childish or anything like that. Just take your medicine, or take your treatment, and don't get worried about being worried, anything like that. Just do the best you can, and maybe you'll get through.

Feldman: Is part of the fear or the problem you have part of knowing what a medical system is all about? I mean, working in a hospital, the VA hospital . . . It can be a pretty frightening Kafkaesque place and suddenly you're at the mercy of it.

Pekar: No, I . . . well, it's just real depressing to be in a hospital, or to be incapacitated. Since I'd been healthy all the way up 'til that time, I didn't know what it was to be weakened or anything like that, and to have my hair fall out and stuff, and lose weight. I was pretty shook up by it. I wasn't prepared for it and that's part of why I fell apart. Fortunately my wife was there to pick up the pieces.

Feldman: It's an excellent story [audience claps] and it won an award too, didn't it? What award did you win for that?

Pekar: Ahh, I won the Harvey Kurtzman award or something, but awards don't mean anything. I mean really. *Forrest Gump* won an award . . . and that's a piece of crap. [audience laughs] Have you ever won any awards, Michael?

Feldman: I've never won an award . . .

Pekar: Well, you should.

Feldman: Broad jump, in the fourth grade was the last one.

Pekar: Well, you should get an award for this show. It's a real good show.

Feldman: Yeah, it'd be a category of one, I think. [audience claps] Best comedy-quiz show on Saturday mornings, I think I could possibly compete for that . . . I'm not sure.

Pekar: It's got the David Letterman show beat hands down. There's just a lot of stupid people out there who don't realize how good this show is, unfortunately.

Feldman: Let's talk about Cleveland for a minute.

Pekar: Alright, let's talk about it.

Feldman: Tell me, growing up in Cleveland . . . if you had grown up in Los Angeles, as opposed to growing up in Cleveland . . . what did Cleveland impart to you? What kind of childhood was it?

Pekar: I have no idea 'cause I only know about growing up in Cleveland. I imagine it would be somewhat akin to growing up in Detroit, Milwaukee, or Chicago.

Feldman: Jewish neighborhood?
Pekar: Well, yeah, it was Jewish, Italian, and black, back where I lived . . .

Feldman: See that's different right there.
Pekar: Yeah.

Feldman: You don't get that in a lot of places. A Jewish-Italian-black neighborhood is not common.
Pekar: Well . . .

Feldman: What food can you agree on, number one? [audience laughs] Even the sausage would be hard to agree on . . .
Pekar: Well . . . there was a certain amount of hostility between the groups. [laughs] I was in a changing neighborhood that had already changed, so it was pretty interesting.

Feldman: What neighborhood was it?
Pekar: It was in the Mount Pleasant area. It was called Kinsman. It was working class area and I got to know the people. Even today, once in a while, like a patient at the VA comes up from those areas, from that area, and says they remember me when and stuff like that . . . and it's real nice. I think it's been a real interesting experience. I really enjoyed the company of the people in the neighborhood. I thought they were great. I'm sorry that they didn't get along any better, but . . .

Feldman: You mean there were fights . . . rumbles . . . actual gang fights, that sort of thing?
Pekar: Well, there was a little . . . there was a certain amount of hostility.

Feldman: Were you involved in any of that?
Pekar: You mean like . . .

Feldman: Actually mixing up?
Pekar: What in racial violence, or something like that?

Feldman: We used to have religious wars in Milwaukee.
Pekar: Oh, is that right?

Feldman: Yeah. We had your Germans against your Irish against . . . everyone against the Jews, basically, but all the kids were fighting out. The parents were sitting around.
Pekar: I got involved in some kind of violence, but not racially based, when I was a kid.

Feldman: And has this all turned up in *American Splendor*?
Pekar: Yes, it does, Michael. Now does that tip you off to the fact that I mind that you're reading it. It's great that you're so well prepared. Now let me point out something else about this show, ladies and gentlemen . . . [audience laughs]

Feldman: Endorsed by Harvey Pekar. Better than Housekeeping . . .
Pekar: That's right. No, I'm amazed that you got the musicians in town here on the basis of listening to their performances. Normally that kind of stuff just goes completely unnoticed. You send a cd or something to the producer of a show, they'll ignore it. They won't even pay any attention to it at all. And the music's been terrific. That fact that you recruited these people says something for you. [audience clapping]

Feldman: It's a big stage and we've got to fill it with something. You know how that goes. The title *American Splendor* . . .
Pekar: If I don't say this stuff about you Michael, who's gonna do it? Right?

Feldman: I know, I know . . . [audience laughs]
Pekar: And I've been behind the scenes.

Feldman: I don't take compliments well. Let's talk about something else.
Pekar: Is your mother listening?

Feldman: No, my mother is not listening actually. She's in a nursing home these days. That would be in my comic if I had to write something . . .
Pekar: Yeah, my parents were in . . .

Feldman: . . . it's one of those difficult things to even talk about. *American Splendor*, the title of it? Where's the *Splendor*? I get the *American* part.
Pekar: It's ironic, Michael. It's an ironic title.

Feldman: Ok, I get you. [audience laughs]
Pekar: In fact, when this thing comes out . . . you mentioned irony in the first place . . . when the thing comes out, there's this new one coming out called *American Splendour* that I did with this English guy and *Splendor* is going to be spelled with a U. [audience laughs] *Transatlantic Comics* is the name of it folks, and it'll be available in two stores in the Cleveland area. [audience laughs]

Feldman: Which two are they, Harvey, just for curiosity's sake?
Pekar: One of them is Mac's Backs on Coventry. I'm not sure actually that it'll be carried anyplace else. My comics are not in great demand [laughs] especially by comic book fans.

Feldman: I think there's probably an untapped market out there. I mean, these are fascinating to read. They really are. They're amazing.
Pekar: Yeah, well, I hoping there's an untapped market and I hope that you can do more for me in that respect . . . [audience laughs]

Feldman: If someone out somewhere across America is interested in picking up a copy of *American Splendor* and is wondering how they can do that, Harvey, how can they do that?
Pekar: Well, they can write to Dark Horse Comics in Milwaukee, Wisconsin . . . I'm sorry, Milwaukie, Oregon. I'm sorry.

Feldman: Yeah, that's a big difference.
Pekar: Let me look in here and see if I can give you the address. [audience laughs]

Feldman: I should have had that ready if I had been . . . yeah, Dark Horse Comics, Milwaukie—that's *ie* by the way—Oregon. Boy, my eyes are bad. Your eye's any better than mine? The little numbers they put in here. 10956 Southeast Main St, Milwaukie, Oregon 97222.
Pekar: Yeah, you can get them there. 'Cause you can't get 'em in Cleveland!

Feldman: Harvey, great to have you here.
Pekar: Michael, thanks.

Feldman: Harvey Pekar! Pick up a copy of *American Splendor*, read about life as it really is! Harvey Pekar!

Harvey Pekar

SHAWNA ERVIN-GORE / 1999

In the last twenty-five years, Harvey Pekar has established himself as an extremely influential comics creator and a somewhat eccentric cultural institution. To be honest, the only thing really "eccentric" about Pekar is his ageless refusal to put up with much crap from anybody—that, and his dedication to sharing intimate stories about his life and his insights into our society through his ongoing comics project, *American Splendor*. Pekar began self-publishing *American Splendor* in 1976 at the age of thirty-four with the help of a few well-known artists, including Robert Crumb.

The series has always been somewhat controversial and not entirely well liked within the comics industry, perhaps because it bears little resemblance to what many people would consider a comic book to be—nobody wears spandex, there's never any intergalactic warfare or international drama, and maybe once has a naked lady graced its pages. Pekar writes mostly autobiographical stories about personal struggles he's faced (the award-winning graphic novel *Our Cancer Year* is a harsh but shining example of how well his stories have worked), but most issues of *American Splendor* also include illustrated biographies or reports on musicians and authors he respects, and intelligent rants about social ills that few people seem to care about.

Pekar recently turned sixty, and what he writes about in his own life has taken a somewhat more melancholy turn, since he's dealing with issues like the onset of old age and the frightening possibility that, like his parents who each died relatively young, he might someday end up with a terrible disease like Alzheimer's. So it would be misleading to say that *American Splendor* is a fun time to be read by all, but discerning readers will always appreciate Pekar's wit and stamina, and the way he crafts compelling stories from relatively mundane aspects of his life. I spoke with Pekar recently about how his life is going and how it's affecting his work on *American Splendor*. Here's what he told me:

Shawna Ervin-Gore: When you first started *American Splendor*, why did you chose to tell your stories in the medium of comics?

Harvey Pekar: I think the main reason was that comics' potential was hardly being scratched at that point. There were some pretty amusing strips, but most comic books at the time were still being written for kids, and it was clear that you could do anything with comics that you could do with any other art form, but less of it was being done. I'd been familiar with comics, and I'd collected 'em when I was a kid, but after I got into junior high school, there wasn't much I was interested in.

More specifically, what stimulated me was I met Robert Crumb in 1962; he lived in Cleveland for a while. I took a look at his stuff, and of course Crumb couldn't do everything, but after looking at his stuff it occurred to me he was doing stuff beyond what other writers and artists were doing. It was a step beyond *Mad*, and it seemed to me that you could do anything in comics. So I started doing my thing, which is mainly influenced by novelists, stand-up comedians, and that sort of thing.

SE-G: How would you describe what you were doing with *American Splendor* when you first started the series compared to what you're doing with it now?

HP: *American Splendor* is just an ongoing journal. It's an ongoing auto-biography. I started it when I was in my early thirties, and I just keep going. Essentially all I've wanted this to be is a journal of a life, because I think that sort of thing is worth recording.

SE-G: What sort of topics have you been exploring lately?

HP: I'm writing about my life. I'm sixty now. My parents both got Alzheimer's disease in their late sixties and died a few years later. I figure that could very well happen to me. So it's gonna be quite a challenge to get through the next few years. My last comic, *The Terminal Years*, set the stage for what I'll be facing. I've got a twelve-year-old foster kid right now, and I've got to support her and my wife, who's unable to work.

The core of my income comes from working as a file clerk at the V.A. hospital in Cleveland, where I make about $24,000 a year. I've got thirty-five years in at the V.A., so I could retire, but if I did, I'd only take in 65 percent of what I make now.

I supplement my pay with freelance writing jobs. My income from that has fluctuated a lot from year to year, although overall it's going up. So deciding what to do about money is a major issue. Just keeping alive and trying to keep my wife and kid alive. The longer I do freelance writing on books and music, the more contacts I make. I've been doing comics for some of the newspapers I write for, you know, on jazz and musicians, and I've been doing some comics online.

My direct income from *American Splendor* has leveled off, and I don't expect it to go up. I don't look for any support from comic book fans, certainly, and comics aren't in the best shape anyway. On top of that, I've probably had my day in the sun. I think I've influenced a lot of comic book writers—I think I've focused a lot more than other writers

Pekar held onto his file clerk job in spite of adversity. Artwork by Alex Wald for "Holding On," reprinted in *The Best of American Splendor*, p. 157.

before me on realistic detail and the details of everyday living. Other people writing about me have said that I've influenced a lot of people, and there are some artists who have credited me with influencing them in interviews, and some of them are a lot more popular than I am today. So that's another reason I think that my day in the sun or my fifteen minutes, or however you'd care to say it, is over. I don't expect that to turn around. So if I'm going to make any money at comics, I'm going to have to get them published—initially, anyway—outside of comics, like in newspapers or magazines, then collect them into comics.

I've always felt that my work has a lot more interest for just about any reader. I think that the people who would be the least interested in my work would be people who read lots of comic books. I'm looking to make money possibly from movie options, too. I've got one going now—I just talked to them yesterday and they said they were working on it. The first idea flopped, and I don't know if they'll ever get around to proposing anything else after that.

The guy at the company that most recently optioned *American Splendor* is Ted Hope of Good Machine. That's the company, as you know, that made such movies as *The Ice Storm*. He's a good guy, and he really likes my work, and he's treated me very well. But I think the chances are against him being able to put together a movie. There are other people who have expressed interest, so I might be able to make money by optioning the rights to *American Splendor* again. If I did it would be helpful, and it might enable me to retire from my V.A. job. I don't expect to make billions of dollars, but if I can't make twenty-five or fifty thousand dollars in one lump, chances are I'll probably keep working 'til I'm sixty-seven, at which time I'll get something like eighty-something percent of my salary, and I couldn't go any higher than that.

SE-G: Do you like your job at the V.A.?
HP: Well, relatively speaking, I think it's been a good job. I've had it so long, I enjoy the people, and the work isn't very taxing. And also, my job involves moving around a lot. So I can do relatively easy, or relatively simple, work—and talk to people while I'm doing it. It's sort of a major part of my social life.

SE-G: And you've been there long enough now to enjoy certain freedoms, like taking phone calls.
HP: Yeah, they're pretty nice about that. It's almost like a family for me now. The employment situation in Cleveland isn't that great, so a job at

the V.A. isn't considered as bad as it might be in a place where jobs are plentiful. So people tend to stay here, and I've got a thing going. I joke with these people—one person, I'll talk about sports with 'em, and I'll talk about music with someone else.

SE-G: Some of these people wind up in your comics, too. Do you ever get feedback from people you've written about? Do you show them your comics when they get published?

HP: Sure I do, and they enjoy it. It's extremely seldom that anybody wants me to change what I've written about them. I can hardly remember any time that's happened. Generally I portray them in a good light, if they're friends. Of course, there are some people that I really dislike that I've written about, and I don't go up to them and ask for their approval (laughs).

SE-G: Where are you getting your writing published elsewhere?

HP: *Jazziz, Jazz Times, Bass Player Magazine*, the *Austin Chronicle*, the *Boston Herald*. In Cleveland, I write for a paper called *The Scene*.

SE-G: And aren't you doing an ongoing thing with an NPR website?

HP: Yeah. Currently I'm writing for . . . it's called *Public Interactive*. I hope that works out. It's a very nice job. And I also do commentary on a local NPR station. I can talk about pretty much anything I want to talk about.

SE-G: Is that weekly?

HP: Nah, it's irregular. Probably once a month. That gig has sort of thinned out, but it gives me a chance to do what some people would call "rants," or "schtick." I talk a lot about politics or whatever comes to mind. They've even asked me to read a couple of my comics stories. I read one on Valentine's Day called "Alice Quinn," about when I was between marriages. Some lady that I'd known as a kid and had a secret crush on, I ran into her at the bank, and we got to talking. She was nice as ever, and I looked at her hand, and she had a wedding ring on. I went over to her house and I met her family, and all that. It was nice, but it's sort of a tearjerker. I went home and felt kinda melancholy. And the next day I got up and went to work.

Harvey Pekar

SHAWNA ERVIN-GORE / 2001

From Dark Horse Comics' website.
© 2001 Dark Horse Comics, Inc.

Harvey Pekar long ago secured his position as the neurotic godfather of autobiographical comics. Pekar has been publishing his searingly honest comic book *American Splendor* for twenty-five years, and in that time his work has inspired everyone from punk upstarts like *Peepshow*'s Joe Matt to best-selling comic-book writers such as Warren Ellis.

    American Splendor is a one-of-a-kind blend of touchingly insightful personal confessions, rants against the downfalls of middle-class life in America, and great retrospectives of the contributions of unsung heroes in the fields of music and literature, all written by Pekar and illustrated by phenomenal artists such as Joe Sacco, Frank Stack, and David Collier. In April, Dark Horse is publishing the next volume of *American Splen-*

dor, aptly titled *Portrait of the Author in His Declining Years*. I recently called Pekar at his job as a file clerk for the V.A. hospital in his neighborhood in Cleveland to talk with him about the twenty-fifth anniversary of *American Splendor* and how his writing has evolved in a quarter-century's time.

Shawna Ervin-Gore: I wanted to start by talking a little about why you chose to start writing comics. It's been twenty-five years since your first issue of *American Splendor*, and I'm curious how you decided that comics would be a good medium for you to work in.

Harvey Pekar: It was one of those things where, you know, I'd read comics—and even collected comics a little—when I was a kid, and I really liked it as a storytelling medium. It can be very effective. But I eventually grew out of the sort of thing I was reading as a kid and didn't have much to do with comics for a long time after that. But I always paid attention to media and eventually people started doing different things with comics, specifically in the '60s with underground cartoonists drawing comics and using the medium to tell stories that were nothing like the superhero stuff I'd seen before.

In 1972, I hooked up with Robert Crumb, who I knew from around town here in Cleveland, and he illustrated a couple of stories that I wrote. They were actually storyboarded. That's how I script comics stories.

Anyway, Crumb liked my stuff, so we worked on a few stories together. I started to see all of these possibilities that would work with comics, and I really got in to it. It was really exciting to consider this new—well, it wasn't new, but using comics like this was pretty new—format as a writer. A lot of comics before the underground cartoonists came along were aimed at kids, or at least they were big on escapist writing. I thought you could do realistic writing in comics the same as you can in any other medium.

SE-G: Were the first stories you did autobiographical, or did you start with broader topics?

HP: No, they were mostly autobiographical. The thing I know most is my own life, and I thought I could write about it in a way that other people could relate to—and I wasn't necessarily thinking of comic-book fans relating to my work, but just anyone who might read. My main writing influences were prose fiction writers.

SE-G: One of the last times we talked, you mentioned that you were also influenced in your writing style by standup comedians. And, as you just said, your scripts for comic stories are all done as storyboards. When I look at your rough scripts, it's easy to see where the standup influence comes in, especially when you put yourself in this sort-of narrator position, speaking directly to the audience. What are you thinking about when you're sitting down at the planning level and deciding where you should be in the panel versus where the rest of the story should be happening?

HP: For the most part I'm thinking about timing: how to break up the dialogue, or if I'm trying to be humorous, how to arrange the panel for maximum effect. Sometimes it's just being thoughtful about where to put the final word when I'm finishing up a rap. So pacing and timing are two of the important things to me. Sometimes I don't end up using as many head-shots in the final product because I like to leave a lot of that up to the artists. I just want to get the words and the pacing in, so I'll storyboard a talking head into the script, but as long as the artist can get the point across and illustrate what I'm saying in the panel, I don't really care if my head's there or not.

SE-G: All of the artists you work with are very competent visual storytellers, too.

HP: That's true. It's also up to me to give them as much reference as possible about the story I've written. I do have a lot of set ideas sometimes, but I always want to discuss things with the illustrators because they can come up with good ideas, too. I don't want to limit them and have it seem like I'm dictating what they do.

SE-G: I'm curious about how you collect your story ideas, say, with the biographical essays on musicians and writers—do you keep a running list of people you want to write about, either real or in your head?

HP: I just keep stuff in my head. I write record reviews and book reviews, so I'm always in the process of doing research, and I'm always running across people who haven't been talked about enough, and I want to talk about them. I've done a lot of stories about writers and musicians—not just jazz musicians, either.

SE-G: Speaking of jazz, what have you been listening to lately? What's on your turntable?

HP: Well, I always try to concentrate on *avant garde* jazz, the stuff that's happening now. That's what critics are supposed to do, or at least, that's what I feel I'm supposed to do. I think it's important to listen to what's going on now and try to write as accurately as possible and present that to readers by saying, "listen, check this guy out." There's this one amazing musician named Joe Maneri, and I've written about him before, even in comics, but he's someone I'm very impressed with. There are a lot of guys in the downtown New York scene, the so-called "new music" scene, and that's what I'm writing about.

SE-G: What about books? In the past you've written about Daniel Fuchs and other relatively unsung or contemporary writers . . .

HP: I just read a book by Stanley Elkin, and I just reviewed something by Gertrude Stein called *Lucy Church Amiably*. I feel the same way about writers that I do about musicians, and I like prose fiction, so I try to keep up with what the more modern and more innovative people are doing, because that's where my head's at. I think innovation is the key thing, or originality, at least. People should have their own voice and should contribute to the vocabulary of the art form they're working in rather than copying other people.

SE-G: With that in mind, how has your own work changed or evolved? What are you doing differently now that you may not have been doing when you first got started?

HP: The focus and content of my stories is changing as I go through different stages of life. Now I'm an official senior citizen, you know. I got my "Golden Buckeye" card from the state of Ohio (laughs) and I'm getting letters all the time from the AARP. So that's a lot of different stuff to deal with. And I'm doing a bit more of the biographical stuff, on musicians and other people, and I wasn't doing as much of that before. I'm also starting to work on some longer biographical pieces now, and I haven't done that very much. One of the stories I'm working on is about a woman I've known for a really long time who went from being on welfare to becoming an M.D. and a fierce advocate of poor people's rights.

Another one I'm working on at the same time is about a guy I work with now who was in Vietnam and what happened to him after Vietnam. It's not a typical Vietnam story, or what people would think of as a typical Vietnam vet-type story, anyway. This is someone I've known for a long time, and I think he's got a really interesting story. So, I'm shifting focus that way, trying to do more different things.

My writing has changed, though. From a technical standpoint, I think it's better than ever.

SE-G: That must come from all the writing assignments you do—the reviews and essays you write—for various magazines, in addition to your comics writing.

HP: Yeah, I think so. Even though my panels continue to be wordy, and deliberately so, I am able to make points now using fewer and fewer words. I'm using language more efficiently now, and that's something else. These are all processes—changes in my writing style—that have taken time to develop, but it's been going on from the start.

SE-G: I think the story in your upcoming issue about your foster daughter, Danielle, is a departure from some of your other autobiographical stories. Even though you've written about very personal topics in the past, like having cancer in *Our Cancer Year*, something about this story feels more vulnerable than other stories you've written. Do you see a difference there, or do you think it has something to do with having a kid in your life.

HP: I don't know. For one thing, I don't really think of Danielle as being a kid—I see her more as being another human being that I live with, and I like her a lot. I'm trying to adjust to her and hope she can adjust to me, and I'm trying to be responsible. I can't say "Wow, it's really dramatically changed my life," but maybe it has. It's been kind of a slow process.

We've been taking care of Danielle since 1997, and I never thought I could do it. I never thought I could handle a kid. Maybe if it was more of a jump, if it was a little baby or something, I couldn't do it. But Danielle was nine years old when she came to us, and she's a real bright, sharp kid. She's got some problems to overcome, but she's doing really well, and we're working together on

Fatherhood brought a new dimension to Pekar's stories seen in his collaboration with Richard Corben, "Halloween Glasses," from *American Splendor: Another Day.*

a lot of things. I think whenever anyone moves into your house and you become responsible to them, it's a big thing and you respond to that.

SE-G: I was laughing reading that story because you mention how Danielle likes Pokémon and *Sailor Moon* and a lot of those "kid entertainment" things. It made me wonder how you, as someone who's essentially a cultural critic, feels about that sort of entertainment for your kid.

HP: Well, you know, I hope she doesn't still like it when she's twenty-five (laughs). It's all right with me. I liked a lot of stuff like that, or the equivalent of that, when I was a kid, too. I just hope she moves on. She's already gotten past the Spice Girls, and she's losing interest in Pokémon, but she really likes Japanese animation and even does some drawing.

SE-G: The thing is that a lot of that can be good. I would expect you to like some of it, maybe not Pokémon . . .

HP: Yeah, some of it's pretty good, and some of it's pretty bad. Did you ever hear of this Japanese film called *Totoro?*

SE-G: Yes! That's one of the best kids' films, I think.

HP: That was pretty good. She's also into *Harry Potter*, I'll tell you that. And that's cool with me. I don't try to shape her tastes or anything.

SE-G: So other than your Danielle story, what else is in this issue of *American Splendor?*

HP: Of course, I've got one story on my guy Toby, who is someone I work with. You might call him a continuing character or something, because I've written about him a lot. He's got some pretty unusual things to say sometimes. I try to make the stories somewhat different from each other. I've also got one in there about the guy who hooked me up with the movie deal. There's always a movie deal (pending for *American Splendor*), I guess, but this one seems better than others I've been involved with. So I wrote a story about the guy who helped me get that going.

Pekar's attitude towards a possible movie was one of taking whatever money he could get for it. Artwork by Gerry Shamray, from "Selling Out," reprinted in *The Best of American Splendor*, p. 29.

SE-G: Tell me more about the movie deal. The last time we talked I think you told me you'd written a script for it.

HP: The producer, a guy named Ted Hope at Good Machine (the company that produced *Crouching Tiger, Hidden Dragon* and *The Ice Storm* for Ang Lee), is working on this. He's gotten some money to get started on the film—not enough to finish it, I guess, but it's a start. I wrote a script for it before, and I don't know how much of that they're going to use. We had one prospect for a director lined up at one point, but then he couldn't do it, so Hope came up with someone else. What he (the director) wants to do is a combination of documentary and dramatic elements. He hasn't formulated exactly what he wants to do yet. He'll probably do the next script, since I didn't envision this in quite the same way. I just hope we can get going on it in the next few months.

Harvey Pekar

"M. PEG" / 2002

From Dark Horse Comics' website.
© 2002 Dark Horse Comics, Inc.

2002 marks the tenth year that Dark Horse Comics has been publish-
ing Harvey Pekar's acclaimed *American Splendor* series and August sees
the beginning of his biggest series so far; the three-issue *Unsung Hero*. It
may also prove to be the most ambitious as Pekar uses all three issues to
tell the story of one man: Vietnam veteran Robert McNeill.

Fans who previously enjoyed *American Splendor* will not be disappointed as *Unsung Hero* delivers the same excellent and off-beat story
telling that they have come to expect.

I recently spoke with Harvey Pekar via telephone from his home in
Cleveland, Ohio.

M. Peg: My first question is how did you find Robert McNeill and hear his story?

Harvey Pekar: Well, Robert McNeill and I worked together at the VA hospital and he was a file clerk. I was sort of responsible for getting him his job, you know, because he had been working on the grounds as a temp worker and he was about to be let go, although everybody thought he was such a hard worker. I tried to get him a gig up in the record room where I was. I don't know exactly to what to attribute it to, but he did get a job there, and we got to be friends. We were actually sort of friends before then—we used to talk a lot.

MP: So these are stories that he told you over time?

HP: Yeah, well, he started telling me stuff about his tour in Vietnam, and he was such a good storyteller, and so intelligent and modest, you know? And I thought I would like to do a series of books about him.

MP: One thing I did notice, in reading this compared to other issues of *American Splendor* is how little of your presence is felt. Is that because he was such a good storyteller?

HP: Yeah, I mean there was no need for me to be messing around, breaking in. I wanted it to unfold as smoothly as possible.

MP: You decided to do three issues on one person's story—in the future do you see going back to the usual mix of autobiography, music, and literary biography?

HP: Yeah, yeah, I just wanted to do as many issues as it took to get Robert's story down, and it took three. But I am continuing to write stories that are autobiographical and—

MP: Are you still doing music reviews and cultural reviews?

HP: Yeah, yeah. I still do that.

MP: How do you decide what artist you want to get to do which stories? It must be hard because you work with some really creative people.

HP: Well, it all depends partly on who's available and partly on how they feel about the book. You know, how they reacted to the stories, and also, how well I think they could do on a particular story.

MP: So when you are writing it do you have an artist in mind, or is it . . . ?

HP: Sometimes. Sometimes I do and sometimes it comes later, it depends. You know, I can't say that there is any hard and fast rule about that.

MP: What about this project?

HP: Well, I had been working with David Collier a little bit in the past, and yeah, David was the guy I wanted to work with because he had had a background in the Canadian Army and stuff. And he really knew what Robert was talking about, and how to illustrate it.

David Collier depicted both Pekar and an older Robert McNeill in *American Splendor: Unsung Hero*.

MP: In an interview a couple of years ago, you said when you first started to do comics, you just wanted to tell stories that you weren't seeing being done. Do you see those stories more now, especially with the influence of *American Splendor*?

HP: Well, I mean, I don't know. I think comics are kind in rough shape now. You know, yeah sure, I see where I have influenced a lot of people, I don't want to sound immodest but, I mean, they have acknowledged the influence. And I am glad that's happened. At the same time, I'm not happy about the difficult times that comics are experiencing currently, especially the alternative comics.

MP: What comics have you been reading?

HP: Lately I haven't been reading many comics at all. I mean, I don't get them sent to me, and so I don't get a chance to look at them.

MP: Do you see yourself continuing writing comics in the future?

HP: Yeah, well, I mean, absolutely. I wrote a story yesterday.

MP: Oh, was that the story for the *Dark Horse Maverick Annual*?

HP: Well, I am writing something for Diana Schutz and illustrated by Joe Sacco. What's the name of the annual?

MP: *Happy Endings*.

HP: Oh, yeah. I've done that. That's already completed and should be on its way to Diana.

MP: I wanted to finish up by asking about the *American Splendor* movie. I see now that the Internet Movie Database is calling it a TV movie.

HP: Well, it was financed by HBO, but the producers were a company called Good Machine. It's going to be on HBO. They put up the money for it. It's got a really good reaction and prior to [it airing on HBO] we will probably be at film festivals and they are trying to get it in theaters, too. I don't know how that is going to work out, but there is a lot of enthusiasm for the movie and for Good Machine. Are you familiar with the Good Machine? They're the company that did *Crouching Tiger, Hidden Dragon*, and *In the Bedroom* and they did some other Ang Lee movies. Are you familiar with that?

MP: Yeah, I think they're pretty well known.

HP: My wife's just told me, that they are doing *The Hulk*, with Ang Lee directing. But, in any event, this thing has got a lot of enthusism and they have got a very good track record. You know, in terms of making high quality films that people really dig.

MP: Are you expecting the movie to bring more exposure to the comics.

HP: Yeah. Well, I hope it brings me good luck because, you know, I mean I want to get something out of it (laughs).

Harvey Pekar's Life Hits the Big Screen in *American Splendor*

REBECCA MURRAY / 2003

From *About.com—Your Guide to Hollywood Movies*.
Reprinted by permission of The New York Times
Syndication Sales Corporation.

Hot off impressive wins at the Sundance and Cannes Film Festivals,
American Splendor began its limited theatrical run in select theaters
August 15, 2003.

Based on the *American Splendor* comic book series by Harvey
Pekar, the film follows the ordinary life of working-class "Everyman,"
Pekar (played by Paul Giamatti). From his daily grind as a file clerk at
the VA Hospital to dealings with artists and his relationship with his wife
Joyce, even the most ordinary situations are encapsulated in this striking
dramatic showcase of a year in one man's life.

Harvey Pekar's a very interesting man to talk to. He's blunt, to
the point, and doesn't mince words. Here's what he had to say about

American Splendor the movie and about the current state of the comic book industry:

Rebecca Murray: How much input did you have in casting Paul Giamatti?

Harvey Pekar: I left that up to [the filmmakers]. I knew I wasn't competent to make the best choice in the matter. I figured they knew more about the acting talent available out there than I did, so I just let them go ahead and do it. I didn't want to try and intrude all over the place.

Murray: So when you pictured your comic book being made into a film, you didn't actually have anyone in mind to play yourself?
Pekar: Not really, I don't go to see a lot of movies.

Murray: Once Paul Giamatti was cast, did he study your mannerisms?
Pekar: No, he studied videotapes of me. He read the comic books. He didn't just say, "Let's take an afternoon off so I can try and get down some of your mannerisms." His idea was to do an interpretation of me, not an imitation.

Murray: What do you think about his portrayal?
Pekar: I'm very happy with it. I like what Paul did.

Murray: Do you think he captured the feel of your life and your comic books?
Pekar: Yeah, I think so, about as well as a movie can.

Murray: Were you leery of what Hollywood might change your life and your comic books into when they first approached you with the idea of making *American Splendor* the movie?
Pekar: No, I wasn't that leery. First of all, I'd heard a lot of good things about [producer] Ted Hope from people that I was confident in. When they said he was okay, I figured he was. When I met him, I was pretty much convinced of it. He has quite an impressive track record. I didn't imagine that the film would be as good as it turned out, but I thought he'd do a good job.

Murray: Did you think it would be more along the lines of a documentary or did you think it would be more along the lines of what it ended up being?
Pekar: I think he indicated in the beginning that he might want a mixture of styles. Of course that came to fruition with Shari Berman and Bob Pul-

cini's script. They had all these ideas; they were thinking along the same lines as Ted. He gave them these comic books and they saw where I was drawn in all sorts of different ways by different artists. They decided they could have more than one version of me.

Murray: Which artist do you believe drew you the best?
Pekar: It depends on what you are looking for. Probably the two greatest all-around artists that I've worked with are Frank Stack and Robert Crumb. There is a guy named Gerry Shamray who has a real realistic style. When he was at his most zealous he would take maybe an average of one Polaroid per panel. He would copy the Polaroids and then he would add his own touches. His work was very interesting from a textural standpoint, too. I thought Jerry was really interesting. I thought Sue Cavey had a real nice lyrical quality to her work. I've worked with some pretty fine people over the years.

Murray: You've stated you wanted the film to remain honest and not have a Hollywood ending. Why was that so important to you?
Pekar: It would have gone against everything that I've been trying to accomplish as a comic book writer. I try and write the way things happen. I try and portray them accurately. I don't try and fulfill people's wishes. Not everything in my book is about unhappiness, but I wanted a kind of an ambivalent ending and that's what I got.

Murray: When you first read the script, what was your reaction to actually being in the film itself?
Pekar: I wasn't concerned about that. I'd been in films before, not a lot, but I've been in a couple of films. I felt comfortable with them. I guess the key is that I felt comfortable doing everything with those people. I liked them an awful lot and I respected their work a lot. It was no problem for me to cooperate with them.

Murray: How has the film's success helped the comic book?
Pekar: I don't know what kind of an effect it's had on the comic book. The film's success so far involves winning a couple of prizes at Cannes and Sundance, and getting some very nice reviews in newspapers and magazines. That hasn't had a big impact on my life yet.

What I want to do is I want to improve my life with this film.

Specifically I'm talking about I'd like to make more money because I have a fifteen-year-old foster daughter and I have a wife to support. I'm already retired and I'm sixty-three years old. My pension is not enough to make it for us. I've got to try and pick up more freelance writing work. I'm hoping that this film helps me do that. I've gotten some pretty lucrative freelance writing jobs out of it so far, but it's stuff that's connected with the film. For example, a six-page story for *Entertainment Weekly* about how the film evolved. I want to be getting work that is more like the work I did before the film. I want to be able to do that on a regular basis. I'd like to find a few good editors that I could work with on a consistent basis. People that saw things the way that I did. I found a couple of people. I'm just hoping I can find a few more and maybe rest a little bit easier about my future.

Murray: How do the people in your life, specifically your wife and your foster daughter, feel about the movie?

Pekar: They are very happy with it, especially Danielle my kid. She's real excited about it. She likes the film. She got a big kick out of meeting all the people that were involved in making the film. She's a little starstruck. She's got a crush on half the cast of *Harry Potter* and half the cast of the *Lord of the Rings*.

Murray: Is she looking down the road at what she wants to do?

Pekar: I think she would normally be interested in being some kind of an artist, some kind of a visual artist. When she first used to come over to our house when she was nine, she liked to work with my wife's art supplies. She's got some talent. She's got the patience to learn a lot of these processes. We just have to see where it goes. I think what she's most interested in doing now is something in visual arts.

Murray: Why was the *Cancer Year* chosen as a focal point for the movie?

Pekar: It was one of the turning points of my life. My life was in the balance. I didn't know whether I was going to live or die. I was very depressed by having the cancer and the treatments. It just so happened that I was moving into a new house at the same time it was discovered that I had this lymphoma. There were just some real important things that were going on, and they were happening simultaneously. Some of them resolved, some didn't. I went into remission for cancer, but I've had it since then. I had it in 2002. I'm supposed to be in remission again.

Murray: Was it tough for you to see that on film? That's a really personal story.

Pekar: That doesn't bother me. There are things that I've done that I'm kind of ashamed of; everybody is like that. I'm not ashamed of having

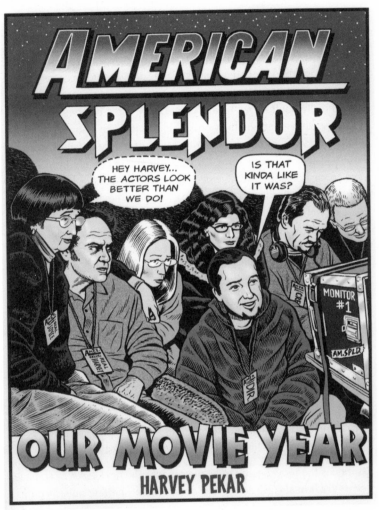

Mark Zingarelli's cover to *Our Movie Year*.

cancer, and I'm not ashamed of having that portrayed. Things like that never used to bother me. Reviewing some intimate details of my life didn't bother me as long as I could live with what I had done.

Murray: How important are events like the San Diego Comic Con to you?

Pekar: I really don't know. I really don't have a lot in common with a lot of the people who attend the Comic Con. It's just like assuming that all people who write prose are the same. My stuff is very different, even though I use comic book form, it's very different in content from what most comic books are like. I've been at comic conventions before and I've been at the San Diego Comic Con a couple of times, primarily just dragging my work across the country to get a booth and set up and try and sell the stuff. Just to try and make a few hundred extra bucks. I never felt real comfortable [at the Comic Con] because I never felt like I had that much in common with the typical superhero fan that comes to these things.

Although I think comics have far more potential than I think a lot of people realize, still there's not a whole lot more being done with them than was done back in the '60s. I would feel much better if the alternative comic book movement was much stronger than it is now.

Murray: Do you think your main audience has changed over the years?

Pekar: I think it's the same type of people. People who are maybe readers of good fiction, who aren't particularly interested in comic books—in most comic books. [They're interested in] maybe alternative comic books but not *Superman*, *Batman*, Mickey Mouse-kind of stuff.

Murray: Is the movie going to be written into the next series of comics?

Pekar: Yes. I'm already doing stuff about it that's getting published in different magazines and books. They just haven't been collected into anything. I don't know what direction to go as far as a publisher's concerned right now. Publications like *Entertainment Weekly*, *New York Times*, *Time Out*—it seems like these kinds of publications are more interested in my work than straight comic book publications.

Murray: Has it always been that way?

Pekar: Yes. I thought that if I was around doing comics since 1972 and I figured I would actually be—and comics would actually be—a little bit farther ahead by this time than they've gotten. Things improved a little bit in the '80s; there was kind of a revival of alternative comics but then they went downhill again in the '90s and they haven't pulled out of it since then. In general, I think comic book industry has been hurt since about 1990. Some of the wounds have been self-inflicted.

Murray: What hurt the industry so badly? Is there one particular event you can point to?

Pekar: The one thing that was the start was when—see, I could be completely wrong about this—one of the major companies, I think Marvel, got an exclusive distributorship with one distributor. So other comic book companies responded in kind, trying to get exclusive distributorships. From that point on, it just seemed like things sort of really deteriorated. At that point, I know that sales started to plummet. At one point Marvel Comics was just about bankrupt. These problems have been with comics for quite some time. Business as well as aesthetic problems, I think. They haven't figured a way out yet. They are certainly as viable an art form as I'd want. I think you can do anything with comics that you could do in just about any art form. I just continue to be kind of disappointed that people don't realize that and try and diversify the kind of work they are doing in comics. Maybe comics aren't as glamorous as some of these other forms.

I always thought I had a great opportunity when I started doing my comic book in 1972. I thought there was so much territory to work in, and so many different ways you could use comics. I didn't use all of them but I was hoping that I would be an inspiration to some other guys to experiment, too. I didn't put the whole thing on my shoulders but I'd hope I'd have some impact. There hasn't been enough change in comics to suit me. It seems clear now that all kinds of things can be done in comics and people just aren't doing them. I don't know why exactly.

The Conversation

STEPHEN GARRETT / 2003

From *Esquire* (August 2003), p. 22.
Reprinted by permission of
Stephen Garrett.

In 1976, Harvey Pekar, a brooding, self-obsessed file clerk from Cleve-
land, teamed up with pal R. Crumb to produce the autobiographical
comic book *American Splendor*. Now Pekar and his rants about daily life
are the subject of a quirky, Sundance-winning biopic from Shari Springer
Berman and Robert Pulcini. *American Splendor*, which opens August 15,
blends documentary footage with an eerily perfect portrayal of Pekar by
actor Paul Giamatti (*Saving Private Ryan, Planet of the Apes*). Esquire
eavesdropped on a conversation between the two Pekars.

Paul Giamatti: People keep asking me. What's *American Splendor*
about? I'd be sad if it were really about anything.

Harvey Pekar: My comic books have always been compelling to me. Why they're compelling to other people I don't know. Sales indicate that they're not particularly compelling.

PG: They're compelling to a select group of people.

HP: I focus on everyday incidents that a lot of writers don't think are worth writing about. I think that that's maybe my appeal.

PG: But it's how you experience them that makes it interesting.

HP: Yeah, well, it's gotta be somebody. It might as well be me.

PG: When you heard I was going to be you in the movie, did you think, the ape guy's gonna play me?

HP: I didn't hold it against you that you played an orangutan.

PG: The orangutan and you—those are the high points of my career!

HP: Actually, I've seen different people play me in different ways on-stage—one of them being Dan Castellaneta, of Homer Simpson fame.

PG: It's difficult playing a real person. People flip out and try to tell you how to do it—a huge pain in the ass. I mean, you were a pain in the ass, too, but in a different way. You gave me crap about my father [the late baseball commissioner and former Yale University president A. Bartlett Giamatti].

HP: I don't remember. They tell me I said you'll never be the man your father was. Did I do that?

PG: That was right when I first met you. That was brutal.

HP: We need people to rein in guys like Pete Rose. Maybe I didn't think you had it in you. You're a terrific actor, but you can't do everything.

PG: Is it true that you never read the movie's script?

HP: It's probably true. I didn't want to go meddling around. I just hope it brings me something, that's all. Money. More work. Actually, I wrote a comic-book story about Sundance. I want you to illustrate it.

PG: I'll try. I mean, I'm not much of a cartoonist, but it sounds like fun.

HP: Maybe we'll get it published in *Esquire*.

PG: How about that!

HP: And they'll pay us for it!

In Depth:
The Harvey Pekar Interview

JOE ZABEL / 2004

From the *Graphic Novel Review*
(January 2005). Reprinted by permission of
Joe Zabel.

It's hard to get used to the idea of Harvey Pekar smiling; he's been for
so long the somber embodiment of pessimism and existential anguish.
Even when celebrity came his way, via the David Letterman show, his
face remained laden with the weight of an all-pervasive gloom.

But with the motion picture version of *American Splendor*, something finally came out right for Harvey. The film was widely praised for.
its excellence, and it was true to the autobiographical saga Harvey had
been authoring all these years.

Most importantly, the publicity of the film brought unprecedented
attention to Harvey's comics, and the reprint volume of his early works
achieved the highest sales he's ever experienced. This has led to a multi-

book deal with Ballantine Books, the first of which is *American Splendor, Our Movie Year*, released early last month in December 2004.

We sat down with Harvey to discuss the first new volume from Ballantine. He was relatively cheerful and delighted to answer our questions.

Zabel: I wanted to start out by asking you just how you go about writing autobiographical stories. I think a lot of people have the impression that it's really simple, like writing in a diary. Is there more to it than that?

Pekar: There's more to it, yeah. For one thing you're not writing straight prose, you're writing for comics, which means you've got to do a storyboard script, I've gotta break up the prose, and I want it to have a certain rhythm. Some stories come easier than others. Something funny might happen to me really fast. If I'm doing something with Toby—Toby is just amazing, some of the stuff he says. When I hear Toby come up with something, I'll just grab a piece of paper and write it right down, because if you don't get it just right, you'll have missed a lot—he puts things so novelly.

There are other stories where I've gone through a long experience, and I have to organize it and figure out.

Zabel: How do you decide where the story begins and where the story ends?

Pekar: Usually I have the parameters of the story in mind before I do it. For example, I have a long story in the new book about going on a trip around the world. I knew I was going to start it by telling the readers just what the trip was about, and then taking them through it chronologically; and it ends when I got back home, it's just as simple as that.

Zabel: That brings up an interesting point—in some of your more ambitious pieces, you know that you're going to write about something before you experience it. I remember when you had just found out you had cancer, we were talking about it; and you knew that you were going to write about it. That book, of course, was *Our Cancer Year*.

Pekar: I had to write about it. What I'm trying to do is write a kind of a lifelong journal or diary, so that someone can follow my life over decades. So when I found out I had cancer, there was no doubt in my mind I was gonna write about it—that's not a small thing! When something big like that comes up, I figure I'll probably write about it, and I try to pay attention to what's going on.

Zabel: A lot of your recent work has departed from autobiography into the area of straight biography, i.e., you writing about other people's lives. For example, you've done a lot of portraits of great jazz musicians. How did you start doing those?

Pekar: I was writing jazz criticism for the *Village Voice*. One of the editors was a fan of my cartoon work. And, well, the prose of my jazz criticism wasn't as lively as what they wanted, and this editor wasn't as much interested in the technical stuff I was writing about. He suggested, "Why don't you do a cartoon thing about that." So I said fine, and I did it. And they paid really good money for it. So I continued writing histories of these musicians who were underappreciated and who had interesting stories to tell. Originally I did them just for the *Voice*; but I like to keep everything I do in print, so I reprinted these pieces in comics. And then other people started to notice the stuff, like the editors of the *Cleveland Free Times*, and they'd ask me to do things like that.

I do these pieces partly for money, to tell you the truth, although I'm obviously interested in jazz criticism. But sometimes I'll need a couple hundred bucks, and I'll start thinking about who can I write about now? Who's coming into town?

From there it branched out to where I was even doing a couple of pieces about baseball for local publications. I thought their readers would be interested, and the editors went along with me.

Zabel: These jazz pieces, they do teach people a lot about music, but they also seem to be very rich in anecdotal detail. For example, the scene where T-bone is on stage doing the split, and the women in the audience are throwing panties and money at him. Where do you find that kind of material?

Pekar: Well, I read a lot about jazz. For the T-bone piece, at the time there were a couple of T-Bone albums that had come out, with extensively detailed booklets in them. Sometimes I'll just write about somebody I'm learning about at the time, where I come across an interesting story.

Zabel: Do you interview some of these musicians?

Pekar: Yeah, some of them I interview, if they're not dead. Especially when I'm talking about experimental musicians, and I want to be accurate about what they're trying to do, I'd just as soon quote them as make an educated guess. Joe Maneri I've interviewed, and Tio Massaro, people like that who are still around.

Zabel: In some cases, you've turned over whole issues of *American Splendor* to telling someone else's story. Starting with Colin Warneford, what can you tell us about him?

Pekar: Colin was a guy from England who just started corresponding with me. He was on welfare, and he said he had Asperger's Syndrome, which is a mild form of autism. He was writing me letters in these really thick packages, twenty-five pages long, handwritten. And he'd include some of his artwork, and I'd think, God, this guy is a good artist!

So I thought I could do something on Colin; his story was really interesting, and I could identify with some of it, the way in school he used to be excluded.

Zabel: We talked about this years ago, and I think your original idea was to have an artist work with him to put together a story. But it looks like he ended up doing his entire segment of that issue.

Pekar: Yeah, he did. I took the text from his letters, and I made up a script and sent it to him, and he illustrated it. I think he's a very fine illustrator, and pretty original. I would have liked to work with him again, but it got increasingly difficult for me to contact him and have coherent conversations with him. I used to talk to him on the phone all the time in Britain, and even though he was on welfare he would sometimes call me.

Zabel: Reading his issue, I was struck by a parallel, or at least some common themes with your own work—depression and alienation. Do you identify with his plight?

Pekar: Very much. I like to think I'm in better shape than him, but I've gone through a lot of the stuff he has. Maybe it didn't hit me as hard.

Zabel: You were mentioning that Toby Radloff might possibly have something similar to Asperger's Syndrome.

Pekar: I don't think Toby's ever gone to a shrink and asked for a diagnosis. But Colin used to send me excerpts from medical journals describing Asperger's, and it sounded just like Toby. The fact that Toby doesn't modulate his voice, how he would take everything literally. And the funny thing is that when I talked to Colin, he sounded just like a normal guy. Colin actually doesn't seem to fit the diagnosis of Asperger's as well as Toby does. But Toby's high-functioning, he's not so afflicted that he can't work.

Zabel: Toby's actually a pretty good conversationalist. I car-pooled with him out to an event with you in Toronto at the Beguiling. I talked to him about all kinds of stuff; for instance, he belonged to an antiquated computer club, and told me all about this subculture of people programming on this model that isn't manufactured anymore.

As a matter of fact, one of the running themes of *American Splendor* is focusing on Toby's life. In some ways these have been the most dramatic developments in *American Splendor*.

Pekar: Yeah, I've tried to keep a running account of Toby in the comics, to keep people up to date with him. He's an amazing character. For a guy who just went through hell when he was a kid, who was just mercilessly picked on in school because he sounded funny, he's putting it together pretty well.

As a matter of fact, they're shooting a movie in Cleveland starring Danny DeVito and Parker Posey; and somebody some kind of way cast Toby in it. A lot of times I've been responsible for setting up Toby with people; I'm talking to some guy who comes around making a movie and I say, "Let me introduce you to this guy I know who's pretty amazing." Now, with the *American Splendor* movie, stuff is getting out about Toby, and people don't have to be told about him—they know.

Zabel: He was in those *Killer Nerd* movies, which you still see ads for on the internet.

Pekar: The way we got involved in that was that in 1988 Tony Isabella and some folks organized this big Superman convention in Cleveland; they were trying to raise money for a statue of Superman. It turned out to be a disaster—they lost so much money on that. Anyway, I was down there, trying to peddle some comics, and my ex-brother-in-law came down there and told me that there were a couple of would-be filmmakers (they were doing commercials for a cable channel at the time). They had access to video equipment, and they were wondering if I would be interested in doing a project with them. I wasn't that interested, but I thought that, every time I introduced Toby to somebody, they've gone for him. So I asked Toby to come down to the convention with me, and these guys came down and met him, and they were just swept away, and they thought right away where they could use him.

It would really be something if he were to go on to slowly build a career in movies; I don't know anybody else like him.

Zabel: Getting back to biography, another one you did was a three-issue saga, *Unsung Hero*, about Robert McNeill, an African American soldier in Vietnam. How did you get to know him?

Pekar: Robert was a patient at the VA hospital where I worked. And then he got a minimum-wage job from the hospital cleaning up the grounds. I'd see him out there, and he was always working so hard; I mean, most people don't kill themselves on these kind of jobs, but he was so responsible. So we got to talking, and I thought that we could really use someone like this in the record room where I worked; so I talked to my supervisor about him, and he eventually got a job there. I'm glad he got into the VA because it's a steady job; and the way George Bush is going, there's gonna be plenty of veterans to populate the VA hospitals!

We got to be friends, and we got to talking, and he started telling me about his adventures, in bits and pieces. And I thought it would make a really good series of comics. So I interviewed him and took down his story. Fortunately, he's a really good storyteller. He gets right to the point, he doesn't mess around. And he hits on interesting subjects all the time.

So it went very, very smoothly. And I got this fella, David Collier, from Canada; and David I guess wasn't used to making a lot of money. Dark Horse paid me about seventeen dollars a page for this project. And I think David got, for the three issues of this series, about $1,500.

Zabel: David did an excellent job on it, too.

Pekar: One of the reasons I asked David to do it was because David, although he's Canadian and they don't have a draft, had actually volunteered and served in the Canadian Army, and he knew something about what rifles looked like and things like that.

As a matter of fact, David's kept in touch and sent me postcards, and he told me that afterward, he got a grant to do some comic book work about war on the basis of what he'd done with me. And the Canadian Government sent him to Afghanistan! I haven't talked to him since then, I hope he's outta there.

Zabel: Yeah, I'm kind of a fan of David's work from the series, *Colliers*, that he did for Fantagraphics. I wanted to ask you about Robert, and also this reflects on the jazz pieces you've done. It seems to me that in *American Splendor*, the experiences of African Americans plays an important part in the story. Oftentimes you attempt to record black dialect, and the attitudes of black people. Is this just a case of working with material you have close to hand?

Pekar: Yeah, not only that, but when I was a kid, I was the only white kid in the neighborhood my age. And I had a nickname—I was called White Cracker.

Pekar grew up in a racially changing neighborhood and worked with African Americans at the Veterans Administration, but he felt the need to address criticism of his depiction of them in "Self-Justification," with art by Frank Stack, reprinted in *The Best of American Splendor*, p. 173.

Zabel: [Laughs.]

Pekar: And my parents had this Mom and Dad store, and I used to wait on them in the store. All my life, I've lived in or near neighborhoods with large black populations. The stories reflect the fact that I had a lot of contact with black people.

Too, I used to think a lot about black/white relations, and why they were so bad, and what could be done and things like that. In my job, I was one of the few white workers at that pay level, and a lot of the people I worked with were black.

Zabel: Maybe it's pretentious, but I think *American Splendor* suggests that there is a black philosophy of life that whites could learn from. Take for instance the Mr. Boats character . . .

Pekar: I don't know if that's the case. But Mr. Boats wasn't typical of anybody. And he didn't really like a lot of aspects of black culture. He didn't like rock and roll—he was a classical violinist. He was for pretty high culture. He used to talk to me about how he'd seen the Chinese Ballet in Toronto and about how nice they danced and all that. He doesn't like a lot of the rough and tumble that goes with urban black culture—he doesn't like that at all. And as a matter of fact, when he retired he actually got himself a farm out in Salem, Ohio. His wife is also a musician, and she teaches too, and he's really proud of the fact that she brings home really good money. He says, "Don't you marry no dumb woman." Mr. Boats is just one of a kind; he just wishes everybody would be more refined.

Zabel: I wanted to ask you about the *American Splendor* movie, and I guess the basic question is, how has it changed your life?

Pekar: Well, it hasn't changed it permanently, but it could. Before the movie, I was with Dark Horse, and my stuff was selling less and less. For a long time they paid me the same rate, about fifty dollars a page for writing. But for the last series I did about Robert McNeill, they reduced it to about seventeen dollars a page. They reduced the money for the artist, too, so it wasn't working for nothing, but we were really vastly underpaid. I accepted it because I thought my stuff would never sell, this is the way it's going to be.

So then they made the movie, and they published a companion volume for the movie, which was the two Doubleday volumes that were published in the 1980s, which they published as a double issue. It was partly because of the popularity of the movie, and maybe partly because they knew how to market the stuff, whereas Dark Horse didn't really know what to do with my stuff. But anyway, this book, to my utter astonishment, really took off, and to date has sold some forty thousand copies, way more than anything I've ever published before.

And the reason it took me aback was that I'd already been on David Letterman, and I thought "this oughta boost sales a little bit," but I didn't see any help coming from there. So I thought there was no power on Earth that could make my comics sell. But apparently that movie did it.

They're still showing the film on HBO, too. It was made for HBO, and that was lucky for me. They had originally made it just to show on television, but when it won the prize at Cannes, there were a lot of distributors who were interested in showing it in regular theaters. So after the theatrical run, it started showing on HBO. It's really had a lot of exposure.

So after this, Random House believed that my other books would do well in the future. So they made me a deal for four books. There's the current new book, *Our Movie Year*, and coming up is a reprint volume, *The Best of Dark Horse*.

Zabel: *The Best of Dark Horse*, will that reprint Colin's piece?
Pekar: Yeah. Dark Horse thought so little of my work that they never secured the rights for anything beyond the first printing. And so I found to my astonishment that when the movie came out, they didn't have stipulation in the contracts, so the work was mine free and clear. So I was able to sell it to Random House. They plan to put it out in January, and it's gonna be about a 335-page book.

They didn't consult me about the stories, they just went ahead and picked them. But they picked a whole lotta stuff.

Zabel: Is the Robert McNeill three-issue saga going to be in it?
Pekar: Well, Dark Horse already made a seventy-seven-page book out of it, published in squareback.

As for the Random House reprint, they didn't pay me a lot of money upfront, because they wanted to sell it fairly cheap, around fifteen-dollar cover price. But it might sell fairly well, especially since it's so big, so we might get good royalties from it.

Zabel: Getting back to the movie, Paul Giamatti has a new film, *Sideways*, which some critics are calling the best American movie of the year. In reviews, he's now considered a major star, primarily because of his starring role in *American Splendor*. Do you think you might go to see it?

Pekar: I might get to see it; I guess if my wife . . .

Zabel: So Joyce might drag you out to see it?

Pekar: Yeah. But I do think that Paul is a terrific actor, and I'm glad he's getting some attention finally.

Zabel: Anyway, moving to the new *American Splendor* book titled *Our Movie Year*—I see that you got Robert Crumb back. How difficult was that?

Pekar: It wasn't difficult at all, once I found out I would be getting paid enough money that artist would be getting paid a hundred dollars a page. I wasn't asking Crumb to do anything for me because frankly I was embarrassed by the lousy money I was getting, and I figured, this guy is trying to make a living—the time he spends for me, he could be spending on more lucrative projects.

But a couple of things happened. *Entertainment Weekly* asked me to do some stuff with them; they were interested in experimenting. Some of that *Entertainment Weekly* stuff is in the new book. And then they asked me if I could get Crumb to do something for them. And they were offering a lot of money, by my standards anyway. So I called Crumb up (I've stayed in touch with him all this time) and I asked him, for X amount of dollars, would you do a one-page story. And he said yeah. So he got paid really good money for the two pieces he illustrated for *Entertainment Weekly*; and I gave him a hundred dollars apiece to reprint them in the new book. So he made out real well.

For the next book that's coming out, which is titled *The Best of American Splendor*, even though it's the best of the Dark Horse stuff, he agreed to do the cover, and Random House paid him good money for it too.

Now I think I ain't gonna be able to get any work from him for a while, because his next project, I dunno if you heard about this, but he's gonna be illustrating the book of Genesis.

Zabel: Adam and Eve and all that stuff?

Pekar: Yeah. That's for Norton. I guess Dennis Kitchen got him that job. I guess they offered him a lot of money, so he's gonna illustrate about two hundred pages of Bible text.

Zabel: Well, I couldn't think of a better artist to do it, actually.

Pekar: Yeah. [Laughs.]

Zabel: Harvey, I wanted to ask you about some of the other artists in the book, starting with Frank Stack. He goes way back in the underground movement, doesn't he?

Pekar: Yeah, Frank is sometimes called the first underground comic book writer, because of his *Adventures of Jesus* in 1962. He did that as Foolbert Sturgeon. Frank is a retired professor of art at the University of Missouri, and he's a really fine all-around artist, watercolor painter, and cityscape artist.

Zabel: He was of course the artist for *Our Cancer Year*.

Pekar: He's a tremendous artist, one of the best I've worked with. In comics, he's kind of a minimalist, but he gets the maximum out of his lines.

Zabel: He has a very loose style, very improvisational.

Pekar: Yeah, and his stuff is real easy to read. I can't say enough about him, I'm really happy to be working with him.

Zabel: Another artist in the book is Mark Zingarelli. I guess he hasn't done a lot of comics, but he did the covers of Sparkle Hayter's mystery series, and a lot of other big-time commercial assignments.

Pekar: Mark works as an illustrator. He tried to make a living in comics, but he couldn't make enough money. His work is bold, but economical. Like Frank, his work is easy to follow and really clear. He did the cover of the book, and I guess there's an interesting story about that.

Zingarelli worked for the company, Good Machine, that produced the movie. He did a cover that was shown briefly at the end of the movie for a book called *Our Movie Year*.

I hadn't intended after the movie to write a book called *Our Movie Year*. But I wanted to continue with my autobiographical series and that meant that I was gonna have to write about the movie, because it was such a major thing in my life.

Mark has given me a b&w copy of the cover from the movie. And I figured, if I was going to write about the movie anyway, I might as well not waste this cover!

Zabel: I'd like to move on to Josh Neufeld. Josh recently published an autobiographical travelogue titled *A Few Perfect Hours*. Have you talked to him a lot about what he's doing?

Pekar: Yeah, I've talked to him a lot, he's based in New York. His work is kind of deceptive; it's not very elaborate, but it gets the job done.

Zabel: Another artist from the book, Gerry Shamray, goes way back with *American Splendor.*
Pekar: Yeah, he started in *American Splendor* #4, and he worked with me for eight or ten issues. Gerry's always done his best for me.

Zabel: He makes heavy use of photography, doesn't he?
Pekar: Yeah, what he does is take a picture of just about every panel, posed with real characters. Then he traces them in a style that uses a lot of lines. In his new piece, he uses some photographs directly. He's technically one of the most accomplished guys I've worked with.

Zabel: Dean Haspiel's also in the book. I guess your introduction to him was that he wrote a comic for his book *Keyhole* about wanting to work for *American Splendor,* but being rejected.
Pekar: Yeah, but actually I was intending to work with Dean. It's ironic that when I finally called him, he didn't believe that it was me, and I got kinda mad. And he did a comic with that scene.

I didn't do a lot of work with Dean, and there's only one page in this volume. But I'm working on a long piece, ninety-six pages, for DC Comics, Vertigo. You see, Dean introduced me to the people who made the *American Splendor* movie, and that got me a lot of money. So I asked him what he would like in return, and he said he wanted to illustrate a really long story of mine. So he proceeded to try to get something of mine placed with DC or Marvel. In fact, I wrote a parody of a Bizarro story, it's about five pages, and I think it's being published next year.

But I wrote this other story, called *The Quitter,* a prequel to the movie.

Zabel: This is the ninety-six-pager?
Pekar: Yeah. This one's really important to me. It's one of the best pieces I've written.

Zabel: A newcomer to *American Splendor* is Ed Piskor, who did one of the longest stories in the new book.
Pekar: Yeah, Ed's a young guy, around twenty-one, from the Pittsburgh area. He's a really hard-working, hustling, ambitious guy. It's kind of ironic that all of this ambition should be in a field, cartooning, that's in really bad shape!

Zabel: He also worked with another underground artist.

Pekar: Yeah, he did a book with Jay Lynch. He's a very promising guy, his stuff is powerful, and he's got a good sense of observation.

Zabel: Another artist in the book, a real *American Splendor* old-timer, is Greg Budgett.

Pekar: I started working with Greg in 1974. He and Gary Dumm always worked together. After several years he started to deemphasize cartooning, and for a long time he didn't do anything for me. But Gary Dumm started urging him to draw again. He penciled a six-page story in the new book and Gary inked it, and I really liked the results a lot.

YEAH, I KNOW. IT WAS SORDID, IT WAS DISGUSTING. I GOT INVOLVED WITH CARLA BECAUSE I WAS GOIN' CRAZY FROM LONELINESS, SO I TRADED ONE KINDA BAD FOR ANOTHER, KNOWING PRETTY MUCH WHAT I WAS DOING, BUT DOING IT ANYWAY. IF I HAD IT TO DO OVER AGAIN UNDER THE SAME CIRCUMSTANCES, I PROBABLY WOULD.

Early artwork by Greg Budgett and Gary Dumm from "Ripoff Chick," reprinted in *American Splendor* (Balla...

Zabel: This brings us to Gary Dumm, a close friend of mine and one of your most longtime associates and a frequent artist for you. He was in the first issue of *American Splendor*, right?

Pekar: Yeah; actually, I did something with him that got published before the first issue. I have a great deal of admiration for Gary as an artist and as a person. He's extremely responsible, and his work just gets better and better. He's doing some really nice stuff now. He's also good to work with—he's always on time, and can meet practically any kind of deadline. He's especially good at working large blocks of text into his work without making it seem text-heavy.

Zabel: I wanted to ask you about one of the longer stories in the new book, illustrated by Ed Piskor. I gather you took a trip around the world to promote the movie.

Pekar: It started out with someone in Australia who wanted me to make an appearance at a book fair. And Joyce said that she and Danielle wanted to go with me. And then somebody in San Francisco wanted me to appear at a comic book convention, Wonder Con, I think.

And then the *American Splendor* movie was opening in Japan, and they wanted me to go to Tokyo to do some promotion for that.

And then they wanted me to do something in Ireland, for a comedy festival.

So what Joyce did was, and I've gotta give her a lot of credit for this, she did some figuring, and got to all of these people, and told them that the cheapest way to do this would be if they all went in together and got this kind of ticket where you can go anywhere you want to. So she sold them on going in on a set of these kind of tickets, and that enabled us to go to New Zealand and Hawaii.

We went to New Zealand mainly because of Danielle and her interest in WETA.

Zabel: WETA? You mean the special effects firm that did the effects for *Lord of the Rings*?

Pekar: Right. The *Lord of the Rings* was distributed by the same guy who distributed the *American Splendor* movie; so we ran into the *Lord of the Rings* guys on several occasions, and we met Richard Taylor, who's the head of WETA. He's a real nice guy, and he identified with Danielle because Danielle has got ADHD, and this guy had dyslexia and couldn't read until he was twelve. But he always had it in mind to do special effects work, and by god, he went out and did it. And he set up what looks like to me a model company. He's real fair, and the people we met out there that work for him, they just loved working for the place, they thought it was tremendous. And they would sometimes take a chance on a guy who didn't have a lot of academic experience, but who had taught himself a lot, like Taylor had.

He and Danielle had a couple of long talks, and he invited us out to New Zealand. So when we were in Australia, we just hopped over.

Zabel: When you visited WETA, what kinds of things did you see? Did you see props and stuff being developed for *King Kong*?

Pekar: Yeah. Not only are they working on *King Kong*, but Danielle got a chance to work on a T-rex that's gonna be in the movie. [Yells to Danielle in the next room] What was that, a clay T-rex?

Danielle: It was plasticine. It never dries.

Pekar: So she got real involved with it, and went out a couple of times to work. And they were so impressed by her enthusiasm and industry that they said if she wanted to she could come back and intern there. So hopefully next year, she and Joyce will go back and she'll intern for a month.

Zabel: In the comic, I guess it was a sequence from Tokyo, it shows you visiting a manga comics shop. What's your opinion of manga?

Pekar: Oh, I was very disappointed. I thought things like *Astro Boy* and the like were cute, but that they're only for kids. And people were telling me, no, in Japan, there's comic books about everybody. There's comic books about garbage men, everything. That everything is covered there; and I thought, "Wow, that's great." And they said that's where they really appreciate comics is in Japan.

Fortunately, the woman who was my interpreter, Maki Hakui, was into alternative comics. She worked for a publisher who had reprinted alternative American comics in Japan.

She took me to a comic book store, and the whole thing was just kid's stuff. There was one book that she told me to pick up, and that was the only one that was alternative comics in this whole store.

It just goes to show you, Japan is held out as a place where they like alternative comics, but it's not true, and alternatives are a very small part of their production.

Zabel: Harvey, I gather you were doing commentaries for National Public Radio. Is that gig still going on?
Pekar: No, most of the people I was working with at WKSU have moved on. What I was doing were the equivalent of blogs. And actually I won a prize. I never actually got anything, but sometimes when people would introduce me they'd say, "and he won such and such radio award." Some of the commentaries turned up on Terry Gross's show, *Fresh Air*. She's always been very supportive of me.

Zabel: I want to turn from that to talk about the recent election.
Pekar: Ohhhh . . .

Zabel: I don't mean to bring you down, but I thought people would be interested in your reaction.
Pekar: I'm very disappointed. I think George Bush has had four years to prove that he was a terrible president, and they still elected him. What's it going to take for them to get somebody good in there?

He's been very hard on poor people; he's giving tax breaks to rich people. He favors large corporations; he's in favor of the trickle-down economic theory. He may preside over the ruination of social security. I was reading in the paper that he wants to privatize it.

And yet these same people, these poor and middle-class white people, just keep on voting for him. Like they're doing it to spite themselves or something. I can understand it; he makes appeals to patriotism and stuff like that. And it's gotten so that the leftist party, which the Democratic Party is supposed to be, isn't offering much of an alternative. Look at all these countries that have had socialized medicine since 1950, and we still don't have it. And now we have senior citizens who are making trips to Canada to get American drugs.

It was awful that he got into this stupid war in Iraq. I don't know what the hell he was trying to prove.

He's just been terrible for the economy. And it's going to hurt the arts. If people don't have much money, that's one thing they cut back on.

Zabel: I'd like to move on to the closing topic. A lot of your writing throughout your career has been about your propensity to worry. In one of your recent comics, you're waking up in the morning, and you think to yourself, "What do I have to do today? What do I have to worry about?" As if that's your goal for the day, to worry about something. After all this time and consideration, do you think you understand it better? Do you know why it is that you worry about everything?
Pekar: I think I know why I worry about everything. But first of all, I think it's bad to ruminate. But recently I found out by accident, if I take some Excedrin headache pills—I'm under the influence of them now, in fact. This is something you can buy off the shelf, so I'm not doing any illegal substances. [Laughs] But it just makes me more relaxed for a few hours, and that's great for me.

Zabel: So you think that the worry is just a chemical state of mind that you can change now with Excedrin?
Pekar: Well, it's not something I can do twenty-four hours a day, because if I did, I'd wake up all shook up. But I'll probably always worry. My mother was a big worrier, and I'm an obsessive-compulsive personality.

Strangely, worrying kind of grounds me. People say, what do I know for sure? I think, therefore I am. With me, it's like what do I know for sure? That I got stuff that I worry about. This is going to go bad, and that's gonna go bad. But that's a lousy way to be.

Harvey Pekar at the 2005 Small Press Expo

Michael Rhode / 2005

From the *International Journal of Comic Art*,
vol. 8, no. 2 (Fall/Winter 2006) pp. 126–62.
Reprinted by permission of Michael Rhode.

Harvey Pekar was the 2005 guest of honor at the Small Press Expo in Bethesda, Maryland. While he sat at a table for most of the weekend, signing material for fans, he also participated in two panel session interviews. The first panel on Friday evening, September 23, was him alone and the second panel on the next day included his collaborators Dean Haspiel, Josh Neufeld, and Ed Piskor.[1] The following is essentially a verbatim transcription of the two events.

Spotlight on Harvey Pekar, Friday, September 23, 2005

Michael Rhode: Harvey Pekar has been doing comics from Cleveland since 1972, so he's got over thirty years under his belt. He's done them through a resulting marriage—Joyce is in the front row here—at least four publishers, two bouts of cancer, and one major motion picture, so tonight I've got a few questions that will hopefully tease out a little bit of the creative process. We're going to start with his new book, *The Quitter*, which is not yet out but which I believe is coming out next week, and I urge you all to immediately rush off to the bookstore to get it. Dean Haspiel, in the second row, is the artist, and they've got these attractive postcards from DC that you can get them both to sign. Is it okay if I call you Harvey?

Harvey Pekar: Yeah, sure.

MR: Thanks. You've got to respect your elders.

HP: Thank you. [laughter]

MR: Your new book, *The Quitter*, is about your childhood, but it's not yet available so most of us haven't been able to see it. I wonder if you can tell us about your background, what your parents did for a living, that type of thing.

HP: Ok, I was born in 1939. My parents were born in Poland in these small towns called *shtetls* around a town called Bialystok. They got married and came over to the States in 1935. After a while my father opened up a grocery store in a neighborhood that had been largely Italian and Jewish, but by the time I was born, I think, it was mostly black. When I was going to school, I was about the only white kid on the street, at least my age. We moved to, after a while, another neighborhood further up this main drag called Kinsman Avenue . . . I don't know . . . what do you want me to [say?]

MR: No, no that's good. Just give us some basic background—that's a world that's far removed from this one.

HP: All right, well, I went to school there in a neighborhood that was kind of a working-class neighborhood. It was Jewish and Italian, there was a lot of immigrants that lived there. In both of the neighborhoods I lived in, I had a real tough time making friends, at least at first, so I was kind of starved for approval. Another thing is that my mother was kind of an obsessive-compulsive person and I think I might have inherited some of that from her, so I was always worrying about stuff— "catastrophising"—and got to a point even as early as elementary school where I . . . things just got too important to me. I couldn't . . . I had to have instant approval for anything that meant anything to me. If I didn't, I'd just freak out. So in order to preserve what little sanity I had left, I had to quit everything that was important to me, including sports and a lot of things as time went on. I gradually found out that I was, believe it or not, a really good street fighter. I used to get a lot of approval for that. In those days, in that neighborhood, that's what got you approval—if you were a tough guy or something. So even though I didn't particularly enjoy beating people up, I used to get in a lot of fights and I gathered a reputation as a tough guy and that sort of sustained me through school . . . something notable anyway. When I came out of high school, I had very good grades, but I had no confidence in my ability to pass math and science courses. I thought I would screw them up completely if I went to college so I didn't even try to go to college. I just got a series of flunky jobs which I held for short periods of time. I worked for various civil service jobs for a while. I went into the Navy and I got kicked out of the Navy because I couldn't wash my clothes right. I guess it sounds kind of comical, but it was a pretty heavy ordeal for me.

MR: Was this the early 1960s?

HP: Uh, yeah, we're talking about the late fifties and early sixties. I went to college for a while finally when I had run out of everything else to do and I started off doing real well in school, but then I got . . . like my best subject in school had always been geography, because I had a real good memory in those days, almost a photographic memory and the geography courses used to just be about memorizing the names of rivers and the capitals of states and stuff so I could manage that. You didn't have to reason or anything like that. So I was just assuming that every geography course I took would be a snap course for me. Instead, when I ran across a geography course that was kind of rough and on the first test I only got a C+, I freaked out. I thought I was coming apart because I only got a C+ so I quit college and I started working other flunky jobs. I was just on the verge of I don't know what—I was running out of ideas. Where to go to? What to do? I finally got another civil service job which was so easy that I could live with it. I didn't use to worry about whether I'd screw things up or anything like that. I could just go in and put in my hours and go home and that would be it. It would be over with. Normally what happened when I went home was I just would worry about everything all the time. So this job really stabilized my life and another couple of things happened that gave my life stability. One was I started writing jazz criticism for jazz publications. I started doing that in 1959. That was at the time . . . this was like the era of the beatniks and it was considered a real accomplishment to get your stuff published somewhere. So when I got my criticism published, I sort of rose in prestige in people's eyes. And then I got married. It was the first of three marriages, but it lasted for about twelve years and gave my life some stability, you know? I don't know—that's about enough isn't it?

MR: Well, that almost carries us up to the questions about the comic books. I think most of the people here at SPX would acknowledge you as one of the fathers of the genre of autobiographic comics, if I can call it a genre. Perhaps you can talk a little about why you started doing comics, and then why you chose autobiographical comics.

HP: Well I started doing comics because I saw an opportunity to really be creative and actually to be innovative as an artist. I was pretty familiar with comics when I was in elementary school. I read them a lot, and after a while I just got sick of them because they were formulaic. So I quit reading them and starting thinking of comics as an inferior art form. I was impressed with *Mad* comics in the fifties.

MR: The Kurtzman years.

HP: Yeah, right. But then I didn't really pay much attention to other comics until I met Robert Crumb who moved into my home town Cleveland in 1962. He was three years younger than me. He was already started on his career and was working on his book that was a graphic novel called *The Big Yum-Yum Book*. I was very impressed when I saw that. Crumb and I used to get together all the time because we both collected jazz records. I was so impressed with this *Big Yum-Yum Book* and later with other underground comic books that I saw coming out that I realized that there was nothing wrong with the comic form, there was nothing limited about the comic book form, it was just used in a real limited way. It was just like mostly for superheroes and talking animals. I thought, "Jeez, comics can be about anything." I was also impressed by the fact there was so little realism in comic books. Over the years, I maintained my connection with Crumb and I continued to follow the rise of the underground comic book movement. I started theorizing about comic books and what else could be done with them. I started thinking in terms of my writing them if I could get someone to illustrate them because I can't draw worth a damn. I started thinking about doing stories that were realistic, and the best realistic stories I could do were autobiographical. It seemed that the more accurately I wrote about my life, the better the story came out. I also wanted to write about everyday life, quotidian life, because I felt that writers in just about every area had ignored a lot of what goes on in everyday life. So I used to write . . . I was thinking about writing stories about working and what it was like to work on a daily basis and how to get along with your boss . . . Writing about the nuts and bolts of marriage and things like that. Finally in 1972, Robert Crumb—he had long ago moved to San Francisco, but he used to come to my house to crash when he would take these trips across the country to visit his friends in all these different cities he'd been in. I had these ideas about experimental comic stories, and I wrote them in like a storyboard style with stick figures with word and thought balloons. I showed them to Crumb and I asked him his opinion of them. He read them and he told me he liked them. He asked me if he could take some of them home with him to illustrate. I was completely floored. I wasn't used to having good luck.

MR: Crumb would have been a big name by then.

HP: Yeah. It just knocked me off my feet because what it did was, in addition to giving me an opportunity to . . . well, okay I'll say it . . . pioneer in an art form that had been used in a severely limited way, it gave me instant credibility because Crumb was illustrating my work so people would think "Oh, Crumb's illustrating this guy's work, he can't be that bad." So, anyway, that's about how I started.

MR: As far as I know, nobody else had been doing your types of comics before except for Justin Green's *Binky Brown*.

HP: (sneeringly) Yeah, well people always point out, "Harvey Pekar wasn't the first person to do autobiographical comics—Justin Green was." Well, yeah, that's true.

MR: That's not quite the same type of comics . . .

HP: No, it's a different type, but people just enjoy saying that. [audience laughter]

MR: Those were collected as *Bob & Harv's Comics*. Let's keep going on Crumb for just a minute. He's left the States for France, but at the same time he's becoming accepted as a fine artist here in the States.

HP: Right.

MR: And your contemporary Art Spiegelman is as well, and I think something similar is happening to your work as well. I'm wondering if you think that's a valid comparison and if so, how do you feel about that?

HP: Well, I think, you know, comics can be a fine art as well as any other art form, so if people want to accept my work and think of it as being on a high level, I'm happy for them to do so. You can admire me as much as you want. [audience laughter]

MR: Ok, you heard that then. I was wondering how you feel the latest version of the trend "Pow, Wham, Zap, comics aren't for kids anymore."

Robert Crumb's cover to *Bob and Harv's Comics* shows both men's typical concerns.

Obviously you're benefitting from it, but do you think it has staying power this time? The large publishers like Pantheon are publishing comic books—do you see this as continuing?

HP: I really don't know. On the one hand, people think comics are in great shape because they make Spider-Man movies and Batman movies, and they think that the wealth is equally distributed throughout the industry. But on the other hand, alternative comics are not getting published very much. Today, while I was just sitting up at my station upstairs [in the Small Press Expo exhibit area], people would come by, maybe to get an autograph or something like that, but also I got given a lot of comics, and some of them were really first rate. Back in maybe 1972 or something like that, they might have been able to get them published, but I think there's practically no chance of the stuff getting published by a fairly large publisher now. I happened to luck out. In the late '90s, my stuff wasn't selling worth a damn. The last paying gig I had at Dark Horse Comics, which I was with at that time, I got seventeen dollars a page so I figured I didn't have much of a future in this as far as ever making enough as I needed to make from freelance writing to retire.

But then, I got this tremendous break. Dean Haspiel over here, introduced me to a movie producer by the name of Ted Hope, who worked for a company called Good Machine. Dean had done some free-lance work for him, and he told me that Ted was interested in making a movie based on my work. Well, I thought . . . I felt pretty confident about getting fifteen hundred bucks for somebody signing an option, but I didn't think there was a chance in hell that anyone would actually come up with the money to make a movie out of a comic book that sold a few thousand copies. But I was wrong. Hope sold the story idea to HBO and amazingly they made a movie out of it. And I think it was a very good movie. I don't take credit for it being a good movie, but I was extremely lucky in working with some very creative people who made an innovative movie. [laughs] And people used to refer to it to me as "your movie" and you know I wasn't responsible for it, aside from providing some of the stories, but it was a really fine movie and a lot of credit goes to people like Hope and the directors Bob Pulcini and Shari Springer Berman . . . But anyway, the movie not only got made and I got paid for it, but it also won some awards like the Sundance Award and a Cannes Award, and HBO decided they could make money on the film by just running it in the regular movie houses and not just showing it on TV. So it had a run around the country and internationally and it got very good reviews. I think in the end of the year 2003, it had been placed in two hundred critics' top ten lists.

I had thought that nothing, no matter how successful the film was, nothing would sell my comic books, like it was just impossible to sell them. People wouldn't buy them. I had been on David Letterman and nothing happened. I was even pretty popular on David Letterman's show and people wouldn't buy them. People wouldn't buy them. I figured this is useless. But they put a companion comic out for the movie, Random House did, and it actually sold real well. Based on that, I got a contract to do four more books for Random House and I got a contract to do *The Quitter*, which is coming out real soon with DC Vertigo. I've been working fairly steadily. I've been getting some pretty good paying comic book gigs although they're becoming fewer and farther between. I think what I need now is I not only need *The Quitter* to become a commercial success, but I need somebody to make a movie out of it. [general laughter] I'm working real hard to accomplish that. I still have my connections at HBO and I'm going around asking like . . . if DC solicits a favorable comment from a writer about my work, then I call the guy up and ask him if he wouldn't want to write a script for the movie or something like that. That's where I'm at now.

MR: The resulting book *Our Movie Year* is for sale upstairs at the CBLDF tables and some other people have it for sale, some of the artists who appeared in it have it for sale as well. I'd urge you all to check it out as well as the movie which I watched again last night. It's really excellent. Harvey's in a lot of it actually. It's not just actors. It alternates between him and the actors which really works successfully although at first it's a little surprising.

You talked about your publishers a little bit. So you've gone from self-publishing to being with mainstream publishers like Doubleday, small publishers like Dark Horse, and now you're with DC. I was wondering—obviously some of that is how life was going at the time—but I was wondering how that worked for you—if they all had something to recommend them, even if it was only keeping your name in public, or if you've had a good experience with some and not others?

HP: Yeah, I've had varied experiences. Well, I first started by publishing my own comic book in 1976, *American Splendor*, and I published that for about fifteen years. I published it because I frankly had more and more grandiose ideas about what I could do in terms of stories in comic books—more complex stories and longer stories. And frankly, there weren't any publishers around that I thought would accept any of these stories. For one thing, if I wanted to write a thirty-five-page story, they were just printing comic books that were like twenty-five pages long or something like that. So I had to decide to publish my own comic and the way I did it was I lived pretty frugally, but I spent a lot of money on rare records. Thousands of dollars on rare records every year. I decided that I would quit collecting records and use the money that I spent on them to put out a comic book. I figured if I could get Crumb to illustrate some of my stories, and I was able to do that for some of the early *American Splendors*, I could at least sell some of the books. I was sure I would lose money on it initially, but I figured I would make back enough money that I could keep publishing if I kept away from my record junkie habit. So I did that for about fifteen years and then in 1990 . . .

MR: Let me interrupt for just a minute. At this time, what was a press run because you had to go to a real printer, I assume?

HP: Ten thousand.

MR: Ok, ten thousand, and that's probably considerably higher than most of the people in the audience would ever have to think about would be my guess. Printing technology has changed quite a bit since the days that Harvey is talking about so he's a real pioneer, and you could imagine having ten thousand of fifteen issues or twenty issues, however many you'd done in fifteen years that you had to keep moving and this is . . .

Joyce Brabner: He kept them in the basement. He didn't keep moving. He kept them in the basement.

MR: Well, hopefully you're trying to sell them to people.

HP: Yeah, I sold them to distributors, but I didn't really . . . I had my day gig and I was just satisfied to go on the way I was. I made enough money on my day job to support myself and my wife. I just kept on doing the stuff. I wasn't hurting for anything because I had stopped collecting records and that was the only thing I really got a kick out of buying. But then in 1990, I found out that I had cancer. I was getting chemotherapy and I was physically too weak that year to publish a comic book, so what happened though was that these two guys that ran these *Teenage Mutant Ninja Turtles* . . .

MR: Was that Eastman and Laird?

HP: Yeah. They decided that they would support worthy comic book institutions and stuff like that and individuals. I checked with them and I was able to get them to publish a comic for a year. The company was called Tundra. And after that . . . Tundra didn't last too long, and after that I got Dark Horse to pick up my comic book and they published it until about 2000 or something. The year 2000 or 2001 . . . something like that. Since then, I've had these experiences with Random House and DC. I didn't really have a real happy experience with Dark Horse. The people there were nice, the editors and everything but they were really interested in putting out comics like *Star Wars* and they didn't give a damn about my stuff. So it didn't get publicized and it sold even less than it had in the late '80s before I went with anybody else. And I wasn't getting very much money from them. But in a way it was good to get the monkey of publishing off my back because that was a pain in the ass. It wasn't like I could just take the stuff down to one printing company and get my comics printed up in Cleveland. Nobody was set up for that so I had to get the negatives shot in one place, and then take the negatives to two printing companies, one of which printed the inside which was in black and white and one of which printed the cover which was in color. Then they'd send them all to a bindery where the finished book would be assembled, stapled, and trimmed. Then I had to pick them all up, take them back home, stick them in my basement, and start soliciting orders and stuff like that. And after a while, I started getting old. [chuckles] I was happy to have it off of my back after a while even though I wasn't getting much money for doing the comics.

MR: And this would be before Diamond was the only distributor in town too, and you have had to deal with several distributors?

HP: Yeah, in those days there were still other distributors.

MR: Ok, I don't want to dwell on this, but *Our Cancer Year*—very moving—I would recommend this to everybody—especially anybody who hasn't read it. Ok, I'm going to ask you one more general question, and then we'll talk about *The Quitter* a little bit and see if we have some time for some questions. The general question is that you appear to have fairly strong political feelings, and I'm wondering why you haven't expressed more of them in your comics, doing something like . . . Joyce mentioned Keith Knight earlier, or Ted Rall, or something like that. I was wondering why you stuck with autobiography all these years, instead of trying something political, say?

HP: If I want to write about a political issue, and I *do* write about political issues, I just write prose articles. I've written about politics for local publications for a pretty long time.

MR: But you don't feel the need to do a comic then?

HP: No, I don't consider that an art form or anything like that. It's like polemics, you know?

MR: Well, there's a long history of political cartooning and some do longer form types of that.

HP: Well, I want to be specific . . . I didn't see where pictures would help me do the kind of things I wanted to do. I thought prose would serve my purposes better.

MR: Ok, well, that's interesting. So let's talk about *The Quitter* a little bit. The new book is on your youth—I was wondering why you picked this topic, and why now?

HP: Well, the reason is . . . there are a couple reasons. One is that my movie was pretty popular and in the movie I'm presented in the middle of life with a job, I'm going between wives. I guess I was about forty when the movie started, or something like that and I presented myself as a kind of an eccentric person, but I didn't really talk about how I had gotten the way I did. So I thought, and I hadn't really written much about my early life either, because when I started writing autobiographical comic books, I was writing about what happened today or the next day or something like that. I started off writing them at the age of thirty-two; I didn't start when I was born. So I just used to keep on writing about what happened to me every year. There was a lot about me that I hadn't written about—from my youth—so I decided that this was some territory that would possibly be interesting to readers if I went into it. So that's what I did.

MR: And you mentioned working with Dean—he had worked with you before—and also he had helped you with the movie. I was wondering if you had particularly asked for Dean when you pitched this to DC? Or had you guys already worked together [on it]?

HP: No, what happened was that when I . . . I got all this money for the movie and everything like that. I felt like I owed Dean something. He'd been responsible for me making thousands and thousands of dollars so I said, "What, *within reason* [general laughter], can I do to pay you back for doing this for me?" So he said he wanted to illustrate a large-scale work of mine, so I said fine. He already had a connection with DC Comics, and the movie had made me a hotter item, and made one of my comic book collections a pretty good seller, so maybe editors weren't as scared to take on selling my work as they used to be, knowing it would lead to financial ruin. Dean approached the people from DC; I didn't have any connection with them at all. He started a dialogue between them and me that he was in on too, and gradually hammered out the idea for the contents of *The Quitter*.

MR: Since you knew you'd be working with Dean, did you pace it to his strengths or is this more of a collaborative process than you may have done in the past?

HP: Once I figured out the style I was gonna write it in, I just went ahead and wrote it and tried to make it the best piece of literature I could, and then I contacted Dean about the style and what I'd like to see in the artwork. I have to say he did a really wonderful job of satisfying my wishes for the artwork for this book. I think just about everybody thinks he did a very nice job on it. Since then, we've done a few other shorter works and they've come out real well too. So I'm really pleased with [his work].

MR: You're doing something for *The Escapist*; I think I saw a color printout upstairs?

HP: Yeah, we did something in that.

MR: So everyone buy that too. I did have one last question. I was wondering where the title *American Splendor* came from. I don't think I've seen that in any interviews.

HP: Well, it has been actually.

MR: Sorry, I didn't do enough research. [audience chuckles] I just found out about this [interview] yesterday.

HP: When I was a kid, and I was reading comics, there was all this patriotism going around, and comics were being called *All-American Comics* and *Star-Spangled Comics* and stuff like that, so that's where I got the "American" from. And then the "splendor" . . . the movie, *Splendor in the Grass* . . . I don't know . . . for some reason that always struck me as an absurd title, absurdly funny. [audience laughs] I just hooked up American and splendor—an American splendor—it's an ironic title. I don't think most people would consider my life particularly splendid. [audience laughs]

MR: You've worked hard at it.

HP: Yeah. That's where the title came from and it's stood the test of time.

MR: Great. You were so concise, we've actually gone through two pages of questions, so let's open it to the audience if anybody has anything. We'll start with the person who came in early and asked questions before everybody else got here and got secret answers that no one else will ever hear.

Audience Member: You mentioned when you were growing up that comics were very patriotic, and after September 11, I see comics getting that way again—Captain America standing on the rubble of the World Trade Center. Now that we're involved in another war in Iraq that seems to resemble, at least on the surface, the war in Vietnam, is there any chance at all that comics might come out . . . That some might grow a backbone and say that the President lied about this, or our leaders lied about why we're in that war?

HP: Well, I've said it . . .

AM: Other people beside you.

HP: . . . and I've written about it. I'm trying to think if I included it in a comic book story or not. I guess I haven't. I dunno. People protested the war in Vietnam in comics. The thing is there's so few comics that're being published now. I mean it's really hard to get an idea what comic book writers . . .

JB: Who asked that question? Why aren't you doing it yourself? Why aren't you doing it yourself?

HP: Aw, c'mon Joyce. [audience laughter]

AM: I'm a journalist, ma'am; I cover homeland security.

JB: Right. OK. And I did journalism in comics for a while too.

AM: I don't write about comics; I write about homeland security.

JB: Ok, well, why not do a . . . I did exactly the same thing. I hooked up a bunch of artists and did a comic called *Real War Stories*, and a comic called *Brought to Light* about Iran-contra issues. Why don't you find yourself an artist and do a comic. You sound eminently qualified; I'd be interested in hearing what you have to say. [Pekar moans] Why don't you do it? You don't have the same kind of problems we had when we started doing comics. You don't have to print ten thousand. You can do a print run of fifty. This is the Small Press Expo—why don't you get up and do it?

Dean Haspiel: Yeah.

AM: I do write short stories . . .

JB: Who illustrates? Talk to this man afterwards. [audience laughter]

HP: All right, all right . . . [continuing audience laughter] You should have asked me that one before.

MR: Thank you, Joyce.

AM: I'm a big jazz fan myself. What's your favorite jazz record and what's your favorite new record?

HP: I don't have any favorite jazz record because I . . . there's so many that I like. I like jazz from every era. I could tell you stuff going back to Jelly Roll Morton and King Oliver and stuff like that I enjoy . . . stuff all the way up to the present. I *do* like to concentrate on what's going on now, on the innovative artists, and the reason is I think those are the greatest artists. Those are the artists that add to the vocabulary of the art form. I would be interested in guys like . . . well, right now, I'm real interested in a guy named Joe Maneri, a Boston musician who's kind of a legend there. He was doing some very far out stuff even back in the fifties; he's now about seventy-eight years old, but he's still one of the most advanced jazz musicians around. So I'm interested in people like Joe and, the thing is with jazz . . . it's like jazz is in real bad shape too in the sense that . . . well, it's in real bad shape period because its share of record sales is constantly going down. It's down to about 2 percent of all record sales now, and people don't give a *damn* about advanced jazz or far-out jazz or experiment jazz or anything like that and they still see things that were done in the 1960s as too far out. Now that's actually true of other art forms as well. There's not much support for avant-garde classic music and James Joyce's books are still as difficult to read for most people as they were when they came out, now, years and years ago. So I don't know what can be done about that. It seems like there's been some kind of a permanent time lag and people don't seem to care for art that's maybe been done after 1960 or something. That's jazz I should say, but in other art forms they don't seem to care about innovations that have been made after 1920 or 1900.

MR: Right, in painting, you're seeing an appreciation of Norman Rockwell in fine art museums, as opposed to his being treated as an illustrator, so I can see your point.

AM: You said you started doing your own comics, and you'd do your small runs, well, they're actually large runs, but now you're going with DC and the larger comic sphere. Do you feel like you still have the same freedom to express what you want?

HP: Yeah, yeah, I have had. I just write what I want. I can only write one kind of way. I wish I could sell out, but . . . [audience laughter] . . . I don't have the ability to. I can't write like superheroes stories. I just can't do it. I mean literally. If I could, maybe I would have done it a long time ago. I've made concessions before about a lot of stuff. I can only just do it the one way and they've got to either accept me or not. When people saw my stuff would sell, with this one Random House book, then they said "Ok, do it anyway you want to. As long as it sells, we'll take it." So right now, my stuff's selling ok, so they're leaving me alone.

MR: There are certainly quite a few long-form comics that are coming out now and I think most major publishers have somebody doing comics now, so it's probably a good time to be coming out with your new book.

AM: I was a huge fan of the movie. I thought it was the best film I saw that year, and I learned about you through the film, but what I didn't know was that you were such a fixture on Letterman at the time. I was wondering if you care to talk about that a little bit?

MR: Gee, the infamous Letterman question.

HP: Yeah, all right. [audience laughter] Yeah, I'll talk about it. Ok, I got on Letterman in 1986

Pekar's move to DC Comics led to a collaboration with expatriate Scotsman Eddie Campbell for "The Czech-Counter" from *American Splendor: Another Day.*

because of a guy named Steve O'Donnell who was Letterman's head writer and who came from Cleveland. I didn't know Steve at the time, but he knew my work. He was responsible for getting me on the show. When I was on the show . . . I thought I'd just be on once. I went on once and I did kind of shtick, sort of a parody of a Cleveland working man, a rust belt guy, the "dese and doser" kind of guy . . . and it went over really well. [sounding surprised] So, they had me back several times, but they always wanted me to act the same. It got old for me. Not only that, my comics weren't selling better, and I wasn't getting much money. Now you talk about compromise, see if he would have given me a lot of money, I'd have probably let him abuse me a whole hell of a lot more than he did. [audience laughter] "You know, no money, then, okay man, we can't talk about this. I'm not getting anything back." So I told him, "You know, look, I understand you want to do a comedy show, but I don't want to do the same crap all the time." I was into political comedy, and at that time General Electric had just bought NBC and I thought that was crazy because GE was constantly breaking antitrust laws and they manufactured at least parts of atomic weapons, and you're letting a company like this get control of NBC News? Certainly they could influence public opinion with that. So I told him that I wanted to talk about that, and he just got all flustered, and he wouldn't give a straight answer. So I said ok, if we don't talk about that, then I'm going to talk about it myself. Solo kind of thing, you know. That happened that night.

I gave him a chance to ask me some questions about this GE/NBC thing and he wouldn't, so after the break, I came back and just started doing a monologue. This was covered in the movie. He kind of freaked out. Said it wasn't appropriate. And I told him I didn't care. I just went on and it developed into a big shouting match. I did it again. I didn't use to do it every time when I came back, but I did it again. Because I had nothin' to lose. "You don't pay me, man. I'm not gonna do what you want." [audience laughter] I didn't care if he kicked me off the show and never had me back because I figured it this way, "At least I'd go out like a hero, or something like that." And that's exactly what happened. You know, the movie got made and they included that stuff about Letterman in, that was one point at least where I looked, I thought, real good and people complimented me, "Oh, he's so courageous" and stuff like that. To me it wasn't even about courage. It was just about not getting ripped off.

MR: Let me follow up on that, Harvey. In the intervening twenty years, there's been far more media consolidation than you would ever have expected in the 1980s. I was wondering if you have any feelings about how the system has evolved since you were making that point.

HP: Well, it's just gotten worse and worse.

MR: So you do think it influences the type of news that we're able to hear?

HP: Yeah.

MR: Ok, Joyce has a comment.

JB: One of the things that's kind of interesting is when Harvey did that on NBC, a lot of people hadn't been thinking about those issues. This was news. Yeah, he got thrown off. Of course, he got brought back on again because he was interesting, and then he got thrown off again. But later on, we saw Tim Robbins doing exactly what Harvey did, as a comedy bit, on *Saturday Night Live*. He did his monologue and he talked about NBC being owned by General Electric, and it was interesting just watching it gradually get into the stream. It was acceptable for Tim Robbins to do it as comedy a number of years later, it just wasn't okay for somebody like Harvey to bring it up.

HP: Well, at least Letterman didn't think it was.

MR: And now it's a part of everyday life, with Walt Disney owning a network [ABC].

JB: And now, what's interesting is you'll see Letterman on with Howard Stern and they'll be talking about this Clear Channel stuff and corporate ownership of the airwaves. It did a complete turnaround, but it took Letterman twenty years to catch on.

HP: Ohhh, it just . . . I dunno. I think he caught on. He didn't want to risk getting hurt by it. He'll talk about it . . .

JB: He'll talk privately about it.

HP: Yeah, he'll talk about any subject as long as it doesn't hurt him. But he felt threatened. Thought that NBC would can him or something like that if he let me go on. Frankly I didn't give a damn. Huh.

MR: Ok, the five minutes sign popped up awhile ago. Does anyone have any questions, or should we have a round of applause and close out the evening? One last question.

AM: When I saw you in the hallway today, I recognized you right away due to your movie. So do you have a little celebrity? Do people recognize you or did that happen before due to Letterman?

HP: No, not too many people recognize me due to Letterman. But the movie, yeah, a lot of people . . . yeah, a relatively large number of people. A lot of times when I go to the supermarket or something like that, someone will know who I am. Or in my neighborhood, or if I go to the airport, somebody will see me standing in line and say something.

AM: Do you enjoy that?

HP: Yeah, sure I enjoy it. [audience laughter]. Because they're praising me usually. The more you praise me, the better I like it.

MR: Well, I don't think we can end on a better note than that except encouraging you to buy *The Quitter* from DC when it comes out in another week or two. Let's have a round of applause. [applause] Thank you very much, and he'll be signing his books tomorrow too, so go out and pick them up and get an autograph.

HP: Ask questions if you want.

Visualizing American Splendor, Saturday, September 24, 2005

MR: Welcome everybody to the panel about Harvey Pekar and his artists. It has a formal title, but I can't remember what it is. Working our way across, we have Ed Piskor who is working on a long format graphic novel with him; Dean Haspiel who has just done with *The Quitter* with him which will be available soon; Harvey himself whom you probably all recognize; and Josh Neufeld's done the cover of the program so you've seen his work with Harvey quite a bit this weekend. Harvey talked a bit last night about his starting with Robert Crumb, probably still his most famous collaborator, would be my guess.

HP: Yes. You guessed right.

MR: Were most of the people in the audience here last night? Maybe you can just go into that again real fast so people will get the background of how you started?

HP: I met Robert Crumb in 1962 and when I saw his work, I realized that my opinion of comics, which had been low for a long time, since about the age of eleven, was probably incorrect. I thought they were intrinsically a limited medium. The reason I thought that was when I got into the later grades of elementary school, I could figure out the story's endings before I got to them because they were so formulaic. So I gave up reading comics. I started reading the *Mad* stuff though in the '50s. And then in the early '60s, Crumb moved into my neighborhood from Philadelphia. We had in common that we were both jazz record collectors.

I got to look at his cartoon work and I was blown away. Here, the guy was actually doing stuff that was meant to appeal to adults, not kids. It occurred to me that you could do anything in comics that you could do in any other art form. Comics were being used in a very limited way, so that superheroes was the main genre in comics. It's not the main genre in movies, or anything else. I figured that comic book companies were satisfied with the sales they were getting from superhero comics and they didn't want to try anything else. There were tons of things you could do in comics that weren't being done. It was a very unexplored medium. I couldn't draw but I wanted to get in on that. I figured that out and I wanted some credit for it. I figured that I'd be known as an innovative and go down in history. [audience laughter]

Josh Neufeld: Your plan worked perfectly.

HP: Yeah, it's going ok. Anyway, I kept up with what Crumb was doing when he became a hippie idol and everything like that and moved out of Cleveland and moved to California. He used to come back to Cleveland for visits and he'd stay in my house. One time in 1972, I had been theorizing about comics and the kind of comics I'd like to do, and I thought I'd like to do autobiographical comics because it seemed like whenever I wrote a narrative it was . . . the closer I came to the truth, the better it was. The more impact it had. So I wanted to do autobiographical comics, and I wanted to do stuff about the dull routine of my everyday existence. Quotidian existence. I did some scripts for Crumb when he was up there using a storyboard style and I showed them to him. I asked him what he thought of them. And he liked them and he said he'd like to take them home and illustrate them. Ok, so that already put me on the map a little bit. Instant legitimacy. When a guy of Robert Crumb's stature illustrates your work, other people sit up and take notice. Crumb got some of his artist friends in California to illustrate my work too. He started talking about me which was really nice, so then guys in Cleveland started to get word about me. I started writing a whole lot more comic book stories. Crumb had his own stuff to do—he wasn't put on earth solely to illustrate my stories. I eventually got into publishing my own comic

Josh Neufeld's artwork for the Small Press Expo advertisement.

which was a pretty long comic, by those standards. It was about sixty pages. I tried to get a group of guys together, (well a group of artists, I work with women too), a group of artists together like a pool of people I could give stories to illustrate to. I dunno, that's about where I left it.

MR: Ok, well let's talk to the people who are actually here at the table. Josh, since he's the longest-serving illustrator at the table.

HP: That's right, that's the truth.

MR: Josh, maybe you could talk about how you started working with Harvey and how you found your experience?

JN: When I came back from traveling, backpacking around Southeast Asia and Europe, for a year, I had during that time gotten into alternative comics. I was really excited when I came back about working in the industry, but I had no confidence as a writer. I started sending my work to various places like *Duplex Planet Illustrated*—David Greenberger's work—and to Harvey just to see if he needed any artists and sort of pimping my own stuff. "I can draw as good as the guys you have working with you"—that kind of thing. [audience laughter] I'm sure other artists are familiar with this. You send your stuff out and you assume 90 percent of the time that you'll never hear anything back, but about a week later, Harvey called me up on the phone which was the last thing I expected. I thought I'd get a letter back or something. [Turns to speak to Harvey]

You said, "Yeah, let's work together. When I think of a piece that's right for you, I'll give it to you," and that really made my year. It did take awhile for us to actually do our first piece together. I think you were at the time still promoting *Our Cancer Year* and getting over having cancer. I think the first piece we worked together on was a piece for the *Village Voice* in 1995 and then it's been sort of steady short pieces here and there in the last ten years or so. It's been great. You really inspired me to start writing my own work as well so I owe it all to this guy [laughs].

MR: I would strongly recommend the audience pick up Josh's book on travel stories, it's an excellent book.

JN: *A Few Perfect Hours.*

MR: *A Few Perfect Hours*—is that Alternative Press?

JN: It was actually self-published through a Xeric Grant.

MR: Well, then buy it directly from him. Let's go over to Dean now, because Josh and you were roommates I think.

Dean Haspiel: No, not . . . okay this is about meeting Harvey for the first time basically?

MR: Right. How you guys started working together.

DH: Josh and I had gone to high school together and have known each other for a very long time. One of my favorite things about Josh is that we challenge each other, creatively. Let me backtrack for one second.

MR: You guys used to do a comic book together.

DH: We did a comic book together, but I'll get to that in a second.

JN: Someplace we were roommates, doing a comic book together.

DH: It was called *Keyhole*, and it was a two-man anthology. Josh told his stories in his half of the book and I told mine. I had a more mixed bag, and then Josh criticized that. [Josh laughs] He didn't like the fact that I was doing crime and superhero and autobio and everything else I was thinking about that week, and he was, like, focusing on, like, one or two things like travel or autobio. By issue 5, he basically told me to stop doing that and just do autobio. [Josh laughs] But we've known each other a very long time, and we challenge each other creatively and that's cool and I don't think I've drawn one professional page without showing it to Josh first actually, in my entire career.

JN: I'm only allowed to give approval. No criticism. [audience laughs]

DH: Yeah, he might have a suggestion, but it's usually a weak suggestion so . . . [laughter] but I appreciate that he feels strongly about certain things.

JN: Well, you saw that first piece I did with Harvey and that kind of got your dander up.

DH: Well, I was going to get to that. [Josh laughs]. One thing was, I grew up reading superhero comics, which a lot of people won't admit, and I still like superhero comics. But in the early '80s, I walked into a store called Soho Zat, in Soho, New York, and I discovered *Yummy Fur* and *American Splendor*, and it kind of blew my mind because I didn't know you could write and draw your own comics, number one, but also they didn't have to be from Marvel or DC. You know, they didn't have to be franchised superhero comics. So that kind of threw me for a loop, and then I started taking my ideas more seriously and then that developed into *Keyhole* with Josh Neufeld. As part of the challenge that Josh and I always had with each other . . . competition . . . Josh had hooked up with Harvey to do some *American Splendor*. I was like, "I draw better than Josh. I could get a job like that." [panel laughs] So I took whatever I had drawn that year and sent Harvey a package of my best stuff, and I never heard from him. I didn't get a phone call or a postcard. I got nothing and I was perplexed by that. He obviously didn't get the mail or something. [audience laughter] So then, I guess Josh had one up on me and I then wrote and drew a two-page story called "American Dilemma" . . .

JN: I think what happened, just to finish, is that you asked me to ask Harvey about your stuff, and I finally got the nerve up, [turns to speak to Harvey] because I was still new working with you and I didn't want to piss you off, so I was like "Did you get something from a friend of mine? Dean Haspiel?" And you were like, [imitating Harvey], "Yeah, his stuff is too stylized."

DH: So . . . [Neufeld laughs] I did a two-page story for *Keyhole* called "American Dilemma" about that problem which was I sent this work off and I imagined in my paranoia how Harvey was reacting to it, which was it was too stylized. I showed examples of the stuff I showed him that I never got a response to. It was basically an autobio piece, thinly disguised as kind of a letter to Harvey begging for work. [panel laughter] So I publish this in *Keyhole*, I send it and I never hear from him. And finally like three or four years go by and I get a phone call, from what I thought was a parody of Harvey Pekar calling me, to give me a gig. A one-page job or something. I'm talking to this guy, and he had woken me up first of all, so I was a little groggy, and it's like a parody. "Hey, don't you want to make some bread, man?" [audience laughter]. I'm thinking that Josh has called me up and for some reason, four years later he's pulling my leg, like this is a joke that suddenly reappears. I keep saying to this guy, "Are you sure that you're Harvey Pekar? Is this really Harvey?" and finally Harvey starts screaming at me, and tells me to fuck off and hangs up the phone. [general laughter] And I'm like, so now the joke turned mean. So I call up Josh and I'm like, "Josh, did you call me up?" He's like, "No, what're you talking about?" and I'm trying to think who else could have done it, and he asks me to describe the conversation. I describe it with some of the verbiage and he says, "Dean, that was Harvey, man." So I said, "Can I get his number? I guess I have to call up and apologize." So I get his number and get Harvey on the phone, and I start to apologize to him. I said, "Did you call me" and he's like "Yeah, yeah, yeah. Dean, what do I gotta to do to prove to you that I'm really me?" [general laughter] And that's how me and Harvey started working together.

MR: Ok. Ed actually tells the story in his book, which is for sale upstairs, but I will let him tell it in his own words here, and then we'll talk about working styles.

Ed Piskor: Yeah, it was basically the same situation as Dean. Just getting back to the whole *American Splendor* thing, how I came to find Harv, or whatever, I saw that documentary in the '80s called *Comic Book Confidential*. I don't know if you've heard of it. There was a little segment on there with Harvey, and in all honesty I was reading *X-Men* and had a crush on Kitty Pryde. [audience laughter] I wasn't too interested in that sort of thing, but it kind of messed with my head a little. I didn't understand the comic.

DH: You're talking about Harvey's comic?

EP: Yeah, yeah. This is around the time that the Doubleday book was put out, so it actually made it to the local bookstore at the mall and I was checking it out, just because I saw it in the movie. And I was waiting for the punch line. I thought *American Splendor* was his superhero name, or something [panel laughter], but there wasn't a scene where he went into the telephone booth and came out with underwear on. I stuck with him and started to really appreciate his stories, because it didn't take too long for X-Men to dry the well for me. I was trying to shop around some of my own comics a couple of years ago, and wasn't having much success, and rightly so because my writing is *terrible*.

JN: *Nooo*.

EP: *Terrible*, Josh Neufeld. So I decided to just starting sending stuff to artists and writers that I appreciated, maybe for some feedback to maybe get some clues to how I could change and get my stuff to professional

sort of quality. I sent some stuff to Harv. The way I found his address . . .
a couple of years ago, there was a Dark Horse book with a photo of you
on the cover smiling and there was a little address . . .

JN: A fake magazine story.

EP: Yeah, like a fake magazine subscription thing. I didn't know if it was
a real P.O. Box or anything, so I had an old issue of *American Splendor* that you put out on your own, Harv, so I assumed that you still used
that. I sent some of my comics to the address on the comic book cover
and didn't hear anything, but I just kept sending them there as part of
a routine. When I would finish a story, I would send it to X number of
people, and he was one of the people who was on the list and I didn't
even know if it was a real address . . . Months go by and I get a call in
the morning. I'm a nocturnal creature and I don't like morning; I don't
function in the morning. Basically it's the same deal as with Dean. The
guy gets on the line, "Hey, this is Harvey Pekar," but there is an Academy Award–nominated flick about the guy not too long ago. I had to
drag my buddies to go see it, and I have a buddy or two who can do a
good Harvey Pekar impersonation [panel laughter] and I knew it was my
buddy. But it wasn't. It was Harvey. He said the same thing he said to
Josh basically–when the time's right, we'll do something or whatever.

JN: Didn't you, in your own thought process, revisit Dean's story . . .

EP: Absolutely.

JN: . . . of thinking it was someone else?

EP: Absolutely. Again, I assumed it was my buddy and then immediately
after it clicked and it was Harv, I just thought, "This is just like 'American Dilemma.' This is just like the Haspiel strip." So about a year goes
by and I do a four-page story for the *Our Movie Year* book. Harv liked
it. I wanted it to be pretty great, so I worked on it constantly. I did it in
a week, but it was literally like twelve- to fourteen-hour days so I could
have a quick turnaround so he could see that he could rely on me. Towards the end of production on the book, he calls me and says, "Ed, are
you interested in doing a lot of work in a short amount of time?" I just
asked for some hint as to what that short amount of time was. What did
we need? Twenty-four pages?

HP: No, no, we did something before that, about the garage.

EP: That was that four-pager.

DH: That's the four-pager.

HP: That was the four-pager, yeah, yeah.

EP: That's the four-pager, right, and you said something like "I need
twenty-four pages in twenty-eight days," [panel laughs].

DH: And just so you know, he gave me the four-pager first.

EP: I know now.

DH: And I was gonna draw it and he says, "Ed's already drawn it." and I'm like "What?!"

EP: I didn't want to step on any toes. I didn't know about it, I swear.

DH: It was *All About Eve*. [laughter]

EP: When he called me that second time to do that twenty-four-pager, it was around my birthday so I decided I'd celebrate my birthday like a month or two later [audience laughter] and I set to work on that twenty-four page comic. I had to pencil two pages a day because I'm still a newbie and he couldn't completely trust that my pencils were in order or whatever, so I had to get everything approved first. And the U.S. Mail isn't the most reliable thing. I got him the pencilled pages, and it's a good thing too, because my drawings of Joyce were so awful.

JN: Is she here tonight?

HP: She walked out.

DH: No, she came and saw you and left. [laughter]

EP: I have to apologize to her publicly for my drawing.

JN: Didn't you drive up to visit him and take actual pictures for reference?

HP: Yeah, yeah, he drove up.

EP: Well, I spoke to Harv. Joyce wasn't around.

DH: Just so you know, a twenty-four page comic written in Harvey standards, is like a fifty-page comic book, isn't it? It's so packed.

EP: It is, it is. There's a lot of words and you can definitely expand the amount of pages by pacing it correctly. But honestly, I didn't want to step on any toes, I didn't want to break any of his panels up or anything like that. I wanted to try to get this thing as good as possible in the twenty-eight days I had to work on it. So, we did that and everything, and the *Our Movie Year* book comes out, and Harv calls and says, "Ed, do you want to draw a graphic novel for me?" There was no question, of course. And that's what we're working on now. It's called *Macedonia* and it should be out around this time next year. The end.

MR: With that lead-in Harv, maybe you can tell us a little bit about *Macedonia*? What it's about? The idea behind it?

HP: *Macedonia* is about the now-independent country of Macedonia which used to be part of Yugoslavia. When Yugoslavia came apart around 1990, it gained its independence, but there was a lot of tensions between the Albanians, who made up about 25 percent of the population, and the Macedonians, who were Slavic and made up most of the population. With that in mind, my movie was going to be shown in

Columbia, Missouri, and they sent me money to come out and talk, lecture, along with the movie. I did that and I met the sister of the woman who was showing the movie and she was a student at Berkeley in California. She was real interested in this Macedonian situation. She was taking political science at Berkeley and she was especially interested in peace studies. She was getting hassled by guys all the time who would say, "Awww, don't you know war is inevitable? What're you wasting your time screwing around with this stuff for?" She came up with the example of Macedonia, where a war had been averted. She wanted to do a thesis on it for college so she was going to travel over there and research why a war hadn't broken out. So I said, "Would you mind taking some notes? I think I'd like to do a comic book story about that." She went, she was there a month, and she sent me back like 140 pages' worth of notes. It was great. She really laid it out—how they had avoided it, what the problem was between the two ethnic groups . . . I used that as the basis of this story that I gave to Ed to illustrate.

Another reason why I did this thing on Macedonia was, I don't know if any of you know Joe Sacco—he's a wonderful cartoonist—and he did some stuff about Yugoslavia too. About the Bosnian War, but Joe does like journalism in comics. He's kind of revolutionary that way, but he tends to feature a lot of violence. So I wanted to do this thing about Yugoslavia, but there was no violence. You know, showing that it was possible to have no violence in Yugoslavia. So Joe Sacco kind of partly inspired me to do this. Ed's doing a beautiful job on it, just beautiful. Ed's just getting better and better, so fast. Well, Dean got real good, real fast too after I got the okay to do [*The Quitter*]. Dean made a quantum leap. He got to be a much better artist.

DH: I think it's the same. [laughter]

HP: No, it's not the same. Bullshit, you don't think it's the same either. [laughter] What're you talking about? Bullshit.

DH: I think I did some good stuff before that.

HP: You think it's the same as the thing we did for *Bizarro*?

DH: Well, that's different.

HP: Aw right.

MR: Dean also did what, one miniseries for Marvel?

DH: I did some stuff for Marvel and DC. I did *Night Falls on Yancy Street*, a Thing miniseries with Evan Dorkin.

MR: Right. So at this point, you had done some longer format work.

DH: Yeah. *The Quitter* is a 104-page book with 96 pages of comics contents and the Thing miniseries is 128 pages. My own personal work I consider to be ongoing, but in terms of one story, this is the second-longest I've ever done. That's the hardest part and I think Ed's dealing with that, keeping a consistency, because that took me about what? Eight months to draw?

HP: I'd say so.

DH: Something like that. Should I talk about *The Quitter* now?

HP: Go ahead, talk about it.

DH: I wanted to do a longer piece with Harvey because I had only done a couple of small one-pagers and three-pagers, and stuff like that. And then I hooked Harvey up with Ted Hope to get the movie done. I kind of had to convince Harvey that there was this film producer who I knew that was interested, could be convinced—talk to him. I think Harvey had some history with other producers wanting to make a movie version of *American Splendor* and it just never panned out, so I think he was a little jaded by the whole Hollywood idea. "Yeah, sure, send a producer my way." Except this guy actually walked the dog and did the job. And did a great job and far surpassed any notions I had for an *American Splendor* movie. I don't know how many of you folks saw it, but it's a pretty unique and great movie. And so, like Harvey will say, he wanted to know how he could pay me back within reason. [laughter]. He taught me the word "reason" through that sentence alone. What he could do for me back?—because he's a *mensch*, he's a good guy, you know? I said I always wanted to do a longer piece with him, and I had some gigs that I was meeting the deadlines on and I got wind that this guy, Jonathan Vankin was just becoming the new editor at [DC's] Vertigo. Vertigo's an interesting imprint. They do their *Swamp Things* and their *Hellblazers* and what not, but they also try to push the envelope in other directions with books like *It's A Bird*. I don't know if you've heard of that book? It's kind of an autobio piece about a Superman writer, and I don't want to give away the punch line, but it's about a disease that a relative has. So I knew that they were open to trying new things. I got together with Jonathan Vankin, and I pitched some ideas, and one of them was doing a longer graphic novel with Harvey Pekar. He was totally excited about that idea so then I called up Harvey and said, "So Harvey, what do you want to do? What do you think we could do here that's longer?" And one of the ideas we had talked about was doing a graphic novel about Jewish boxers.

HP: Yeah.

DH: And Joyce was in on that. Weren't you in on that a little bit? With that idea? [speaking to JB in the audience].

JB: Well, that's what we . . .

DH: That was the original idea.

JB: They wanted Harvey to do superheroes, and then it was going to be guys in tights, and then we wore it down to guys in trunks, and then we simply made it Jews in trunks, [audience laughter] and I got him all these books, and pretty soon it just turned into Harvey beating people up. [audience laughter]

DH: Basically, Harvey beating people up. That's true. Which nobody knows about. Anyway, I think what they were really concerned about was, "Can Harvey fictionalize?" or write fiction. And you know what? Harvey can't write fiction. Ok, I think you tried to and you dabbled in it, like the *Bizarro* thing, but the *Bizarro* thing's still about you anyway.

HP: Yeah, everything's about me.

DH: Everything's about you. And I think ultimately he just returned to what he does best which is write about himself. Only, he hadn't written about the first thirty-some odd years of his life, ergo the origin of Harvey Pekar which is this "prequel" to *American Splendor the Movie* in a way. What a fascinating story. Who would have known that Harvey had a really good right hook and beat the hell out of people? If you follow his work, it's just a fascinating "how did that happen?" It kind of explains where he is today, but how did he get there? And that's not the only thing the book's about obviously, but I guess I'll have to let Harvey talk about that. It took me about eight months to draw. I remember sitting down—I had gotten this sixty-two-page, handwritten manuscript, of this man's origin in life. It was the most daunting thing I ever had to read and consider in my head—to interpret someone's life. If it was Superman, there's a lot there, but to me, I was kind of afraid to draw from birth to the first thirty-some odd years. And then it jumps about twenty-five years, and you can read all that work in the comics that have already come out and been collected, and then it has a nice little denouement. What I realized I had to do, and I had ninety-six pages to turn this sixty-two-page manuscript and pace it into graphic novel form. I realized what I had to do was to make it kind of my story so it could be yours, the reader's. To universalize it in that way, still maintaining it being Harvey's life and I hope I achieved that.

HP: Sure, you did a real good job.

MR: Dean, you talked about getting sixty pages from Harvey, and Harvey, in the movie, it shows you drawing stick figures and doing breakdowns for people. Is that still the way you work?

HP: Yeah. It's still that way.

MR: So let's turn it back over to Josh who hasn't talked for a while. Josh, how did you feel when you first saw Harvey's script and how do you feel now when you get one? Are you more comfortable with knowing the way Harvey works and what he'll be looking for in your art?

JN: I think probably my comfort level is fairly similar because I had a whole history of all the other comics he had done to sort of see the treatment that artists had generally given to his work. Other than Dean I think [chuckles], everybody else pretty much tries to keep the work static . . . not static, but unstylized and straightforward . . . very much like the mundanity or quotidian aspects of life. It's important for the artist to also translate that, and keep that aesthetic as part of the work, so I didn't feel like I was under any obligation to be really dramatic or experimental in my layouts. I just wanted to keep it very human and really use the art to serve the story more than anything else. That was something I was really comfortable doing. I think that the thing that's really different and fun about working with Harvey is that you do get these breakdowns about how he wants the story to work which is basically these figures that look sort of like a chair with a head on it and just some word balloons above it. It's very basic, but there's a lot of room as an artist within that to work in terms of what sort of details you want to add and how you want to augment the surroundings. For me, it's a nice challenge. It's like collaboration at its purest form. Harvey's also incredibly generous; he pretty much loves everything anyone does for him and he's very easy to work with on that level . . .

DH: Well . . .

JN: . . . except for Dean. [audience laughter]

DH: No, no, *The Quitter* was a great experience for me. I don't think we . . . except that he changed my art style and made me better . . . I don't think that we had any differences . . .

JN: You had further to go. It's ok.

DH: . . . but I remember the second job I did for Harvey, way before *The Quitter*. It was a one-pager and I remember we had a forty-five minute argument after I drew it about what I had drawn. Basically, I had drawn Harvey overhearing a black guy talking to a black woman, and he did not like the way I drew the black people. He thought I was a racist.

HP: No, that wasn't it. I thought you drew them as being way too old.

DH: Oh, is that what it was? [audience laughter]

HP: Yeah. I take part of the blame for that because I should have mentioned their age because it came out way different with their being old, than with their being young.

DH: I remember that my argument back to you was "I may be drawing them in a way that you're uncomfortable with, but look at the way you're writing them" because I remember the dialogue was pretty . . . anyway, we have . . . [audience laughter] . . . that was the only static I've ever had with Harvey.

HP: Well, one page ain't bad.

DH: [quickly] That's not so bad. [audience laughter]

MR: For Harvey, Ed and Dean—for both *The Quitter* and *Macedonia*, the backgrounds may be more important than just a stick figure would convey, and I was wondering how you worked through that. If you provided Dean with pictures of people and the time period.

HP: Nah. Ed got pictures. You should work with picture references if you could. The woman who wrote the notes for Macedonia also provided a lot of pictures, right?

EP: She did a lot of work on this thing, yeah. How many pages of notes did she give you?

HP: About 140.

EP: 140 pages of notes. She sent me about close to 100 photos and on the back of each photo she sort of plotted out her course in the story. She'd label it "1" and then she'd write what pages of comics this covered, so there's really no excuse for me to screw this thing up. [audience laughter] I need all the help I can get with this *Macedonia* story. I've never been out of the *Eastern* time zone [louder audience laughter].

HP: As far as with Dean, I was trying to get him to come to Cleveland to take pictures and stuff like that, but he never came so I just went over it with him on a panel by panel basis, talking about what the houses were like and giving him a verbal description of them and everything. It was ok. It worked.

DH: In terms of reference, in a ninety-six-page story, there are some pictures of Harvey in the graphic novel that show him when he was younger, being a kid to a teenager, and in his early twenties. I didn't even get to see these pictures until I was on page fifty. Once I saw them, I was like "Oooohhh."

HP: So you did a good job anyway.

DH: I did an okay job interpreting what I thought you might look like . . .

HP: You did a good job. [audience laughter]

DH: . . . so I had to keep that consistent, but Harvey definitely told me . . . well, I had some questions about "what do you mean like a double house?"

HP: Yeah, a double house.

DH: I had some questions about some stuff he was writing about, but honestly the Internet, you know, was very helpful.

HP: Yeah. [audience laughter]

DH: I typed a lot of [queries] about Ohio, a lot of Ohio in the 1940s and '50s, and certain cars and whatnots to try to maintain that feel and get that vibe, but to me, as Josh was saying before, Harvey gives you a lot of leeway to dramatize the story visually. He basically sets the pace, but like I said, with my sixty-two-page manuscript, I had to pace things a little differently. I would even cut a panel he wrote in half, or into three panels sometimes, or take four of his captions and make that into one big panel. I had laid out the entire ninety-six-page comic in five weeks and then we went over that. Once that was all settled, I went into execution mode for about seven months, and it was just all craftsmanship after that.

JN: If I can just add something to that . . . as someone who tries to tell my own stories as well, working with Harvey's been amazing because what comes across very effortlessly to him in scripts—the way they seem like you wrote them down without thinking about them very much—when they're actually translated into comics, you realize his understanding of pacing, narrative, how to use silent panels, just not using a lot of the crutches that I know I certainly rely on a lot when doing autobiographical comics. For instance, I use lots of narrative captions that kind of explain or tell the story rather than just showing the story. It's a real skill that he has, it's, I think, very understated, and it's taught me a lot about the craft of comics.

HP: Thank you.

MR: Okay, I'm going to ask a self-indulgent question now. In the real world, I'm actually a museum archivist, and I'm wondering what happens to all these scripts? Do people send them back to you?

HP: No, no, I don't . . . I make xeroxes of them and I send them to the artists. I lose them, you know? [audience laughter] And I *know* they're going to be worth money, or they are worth money.

JB: We have them. Every so often, some guy with a ponytail and an MBA shows up and says they want to archive the stuff, and the rule is they have to wait until he's dead, and I need them to move all of the crap out of the basement so you can get to the file cabinets where the stuff's being stacked. They were asking you for . . . you've had a couple of universities hit you up for your papers before . . . it's like you're still using them, you know?

JN: As an obsessive myself, I have copies of every script and everything that Harvey's done, and every sketch I've done.

JB: There is a living room under the mess. [audience laughter]

JN: I keep mine in a filing cabinet, but that'll work too.

MR: The Ransom Center, down in Texas, pays a lot for archives. Okay, I've got one more question for Harvey and then we're going to open it up for questions from the audience. I had asked you upstairs approximately how many people you thought had drawn you over the years?

HP: Yeah, I don't know. Maybe around thirty. That's just a wild guess.

JN: I think it's more. I think it's like fifty.

HP: I dunno.

JN: There's a lot of one-timers.

DH: About a year or two ago, Josh Neufeld e-mailed me . . . I don't know why he does this because I don't know where he finds the time to do this . . . but you had gone through every Harvey Pekar story and in an Excel file,[2] figured out all the artists, how many pages they did, all this stuff, and I'm like "Why did you send this to me? And number one, why do you do this?" [JN laughs] Nobody's paying him to do this. [audience laughs]

JN: I told you I was obsessive.

DH: He's got a disorder, but it serves that question.

HP: So how many were there?

JN: I don't remember, but it was like fifty.

DH: It was probably like fifty . . .

HP: Awright, so he knows better than me.

DH: . . . he made an educated guess.

HP: He knows better than me. It's fifty.

MR: The final question–I know people send you submissions—these guys were talking about it—out of the blue.

DH: Just today an artist drew him.

HP: Yeah.

MR: I was wondering if you enjoy it after all these years. If you still feel a certain *frisson* when you open the envelope.

HP: It's nice. See now, I've got a group of people, not only do I think I'm working with a group of really accomplished artists, there are several more guys that I work with too. These are really, I think, top of the line people.

MR: Why don't you mention some names?

HP: Well, like Frank Stack, every once in a while I work with Gerry Shamray, a guy who I've worked with since 1974 is Gary Dumm. I've worked with some really good people that I don't work with anymore. Along the way a bunch of good people.

JN: Joe Sacco too.

HP: Joe Sacco. Yeah. Joe Sacco's excellent. [Hesitatingly] I don't really need artists as badly as I used to. It used to be a real hassle for me to get together enough artists to do a sixty-page book, but now these guys are so good, and they work pretty quickly. A lot of times I'll get stuff from people that's really pretty good stuff, but these guys have been working with me for years. Even Ed, you've been working with me for a couple of years, right?

EP: Two.

HP: Yeah.

JN: Which is like half Ed's life. [audience laughter]

EP: I shave every Friday.

HP: I feel like my primary loyalty is to the guys I'm working with especially now. A lot of these guys, when I was putting out my own stuff, I didn't pay them very much money at all. I couldn't afford to. And now that I'm making more money, I figure it should go to them. I get good stuff from people, but I have kind of an ambivalent feeling. It's like "It's good, and it's good enough for me and everything like that," but still if I give the assignment to this guy, then I take money away from that guy. So it takes a lot for me to start working with a new artist.

MR: I'd like to follow up that actually. Something strange occurred to me—has anyone ever sent you bizarre submissions, like funny animal Harvey Pekar or all-nude *American Splendor*? [audience laughter]

HP: No, really I don't think I've ever . . . I don't know, somebody might have sent me something, in all the years I've been doing it, somebody may have that I can't recall.

JN: There were the Chester Brown drawings of himself as a bunny talking to you.

HP: Oh yeah, yeah. [audience laughter]

JN: Those are classic. [chuckles]

MR: Okay, Chester Brown. Does anybody on the panel want to say anything, or should we just open it up to questions? In the yellow. [pointing at audience member]

AM: Harvey, how did you learn, or teach yourself, storytelling through panel and comic form?

HP: Because I was real familiar with comics. I just automatically did it that way. When I thought to do a script, I didn't write a theater-type script. Most comic book writers will write a theater script, but I thought if I divided the page into squares or rectangles, put captions where they belonged at the top, and then had the dialogue coming from the characters, plus a little description in the panel of what I wanted the panel to look like or something like that, I thought that would be easier. And also, doing it in a storyboard way helps you time the story better and pace it better than if you're doing it in a theater script way.

Englishman Hunt Emerson seems like another unlikely collaborator in his artwork for "Through the Generation from *American Splendor: Another Day.*

MR: Surely somebody must have a question. Tough audience.

JN: Or we're that thorough.

AM: This is about your movie. I saw it a while ago. Are you pretty happy about the interpretation of the director and all the actors?

HP: Oh yeah, yeah. I thought they did a wonderful job. Especially in fact of the fact, from what I can tell, what other comic book artists say, they really dislike what the film industry does to their work, but I had no problems. It was just unbelievable. It was great. The people from HBO that financed the film didn't even come out to watch it be shot. It was left in the hands of the producer, Ted Hope, who is a super-competent guy and knows the movie business backwards and forwards, and recruited a wonderful staff. Together they got together a really good cast. I could have never dreamed, like Dean suggested, I could have never have dreamed it came out as good as it did. It came out wonderfully.

AM: Do you mind if I ask Joyce as well? What did you think?

JB: Well . . . we got paid. [audience laughter] That was the bottom line on it really. But we did see *American Splendor* produced theatrically about four times and I had a pretty good sense of how it would play, plus a couple people have done some filmic adaptations of bits and pieces. So I had a lot of confidence because we weren't just working with an individual director. We were working with a husband and wife team. They kind of got the idea that *American Splendor*, because they're also building this on *Our Cancer Year* the book that Harvey and I did together, that this was really a movie about marriage. It wasn't just about some lonely guy doing his comics on his own. It really was about marriage and was about a relationship. The sessions that we had together, the meetings talking about setting it up and the script line—yeah, these were very, very good listeners. It was spooky because we had some near misses with other directors, other people that had options, and they kind of wanted to do this freakish thing like, "Oh look, a working class guy with a library cart. How interesting." [laughs] Or the people who couldn't understand the difference between comic book and comic as in stand-up comic. We knew almost from the jump . . . Harvey didn't know this. Harvey didn't catch on until much later, 'til after he had seen the movie a few times, that this was a good thing . . . he thought this was pretty depressing . . .

HP: Yeah. I'm way slower than she is.

JB: . . . but it just felt right this time around.

HP: Is that a dig?

JN: If I could follow up, just on that question, as an artist I've always found it fascinating . . .

HP: [continuing] 24/7.

JN: . . . to compare all the ways the different artists in a book illustrate him and Joyce and other recurring characters. I think that often gets overlooked in critical discussions of his work, the way each artist brings whatever they have to the table, all working to the same goal, but bringing their own styles or visions. I think that was to me one of the most *vital* aspects of the movie—what they understood about this idea of the multiplicity of Harveys that there are out there. There's the real Harvey playing himself, the actor playing Harvey, the actor playing the actor who played him theatrically, the cartoon versions of him in the movie, and of course, lots of shots of the different artists who have drawn him over the years. That was the meta aspect of the movie that was an unspoken part of it, but really vital to the overall thing that is *American Splendor*. That was something I really loved about the film.

Sari Wilson, JN's wife: [hoarsely due to illness] My question is for Harvey—how do you decide which artist for which story—do you ever write a story with an artist in mind?

HP: No, I try and write the best . . .

DH: She sounds like Harvey. [audience laughter]

HP: 24/7. Man, 24/7 from all angles I get it. [continuing laughter] I try and write the best stories I can, and then I think about matching them up with an artist. Some guys aren't going to be available, so that cuts it down a little bit. Then some guys do comedic stories better than others, some guys do serious stories better than others, some guys may *know* a particular area in the city or a geographical region better than others so they have a better feel for what they're doing there. I take all kinds of considerations like that into account, but I'll tell you [enthusiastically] working with the guys I'm working with now, I think I would feel pretty confident about giving them any kind of story. I think that they're versatile and they're real bright. There might be a little difference, maybe one would be better than another on a particular story, but everybody can handle them at least competently. I feel real lucky that I'm working with such good people.

AM: In the movie, it portrayed that you and Joyce met through a visit and not long after you got married.

JB: We decided to get married the day after we met.

AM: Now the question is, how did you make that decision?

JB: Harvey will marry anything. [audience laughter] I was available . . . I was female . . . [continuing laughter] Our second day we picked out rings and on the third day, we got married. We did talk, and we did correspond. This was before the Internet—it was actual letters and phone calls. It helped that we had both been married before and learned what really counted.

DH: I'd like to draw those letters into a graphic novel.

JB: You know, I cut up a bunch of the phone bills and made them into a Valentine.

DH: Wow. [audience laughter]

JB: Yeah, we just figured we could negotiate and work it out later. We didn't have this naive assumption like "Oh, you like the Beatles. I like the Beatles. We've got so much in common." [audience laughter] We just figured it was going to be a struggle every bit of the way, and that we would fuck it up, and just didn't take anything for granted.

AM: That's very impressive you'd make the decision that heavy in two days.

JB: We've been married for what . . . twenty-something years? Twenty-three years?

HP: We corresponded and talked on the phone for months.

JB: It was four months we corresponded. I met you in March and we were married by May.

HP: Yeah. Yeah. But we had corresponded . . . [JB also talking]

JB: As soon as we decided to get married I went home.

HP: It was August of the year before when we really started corresponding though so there's that time.

JB: Something like that. All I know is that we argued. We argued and then one day I called him up and told him to sit down because I was ready to settle it. And then I was traveling through town and agreed to stop off in Cleveland. The next day we were together.

HP: [simultaneously] Ayiyiyiyi . . .

DH: Wait, you used "argued" in the past tense? [audience laughter]

HP: I dunno. I don't resist anymore. I don't resist anymore.

JB: Dean, this is the future for you too—just watch it.

DH: I know, I know. [audience laughter]

HP: [to Dean] It's stupid, it takes two to make an argument.

DH: It's true, it's true.

AM: My wife and I dated for eight years before we got married. I don't understand it all, but everything worked out. Harvey, the question I have is you've been doing for the last several years, a lot of stuff that isn't autobiographical like *Macedonia*, some biography and stuff like that. It's kind of an amorphous question, but how is your working process different? Do you find that it's very different stuff to write or does it work the same way with different names?

HP: It's like, in the beginning, when I'd write all these stories in the first person, but still I'd feature other people and so . . . when I wrote the thing *Unsung Hero* about the Vietnam guy, I interviewed him and I wrote down what he said. That's the way I used to do it when I would be the protagonist of the story. I use pretty much the same methods. I had used them previously in some of my earlier stories when I would talk about somebody.

AM: This kind of follows on what you both said about meeting and marrying—the personal stories you write are so stark and real and taken from your life and exactly the opposite from what many authors do where they try to fend people off and keep their own privacy. Your books are kind of like the original Osborne show; you're inviting people into your home and your personal life, and you have more control than maybe you would if you let a person with a video camera in, but it's so personalized. I was wondering if you find that weird stuff comes down to you as a result? People read your books, and they pick up something, and they meet you . . .

JB: That's how we got a kid. We fuzzed it a bit in the movie because Danielle was young, and we fuzzed it a bit in the stories Harvey wrote. First, it's how he got a wife. I had a distribution problem and I couldn't get copies and I wrote to him asking about getting copies for my store and we ended up corresponding and marrying. Yeah, once somebody knocked on the door and they wanted to show Harvey some comics and they brought this little girl along. The little girl asked me if I'd be her mother and if she could move in and that's how we got our daughter.

MR: Was it really Frank Stack?

HP: No, it wasn't really Frank Stack. No, Danielle didn't want it to be her real father.

JB: Danielle will talk about it now, and eventually Danielle will do her own comic about it. She's doing comics now.

EP: She'd better. And she'd better not draw the characters like *Sailor Moon*. [laughter]

JB: That's for her to tell, but yeah, that was one. Actually, I said that to Neil Gaiman. He asked, "What's the weirdest thing a fan ever gave you?" and I said, "Well, we got a kid." [audience laughter]

AM: Do people come up with reinterpretations of your personal stories where they think something else is so important that you never even noticed?

JB: Oh, sure. I've had about five women pull me aside and say, "I'm the one that broke his heart in that story about the bakery" like that's the way it was. The real one has no idea that she is in this, but all these women like to make claims about meeting Harvey.

JN: Your question is interesting as an artist too because sometimes I'll get a story from Harvey that I'll illustrate and then I'll have this weird feeling, if it's a really sad story about his cat or something, or a personal thing that people talk about, because it's not like we socialize on the phone that much, other than when we work together. So I'll do the story, or I'll be working on it and then I'll have this kind of strange feeling like I'm prying if I actually ask him anything about it beyond the parameters of the story itself. Is this fiction? I know it's not fiction, but are we intimate enough to talk about this stuff—how you felt about something? So I always get this weird shyness around it, so I just try to go with my own feelings about it, and then sort of leave it there.

DH: That happened to me with *The Quitter*. I just realized right now, you're right. Harvey is so personal in his writing, that you don't . . . well for me, it's just like "that's the story," but when I had *The Quitter*, right before it went to print and it was all in front of me, there's stuff about his parents all throughout the book. I'm not giving too much away—it's not like *Star Wars* or something and Darth Vader's his father. I wanted to know more about what happened to his parents, I was like "Wait, it's not in here." I drew it and I took eight months and it occurred to me I wanted to know more. I asked Harvey because I had this question about it and it messed me up when he told me the answer. I was like, "Why isn't this in the book?" but why didn't it occur to me to think about that when I was doing it too? So it's weird how it gets blurry.

AM: Harvey, are you still in contact with Robert Crumb?

HP: Yeah, very occasionally. He's in France. He comes over here, but he avoids the Midwest where I live. It's too depressing. I don't blame him.

AM: What do you think about his film, *Crumb*?

HP: I thought it was very good. I will say that, you know, his years in Cleveland were left out of there. 1962–1966 and those are really crucial years for him. That's when he got married. Well, that's when he first started going out with girls and got married, when he first had a job, when he first lived on his own and that stuff wasn't covered. I think I know why. Because Terry Zwigoff, who was the director, actually wanted to interview me about this stuff, but when he called me up and wanted to interview me, he was in New York and I was in Cleveland . . .

JB: You were going through chemo . . .

HP: Maybe I was sick . . .

JB: He also didn't have any dough to fly out . . .

HP: He didn't want to spend the money to come to Cleveland, and I didn't want to spend the money to go to New York, so I don't know.

JB: . . . because nobody thought the movie was going to go anywhere, anyway.

HP: Yeah, that's the reason Crumb went along with it in the first place. Terry made a film before that on a string band called *Louie Bluie*. I've never seen it; I guess it was very well done. I've since learned that he's a very good director. It was one of a million real good documentaries that nobody ever watches, and I figured this was going to be another one. And Crumb figured this was going to be another one too. That's why Crumb gave his consent. When it became a semi-hit, he was walking around in disguise with a false beard on and stuff like that. [audience laughter] Yeah, he was. He didn't want to be bothered. He can't *stand* being bothered by the public. Hates it.

AM: I have a question a little bit related to that. When you became more successful or found more interest directed at you without having to search for it or struggle for it, do you find that changes your ideas of the kinds of stories you want to tell in any way? Or does that change your perceptions?

HP: I'm so obsessive-compulsive that I haven't accepted the fact that in the minds of many people, I've made it. I'm always worried about where the next dollar is coming from and all that. I'm always "catastrophising"—thinking the worst. That's the way I operate, and it's kind of pathetic I guess. [laughs] I know I should feel a lot more comfortable and better about myself than I do. I take a lot of pills, but I still can't do anything about it. I know it's not rational, but that's the way I'm programmed and I've just got to work around it.

AM: Harvey, I was wondering if you still did critiques on comics. Years ago you did something for the *Comics Journal* on *Maus*,[3] and I know you got a lot of angry mail. I liked a lot the way you attacked it literally, and I know a lot of people did at the time, because I was in art school studying to be a comics artist. People didn't want to touch that because it won the Pulitzer Prize and it was a literary fad. I thought you were very bold for saying some things didn't work on a literal level and some things it borrowed a lot from. It was refreshing to see. People were still having delusions about comics and you actually treated it on the same level as a work of fiction. If you're going to do it, it should be capable of being compared . . .

HP: Yeah, a lot of people really got mad at me because of that. I feel like, and I may be completely wrong about this, but I feel that some of them are still thinking "Oh why does he have this attitude towards Spiegelman? What's behind it?" or something like that. But I thought the work was flawed, seriously flawed. And I come from a very similar background and I found it kind of offensive in some ways. My parents are from Europe too. They didn't go through the Holocaust. They came to America just before the war. Well, that's all I'll say about it.

MR: I think the question was also if you're going to do any more types of criticism like that?

HP: Yeah, I do book criticism now. For *Book Forum* I wrote a couple of reviews of graphic novels, but I'll tell you the truth. There aren't really a lot of good graphic novels that I see. But on the other hand, today at this show, people are coming around and giving me their work that they self-publish and a lot of it is *really good*. Just for what it's worth to you, if you despair about the future of comics, there are still plenty of really good people out there. It's just that they can't get their work out.

JB: Harvey, what's that anthology you're supposed to be editing?

HP: Houghton-Mifflin has hired me. For many, many years, they've been putting out *Best Short Stories of 1951, 1952* like that. They've hired me to do a best graphics stories of the past year or so, so I'm going to be working on that. Somebody else is going to screen some of them out and give me what they think are the 125 best short stories and I'm supposed to choose between them. I have kind of an ambivalent attitude about that, because in a way, I feel funny about judging. Saying this work is better than that work in other words and including some and not including others when there's just a hair's-breadth of difference. But on the other hand, they *are* paying me well. [audience laughter]

MR: I'd like to let that lie as the perfect ending, but I am going to ask another question. Are you excerpting from longer works like the *McSweeney's* that Chris Ware[4] put together, or do these have to be short?

HP: I dunno yet what's going on because the person who's working with me and getting the preliminary group [of stories] together has not done it yet. I don't know if she is sure yet how she's going to work it. I asked her if she was going to consider one-panel entries and she wasn't sure. So I guess I'll just have to work with it when I get to it.

MR: We've gone about fifteen minutes over, so I suggest we let everyone go back upstairs so you can buy their books. They're all up the stairs next to the Comic Book Legal Defense Fund table. Thank you.

Afterword

Since these interviews saw print a year after being conducted, the artists provided updates on their work. Earlier this year, Pekar published *Ego & Hubris: The Michael Malice Story* with Gary Dumm. Both Haspiel and Neufeld are doing stories online for the electronic artist community Act-i-vate which can be reached at http://act_i_vate.livejournal.com/

HP: Well, I'm writing comics books. I've written three and part of the fourth *American Splendor* issues for Vertigo. I've just finished *Macedonia*, I'm working on a book about SDS (Students for a Democratic Society) and a book about the Beat Generation, all in comics format.

DH: What I'm currently working on: I'm drawing *Immortal*, my free weekly comix strip[5] while concurrently adapting R. L. Stein's "Revenge of the Lawn Gnomes" for Scholastic Graphics' *Goosebumps: Scary Summer* graphic novel and illustrating more Harvey Pekar stories for Vertigo's *American Splendor* miniseries. After that? I'm collaborating on a kids book with legendary underground cartoonist/writer, Jay Lynch, for editor Françoise Mouly at Raw Jr. Come 2007, I buckle down and illustrate *The Alcoholic*, an original graphic novel written by my friend/ author Jonathan Ames for Vertigo.

EP: What I'm working on nowadays . . . Harvey and I just wrapped up our graphic novel, *Macedonia*, for a release during late 2006, early 2007. Pekar and I are maintaining our working relationship with a bunch of projects that are too early to speak about. And Jay Lynch wrote a few strips that I ended up drawing and they'll see print in the pages of *Mineshaft Magazine*. Check out my website at www.edpiskor.com.

JN: Collaboration has always been part of my comix repertoire, and *The Vagabonds #2: "Of Two Minds"* (coming out in October, at SPX) continues that tradition. In it, I illustrate stories by (among others) Harvey Pekar, *Duplex Planet*'s David Greenberger, award-winning poet/ memoirist Nick Flynn, literary cult figure Eileen Myles, artist Martha Rosler, Lennon/McCartney, and the New York downtown theater company The Civilians. A good collaboration is an ongoing conversation between writer and artist, each challenging the other, and the result truly is "Of Two Minds." *The Vagabonds* is published by Alternative Comics.

I'm also doing a new four-pager with Harvey P. for the third issue of the four-issue *American Splendor* Vertigo "miniseries". And I'm doing a new two-page spread collaboration with poet Nick Flynn for a literary journal called *World Literature Today*. I also just finished a short piece for the urban free daily paper, *Metro*, about my worst job ever. In addition, as a member of the online comics studio, Act-i-vate, I'm working on a long-form comics story about my experience as a Red Cross volunteer following Hurricane Katrina (which I wrote about in non-comics form in my blog/book, *Katrina Came Calling*). My website, JoshComix .com, has info about most of these upcoming projects.

Notes

1. Ed Piskor has made a home video of the second panel available at http://edpiskor .com/splendorpanel.html.

2. Online at http://joshcomix.home.mindspring.com/and/pekar_artists/.

3. "Maus and Other Topics," *Comics Journal* 113, December 1986, p. 54–57.

4. *McSweeney's Quarterly Concern* Issue 13, McSweeney's, 2004.

5. *Immortal* can be seen at Haspiel's website at http://www.deanhaspiel.com/.

Harvey Pekar Interview

Scott A. Rosenberg / 2005

Previously unpublished interview from the
Small Press Expo. Printed by permission of
Scott A. Rosenberg.

Harvey Pekar: [about some mustard] You want to take them home with
you? You can tell them they gave it to you. You can tell them you've
been elevated in status. They just give this stuff to VIPs.

Scott A. Rosenberg: What made you decide you wanted to tell your de-
finitive childhood story?
HP: Dean Haspiel, who illustrated the thing, hooked me up with the
guys that made the movie. So I said, "Dean, you got me a lot of money,
what can I do for you, you know?" He said, "I'd like to illustrate one of
your longer works," and I had to come up with a longer work for him to

185

illustrate and I thought, you know, it would be a good idea to do a pre-quel to the movie to cover my early life. That's why I did it, so people could see how I got to be the mess that I am.

SR: Was it tough for you to go back to all that?
HP: No, I obsess about that stuff. I go back to it anyway, might as well make some money off it.

SR: What made you decide to take bring it to DC Comics?
HP: Dean had a connection there. That's why I brought it to DC.

SR: Did you ever think you'd be working for DC Comics?
HP: It wasn't at the top of my list. No, I didn't think . . . you want that? Mind if I sign this?

SR: No, please.
HP: How do I sign it?

ATTENDEE: Kevin. I was working at a bookstore and someone came in and ordered that and never picked it up. Someone came to me and said, "you like comic books, you want to buy this?" I said OK. It was great, I was really happy.
HP: See that, you can talk to him too. [Points to one of his artists.] That's Josh Neufeld.

SR: Definitely. Working for DC, do you ever have a desire to maybe one day write *Superman?*
HP: No. This is the closest that I've come. You want to take a look at that? [shows an *Escapist* comic]

SR: Absolutely. How was it working on a different character?
HP: It's a satire. I also did a satire on Bizarro.

SR: How has your life changed since the movie came out?
HP: It hasn't changed at all. I still work . . . well, I don't work at the same place, I retired, but live in the same place, my lifestyle is the same. If I get any extra money, I put it aside for my kid for school. I live kind of a dull life.

I'm getting recognized more, supermarkets and everything, you know.

SR: Do you like that kind of stardom?
HP: Yeah! I can handle a lot of that. I was very underrated until recently. I was very underrated. Now I can take lifetimes of praise and it wouldn't throw me off. I can handle it.

SR: Do you think that *Quitter*, coming from a big huge publisher, is going to put you more in the spotlight?

HP: I'm with Random House anyways. I was with Random House before this. They're bigger than DC. It will help. They do advertising and stuff like that. They do a lot more of that than the small companies I worked with before. When I self-published, I didn't have time to advertise.

SR: Did you approach *Quitter* any differently than you approached *American Splendor*?

HP: No. It's the same general approach. I could have called it *American Splendor Presents: The Quitter* if I wanted to.

SR: Why'd you choose not to?

HP: Because I just decided I was calling everything *American Splen-*

Dean Haspiel's cover for *The Quitter*.

dor, everything was *American Splendor*. I just decided I would take a break from *American Splendor* and just call it what it was and not have *American Splendor* in there.

SR: Do you think that this is going to make people look at you differently?

HP: I don't know. I can't say. I mean, it shows a side of my life that they're not familiar with. But I don't know if they'd look at me any differently.

SR: They sent me the book yesterday, so I'm not fully done with it— I don't know how it ends. But do you still have any of those fighting tendencies?

HP: I haven't punched anybody in a long time.

SR: Do you want to?

HP: No. That was just to get recognition. I'm OK. I'm a nice guy. You read that I'm a curmudgeon and stuff like that. Not true. I'm a nice guy.

SR: In the notes that they sent with the book, they call you a curmudgeon.

HP: Ahh, everybody's calling me a curmudgeon. I'm so sick of that. Do I seem like a curmudgeon? Am I giving you a hard time?

SR: No, absolutely not.

HP: You want an interview, I do it right on the spot. That's not a curmudgeon. I don't complain.

SR: How would you describe yourself?

HP: Well, I think I'm a pretty nice guy, you know. Maybe I'm not the salt of the Earth, but I think I'm a reasonably nice guy. That's the way people generally regard me that know me. [Pekar turns to Ed Piskor, one of his artists.] Would you say that I'm a nice guy?

Ed Piskor: Very nice guy.

HP: You see that? There you go. I give them work.

SR: How does it feel to know that this work inspired so many people here at SPX?

HP: It makes me feel good; I just wish more people knew about it. I wish they knew about the impact I had on comics.

SR: How do you think it would have been if you had to debut *American Splendor* nowadays?

HP: I don't know. Would it have gone over better? I probably would have a harder time.

SR: How is it working with so many amazing artists over the years?

HP: It was great, I like it. It's great to work with these guys.

SR: Are you still having people coming to you all the time trying to work with you?

HP: Yeah, look at that. [He points to a large pile of comics on the floor behind the table.]

SR: Do you read comics?

HP: Not a lot. There's not a lot published nowadays that I can really get into. I'm not into superhero stuff or any of that stuff or genre kind of stuff.

[He signs a book for an attendee.]

This is a typical Harvey Pekar transaction, everybody's happy, you know? I do what they ask me to do, I don't argue with nobody, I just go ahead and give them what they want.

SR: Do you think that the film gave you a fair shake?

HP: Yeah, I thought it was a wonderful film. I can't take credit for the film. I feel kind of bad that people think—they talk about it as "your" film, because actually, I didn't write the script and I didn't direct it or anything like that. Granted, I wrote stories that they were based on, but I mean it was done in such an innovative way. It actually has helped the careers of a few people like Paul Giamatti. You may not know too much about them, [the writer-directors] Shari Berman and Bob Pulcini. They've been getting a lot of work lately.

SR: Is it kind of surreal seeing your story up on the screen?

HP: I've seen my story in comics. I've seen my stories put on stage three times. I'm kind of used to it. I don't want to say blasé or anything, but that's the way it is.

SR: What comes after *The Quitter?*

HP: That's one book over there. Want to look at that book? That's a new thing I'm working on that Ed [Piskor] is illustrating and it's about Macedonia, and the peace between Albanians and the Slavs that was made in Albania.

SR: What brought you to do that topic?

HP: Well, I'm interested in politics and also there's a guy by the name of, maybe you've heard of him, Joe Sacco. He was trained as a reporter, and he did political kind of comics and he did this stuff about Yugoslavia, but it was all war stuff about Bosnia and stuff like that. I met this woman and she said she was taking political science at Berkley and concentrating on peace studies. People would give her a hard time, saying why are you wasting your time with that stuff? War is inevitable. So then she hears about this situation in Yugoslavia where war was avoided in Macedonia. I met her just before she was going to go over there to get the materials to write her thesis on it. I asked her, if you take notes, I was thinking I might like to do a story like that. So she sent me 140 pages of notes. With that, I could go a long way. Want to see it?

SR: Yeah, I'll take a look. Are you in this one?

HP: Am I in this one? A little bit. One page. That's probably going to be it. I want to show how the book came about, so I show myself talking to her in Missouri where I met and calling her and asking her if she would take the notes for me. That's in there.

SR: Do you have any interest in doing fiction?

HP: Nah. I'm interested in it in that I read it. I write book reviews about fiction. But I prefer to write autobiography. All my writing is based on stuff I do in my life. My writing seems better the more accurate it is. [To attendee] You want me to sign that?

ATTENDEE: Can I get a picture with you?

HP: Look at that. That seem like a curmudgeon to you? They call me a curmudgeon. Am I a curmudgeon? Look at that, they're toasting me. I'm the toast of Bethesda. What else you want to know?

SR: Are there any topics in your life that you deem taboo?

HP: I tell you the truth. The one thing, sometimes, I don't write about quarrels or disagreements I have with my current wife, you know what I mean? That's the one thing I'm kind of careful about.

[Signs books for more attendees.]

This is breaking up the interview, but on the other hand, you get to see me in action.

SR: How do you pick your artists if you're not reading a lot of comics?

HP: I'm mostly working with guys I've been working with for a really long time. I haven't completely stopped reading, but I don't read them that much anymore. I've built up a stock of guys, a group of artists over the years that are still interested in doing my work. Crumb in '72, Gary Dumm in 1974—I'm still in contact with them and I really like them and I like working with them. I know what I'm gonna get when I work with them.

Dean Haspiel: Can I interrupt for one second?

SR: Please do.

DH: Dan [Goldman] is an artist. You met him. He's an artist and he's something I think you might want to work with. He did an example.

HP: That's pretty good. What do you think?

SR: Nice.

HP: It could use more hair! But there's no disputing the truth.

DH: Dan Goldman. He's got a nice Jewish same. Got that Harvey? I'll remind you about him later.

HP: See if I wasn't a nice guy, Dean wouldn't introduce me to that guy.

SR: How does it feel seeing all these people drawing you and coming up and giving you samples like that with you on it?

Pekar took note of Dean Haspiel's explanation for his shirtless status at conventions and used it in "New York City Signing," from *American Splendor: Another Day.*

HP: It makes me feel good. What can I say? I didn't get enough credit when I was a kid. I've always been starved for praise. Now I love it. My name is still in the phone book—not that I get that many calls anyways. That's another thing that hasn't changed too much. I don't get swamped with . . . I left my name in the phone book so if somebody saw my movie on HBO—not my movie, the movie—and they want to call me up at 4:30 in the morning and want to say, "Boy, I just saw that movie; that's really great, I loved it," as once in a while happens, they have the opportunity to do that and I wouldn't miss out on that call.

SR: Do you get a lot of calls like that?
HP: I don't get a lot of calls like that. Once in a while I get a call like that. I want people to know how to reach me. If they want to praise me, I want to be around where they can find me. I can't get enough praise, like I said.

SR: I had heard from one of the guys who was with you yesterday that was taking you to Barnes and Noble. What's your opinion on manga and that kind of growth in the comic industry?
HP: I heard all this stuff about how great Japanese comics were. The first stuff I saw was *Barefoot Gen*, which is very good. You know what that is. You sound like you really know a lot about comics. The other stuff I saw in the area is these cartoons on TV. Big-eyed people, like *Astroboy* and stuff. They were wild. I thought they were kind of cute. I didn't exactly think they were adult stuff, you know. All these people kept telling

me, "Man, you ought to go over to Japan, they got every kind of comic for everything. Everything is over there." It just so happens that to publicize the movie, I did go over to Japan and they took me down to a comic book store and all I saw in these comics was big-eyed kind of people. I can't read Japanese of course, but from what I could tell, it looked like there wasn't really much variety and this was verified to me by a Japanese alternative comic artist who told me that he had a really hard time getting stuff published in Japan. I have frankly yet to see—aside from *Barefoot Gen*—any Japanese comic that really impressed me. I saw that cartoon movie *Totoro*—I thought that was good. I mean, a lot of it is really sentimental, cutesy. I'm not one of the people that's going around singing the praises of Japanese cartoons. I'm not saying they're not out there some place, but I haven't seen them yet.

SR: Would you ever have someone who draws in that Japanese style draw a story of *American Splendor?*

HP: If I made enough money. Otherwise, no—that stuff doesn't fit my work, unless I were to deliberately write a kid's story. My normal stories that I write is not meant for kids and like I say, we do a lot of stuff for money. Every man has his price they say. That might be true. Maybe it's world peace, I don't know. Maybe it's not money. But I would not generally look for a guy that drew like that.

Interview with Harvey Pekar

ALAN DAVID DOANE / 2005

From *Comic Book Galaxy* (October 5, 2007).
Reprinted by permission of
Alan David Doane.

Alan David Doane: Comic book readers have known about Harvey
Pekar for many years following your life and times through your series
American Splendor. The greater public at large learned about your story
through the *American Splendor* movie a couple of years back. Tell me
what effect the movie had on your life and your approach to your
comics?

Harvey Pekar: Like I say, I'm just living the way I used to live. I live in the
same house, I eat the same food, I dress the same. Y'know, there's not
much difference. I'm trying to do as much writing as I possibly can—you
know, comic book writing and prose writing because I do reviews and
some essays.

Doane: Which do you enjoy more—the comics writing or the prose writing? Or is it just two totally different . . .

Pekar: I mean comics writing is more important to me than prose writing most of the time because in comics writing I feel like I sort of have kind of an innovative style, and I want to extend that. It's important to me to do kind of new things. The prose stuff that I do—stylistically it's pretty straightforward, although I get really worked about some of the stuff, you know, like politics or music reviews or book reviews—things like that. But nobody would have heard of me if it hadn't been for comics. I'm very lucky, and very thankful that I got a few breaks that enabled me to have a career in comics.

Doane: Since the movie came out, there have been quite a few really big collections of your previous comics work in addition to your new book, which we're going to talk about in a few minutes. Do you think these collections are helping you to expand your readership?

Pekar: Yeah, I know they are because they're selling fairly well, and that's something I should say—since the movie, my book sales have *really*, you know, *skyrocketed*. I mean going from practically *nothing* into respectability. I mean I actually for the first time in my life, and I've been doing comics for many, many years, I'm actually making royalties. I feel like that's quite a luxury.

Doane: Yeah, but it's a luxury you've certainly worked for with all the years . . . just from reading your stories . . . all the years of worrying about paying bills and trying to make the comic successful, it must be quite gratifying.

Pekar: Yeah, it is very gratifying, but it's like I'm too old to really believe it. You know, every time I get a check or something like that, it's a joke. I go back into my old way of thinking, my pessimistic way of thinking, which is not good. But I dunno. I guess after you get to be a certain age, some people can't change.

Doane: Have you received any feedback from new readers? People that have maybe started picking up your stuff since the movie came out?

Pekar: Oh yeah, I get a lot of positive feedback all the time. Yeah, from new readers. And I enjoy it. My number's in the phone book, so that in case somebody wants to call me after they've seen the movie at 4:30 in the morning on HBO and tell me how much they enjoyed it, they can do that. I hate to miss out on some praise, you know.

Doane: Sure, I think all creative people like to hear what people think about their work. Who do you think the average reader is that you'd like to reach with your comics work?

Pekar: I think I have a larger audience in the general book-reading public than in the comic book area, because comic book fans are, for the most part, superhero fans and my stuff is not about guys going about in spandex suits, punching people and stuff. And so they tend not to be all that interested in my work. I mean, it's not escapist, and that's what they're really looking for is escapism. General readers—since my stuff has come out in trade paperback and it's been available at regular bookstores—that's when my sales really started to go up.

Doane: Your work is sort of the opposite of escapism—really completely immersing yourself in the human condition rather than trying to forget about it or ignore it.

Pekar: Yeah, that's what I try to do. You're exactly right. Thank you.

Doane: And I have to say, one of my favorite scenes, and maybe this is a chance to ask you about that, one of my favorite scenes in the movie is that scene right at the beginning with little Harvey going trick-or-treating in just his regular clothes and all the other kids dressed up in superhero costumes—that seemed to me like it was a comment on your place in the comics realm.

Pekar: Yeah, well, actually, I didn't script that. I just told them . . . the credit for that scene should go to Bob Pulcini and Shari Berman, the writer-directors. But what I told them was when I was a kid, I didn't go much for playing around and for frills and stuff like that. I used to go trick-or-treating with the other kids, but I wouldn't wear a costume, you know, because that seemed like it was kind of childish or something, or I was above it or something like that, so that's where they got the idea for that.

Doane: You know, my kids have seen *American Splendor* and loved it, and now the funny thing is they probably would wear a Harvey Pekar costume.

Pekar: [laughs] Well, let me know if you can find any anyplace.

Doane: I don't think that would be that hard to make. Let me ask you, Harvey—Paul Giamatti did such a wonderful job in the movie channeling your character, and I'm just wondering, did you stay in contact with him? Did you enjoy his performance?

Pekar: Oh, I enjoyed it. Yeah, he's great. Yeah, I've stayed in contact with him, although, you know, the more time that elapses between the end of the movie's run and the present, the less I see of him, or have contact with him and the other people in the movie. That being said, I just had breakfast with a couple of HBO employees. I mean, it was just a marvelous experience making that movie. I get asked a lot of times about how Giamatti went about learning to play me, and how he did such a great job, and people assume that he came out to Cleveland, you know, a few weeks early or something, and just *shadowed* me all the time, and you know, picked up my gestures and things like that, but in actuality, he just got that from videotapes of me, I guess on the Letterman show, and the written work that I've done. He's really a master.

Doane: Yeah, that one scene in the movie, where he is watching you . . . he's sort of semi-off-stage and watching you . . . he seems to be taking such delight in being in your presence that you got the feeling that he really developed a great affection for you. I think that really came through.
Pekar: We like each other a lot. He's very nice guy, and a real likable guy. There's no doubt about that, and still, although he's gotten more acclaim, still an underappreciated actor, I think. I think he's one of the best out there.

Doane: Yeah, I think the first movie I saw him in was the Howard Stern movie, if you've seen that. He played this vile character, but he did it so well.
Pekar: Yeah, yeah, the guy where he put on a slight southern accent. Yeah, I remember that.

Doane: And then when you compare that to the performance in *American Splendor* . . . and then the performance in . . . I can't think of the name of the movie . . .
Pekar: *Man on the Moon*?

Doane: No, the movie about wine that he was in a couple of years ago.
Pekar: Oh yeah, that one.

Doane: Yeah, a lot of range there. A great actor.
Pekar: Yeah, yeah, he is. He's wonderful.

Doane: Well, your new book is *The Quitter*. It's published by Vertigo Comics and with illustrations by Dean Haspiel. It's described at one point, I think maybe on the back of the book, as sort of a prequel to the movie and having just finished it last night, that seems really apt. It does cover the period from that Halloween scene up until where the rest of the movie really begins, covering a large chunk of your childhood and

really filling in a lot of holes. Can you tell me how the idea for finally doing a long-form autobiography like this came about?

Pekar: Yeah. Actually what happened was the illustrator, Dean Haspiel,
was the person who put me in touch with Ted Hope who was the
producer of the movie. He was doing some freelance illustration work
for Hope and he told him that he had done some work me, and Hope
said that he liked my work and he'd be interested in doing a movie based
on it. So, my wife and I called and we had a deal with them. I thought,
"Good, we're going to get some option money." I didn't, in my wildest
dreams, think that we'd be able to sell this movie because who's going to
invest a couple million dollars in a movie based on a comic book that sells
maybe three thousand copies a year. But amazingly, Hope was able to sell
HBO on the thing, and it's like a storybook kind of tale after that. I mean,
it won awards and everything, so at the end of it all, I called up Dean and
said, "Look, I really appreciate your tipping Hope off to me. Is there
anything within reason that I can do to pay you back?" And he said,
"Yeah, let me illustrate a long work of yours." So I said OK, but I didn't
offhand know of anybody who would be interested. He had contacts
with DC Comics, more specifically with their Vertigo line which is
supposed to be their more intellectual kind of stuff, and because people
were still talking about the movie, he was able to interest some editors in
my doing something. At first, I thought . . . they were telling me that they
wanted me to do something that was fiction, y'know, and they even said
something with a romantic interest and stuff. I tried to do that, you know,
like write fiction based on my own experience, but I just saw where for
me it would work so much better if I just was as accurate as I could be
and didn't gloss over anything. So I wrote the comic like that and just
hoped that they would see that it was better that way. And happily
they did. They liked it a lot and they really got behind it and the promotion
they've done with this book is just incredible. I mean, you know . . . they've
gotten it publicized so well and sales so far have been just terrific, even
before the thing's been released. I mean, it's *staggering* to me.

Doane: I have to say, that it's surprising—you mentioned that Vertigo's
sort of the intellectual line of DC, but even for a Vertigo title, it really is
a strikingly touching and human work that really offers some profound
insight into your life. I for one am grateful that they published it. I'm
grateful that you took the time to write it.

Pekar: Well, I think that Vertigo's looking for more stuff like it, in case
anybody out there is interested. Some of the stuff that they've done

actually hasn't really varied that much from standard comics, but I know that the editors there would like to develop a lot more independent lines. I'm hoping that comics do continue to expand. I was just at a Small Press Expo a couple of weeks ago and I saw some *really* fine stuff out there, but it was like it was all self-published or the publishers were really small, and I wasn't aware of anybody. Guys were coming up to me and handing me examples of their work, and when I got it back home and got a chance to look at it, I was really impressed, but then I was kind of *de*pressed because nobody knows about these people.

Doane: But is that not where you were in, say, 1975–1976?
Pekar: Yeah, that's where I was . . . well, I actually thought with the coming of underground comics in the late '60s, well mid-'60s actually I guess it started, that comics would be forever changed. I thought when people saw that you could write about just about anything you wanted to in

> JUST PLEASE TELL ME SO I KNOW WHAT'S GOING ON. YOU KNOW I'M A COMPULSIVE WORRIER, AND I'LL WORRY ABOUT YOU IF I HAVE NO IDEA WHERE YOU ARE.

Pekar's worries about his daughter are captured by Haspiel's art in "The Day's Highlights," from *American Splendor: Another Day*.

underground comics, they wouldn't be so under-utilized. *In fact,* nothing much has changed, and that's pretty distressing for me, that still superhero comics are at the top of the heap, you know, like so many years later. Ok, if people want to like superhero comics, that's fine, but the superhero sub-genre doesn't dominate any other art form, and it certainly shouldn't dominate comics.

Doane: And I think we're really in a transitional period right now, and have been probably for the last couple of years, where the greater comics industry, including stuff like the stuff that you do, is expanding into areas like mainstream bookstores and libraries, but the comic shops are kind of entrenched and dug in and continuing to emphasize the superheroes. Meanwhile, also comics from Japan, I think, is another area that's seeing some expansion everywhere except the comics shops. I dunno, I'm starting to see a pattern where perhaps the comics shops are going to be the ones that are left behind as everybody else gets into all the other kind of comics that are out there.

Pekar: I think they have been hurting. I know a guy who worked with one and lost his job—the place went under. Statistically, there are a lot fewer comics shops now than there were maybe a couple of decades ago. It looked like there was going to be a kind of revival in the eighties, but then it just slowed down again.

Doane: Well, there's got to be hope though if DC sees a place for *The Quitter* in its lineup, don't you think?

Pekar: Well, but people have to offer them stuff like that. And they have to accept it to. Some of the stuff that I saw, that I was impressed with, would impress a lot of regular comic book readers as being pretty avant-garde. There's a lot of free-association and things like that in it, and I mean, people haven't even accepted James Joyce's *Ulysses* after all these years and if they see stuff like that in comics, they're going think it's not commercial. There are these commercial considerations. A large company like DC will just go so far; they want to see something proven. If my movie hadn't gone over as well as it did—it made some money and got a lot of artistic approval—if that hadn't a happened, I wouldn't a had a chance with DC.

Doane: But I do think it's an incremental thing though. I think that because *The Quitter* is a success, maybe next year they'll print two or three like that, and year after that, maybe four or five, if it continues to resonate with readers.

Pekar: Well, I hope so. But then on the other hand, I look back on all the good work that was done in the late '60s by people like Robert Crumb, and Frank Stack, and Spain Rodriguez, and really first-class stuff. In my opinion, that was the most fruitful of periods in comic history and yet nothing came of it. The hippies that supported the movement became yuppies after we pulled out of Vietnam and it just went down again. So I'm not takin' anything for granted. I'm gonna to try to take advantage as much as possible of the opportunities I have to write varied kind of stories, like I'm doing one about a woman who went to Macedonia to find out why there was peace there, and there wasn't peace anywhere else in the former Yugoslavia. I'm trying to do quite a variety of things, but I dunno, a lot of people are sort of afraid of that thing. Especially the publishers are afraid of them.

Doane: Is there any chance perhaps, some of the artists whose work you encountered at the Small Press Expo, maybe you'll do some work with some of them?

Pekar: Well, that would be just . . . if I did, they would just be illustrating it, I'd be writing the stories. I sincerely think that some of those people out there are very good and deserve to be recognized nationally. But with all avant-garde art in the past century, it's been very hard for the general public to accept. I mentioned *Ulysses*, I could mention Arnold Schoenberg's work—a hundred years after he started doing the stuff— it's still not accepted—atonal music that is. People still don't like non-objective paintings. There used to be a time lag that used to be overcome between the time a piece of art came out, a challenging piece of art, and the time the public would be able to figure out where it was coming from. But now, it's like a permanent time lag. It's like there's just no acceptance by the general public of anything that was done after like 1925 or something.

Doane: At least as far as comics go, I guess maybe I have a little more of an optimistic view, and again, looking at this as kind of a transitional period over the last couple of years, where we've seen companies like Fantagraphics and Drawn & Quarterly start to pick up business in the bookstores and start to make some inroads with libraries and things like that. I really think that there's an awful lot of good comics that are being published today especially by companies like Fantagraphics, Drawn & Quarterly, Pantheon, the publishers that you've been working with . . . I've been reading comics for over thirty years and it does seem there's always, if you know where to look, and it is sometimes hard to find it, but there always is good quality work being done and it seems to me we're seeing a lot more mention of it in the media and the press in the last couple of years, and that kind of gives me hope, I guess.

Pekar: Well, I hope you're right. I have a tendency to be pessimistic, and I hope you're right, and I'm not convinced. I'm just going to try to do as much as I can to put out good work. I also try and interest editors in some of these young artists I run across and I hope that some of their work will be more widely read.

Doane: Well, as far as your own work, what does the future hold for *American Splendor* as a brand? Will there be any more single issues? Or just books for a while?

Pekar: Yeah, I think so. I'm working on something with DC . . . we've just laid the groundwork for a deal . . . they wanted me to do like four thirty-two-page comic books a year, and maybe collect them at the end of the year, or something like that, in a trade paperback. So I *need* a place to do shorter stories—that's mostly what I've done are shorter stories—but I want to continue to write, now that I've had the opportunity, continue to write the longer pieces too, and I have two more works, longer pieces, in the process of being done and I plan to write more.

Doane: I'm very, very glad to hear that, as somebody who's been reading your work for about twenty-five years now. As long as you keep writing it, I'll keep reading it.

Pekar: Well, thanks a lot. I appreciate that very much.

Doane: It's really been an honor and a pleasure to talk to you Harvey. I appreciate it and best of luck with the new book.

Pekar: Thanks very much for your kindness. Take it easy.

Doane: Thanks, you too.

Harvey Pekar:
The MrSkin.com Interview

PETER LANDAU / 2006

From MrSkin.com.
Reprinted by permission of
MrSkin.com.

Harvey Pekar is not a cartoonist, but his comic book *American Splendor* is one of the most influential of the underground movement. His slice-of-working-class-life stories have been illustrated by a revolving door of talented scribblers, including his old record-collecting friend Robert Crumb.

Just like Crumb, Pekar gained wider recognition for his work with the release of a critically acclaimed and Oscar-nominated movie named after his autobiographical comic *American Splendor*, where he was played by Paul Giamatti, as well as by himself. He continues to lay out his stick-figure storyboards and gets artists like Gary Dumm to illustrate his grumbling tales of life in Cleveland.

Pekar and Dumm have just published *Ego & Hubris: The Michael Malice Story* (Ballantine Books), but the story takes place far from Cleveland and barely features the cantankerous Pekar. It's another real-life tale, but about an aggressive and smart young anarchist and libertarian.

The character couldn't be farther from Pekar, yet his story fits neatly into the Pekar oeuvre, a body of work that is growing. There's another book from Ballantine coming called *Macedonia*, and DC Comics is scheduled to resume publication of Pekar's flagship title *American Splendor* this fall. He's also working with Paul Buhle on books about the Students for Democratic Society and the Beats.

Even though Pekar knows nothing about the internet, he was more than happy to spend some time chatting with Mr. Skin about his achievements. While his work isn't known for its "fast-forward to" scenes, he still has a warm spot for Italian actresses.

Landau: Is *Ego & Hubris* the first time you've worked on a story where you were not the main or an integral character?
Pekar: No. I did a book for [comics publisher] Dark Horse and I did it about a soldier, called *Unsung Hero*. But it didn't sell very well—none of my stuff did for Dark Horse. That was nonfiction, biography.

Landau: What made you return to another story like that?
Pekar: I frequently, although I haven't regularly made people other than myself the protagonist of my stories, I've done that fairly often. Well, I just ran across this guy and he seemed real interesting. As a result of *[American Splendor]* there was more demand for my work, and I thought he'd make an interesting topic to write about.

Landau: Michael Malice doesn't seem like the kind of guy you'd want to work with, let alone devote the time and effort to tell his story, so what was it about him that compelled you to take on the task?
Pekar: I take it that you were not too crazy about the guy.

Landau: I thought he was fascinating, but not the most likeable character.
Pekar: In the first place, he doesn't act vindictive all the time. And he's a smart guy, and we were both interested in politics, although we have pretty widely differing philosophies. The guy was willing to take unpopular stands and take on authority figures; I liked that about him, I thought that was interesting.

Landau: There's definitely something to be said about accepting and be-friending people who don't share your opinions, that's admirable, I'm just curious why you wanted to write a book about someone like that.

Pekar: Like I say, he was worth writing about. I thought he was an un-usual person. Another thing I like about him, if you get into discussion with this guy, a lot of times if you disagree he has good arguments on his side and makes you reexamine your position and not just take the things you say for granted. I thought that was good.

Landau: How does Malice feel about your portrayal of him?

Pekar: He's seen it. He's fine with it. Look, I did this thing like a Studs Terkel book, so those are [Malice's] words. If he didn't like it he would have only himself to blame. He said what he wanted to say and put for-ward parts of his personality that he thought most interesting or compel-ling.

Landau: How did you feel about the film version of your life with *Ameri-can Splendor*?

Pekar: People interpreting my work are not new to me, and it wasn't new when the movie came out. It's been dramatized in the theater be-fore. Cartoon artists and illustrators had drawn me in various ways, so I was not particularly surprised like that when they made the movie.

What's surprising was how good I thought it was. For the kind of money they offered me, it would have been OK with me if they screwed up the material, you know? I'd just cry all the way to the bank, I guess.

But it was an amazingly good job, considering a lot of comic-book artists complain all the time how badly the movie industry treats their product and how little respect it has for it, I was very pleased. I just couldn't get over the fact that these people not only made a good movie, they made a movie where they were experimenting.

Landau: Were you aware that they wanted to include you in front of the camera?

Pekar: Not immediately, no. It's OK with me. I've been in a couple of movies before and I'm kind of a clown or a ham, whatever you want to call me. I was in documentaries. In a sense, I was playing myself, which is what I do all the time anyway.

Landau: Do you get recognized on the streets now?

Pekar: Yeah, people recognize me. It's not like going to an airport and a crowd of people rushes over to me and asks for my autograph, but maybe I'll sit down and I'll notice somebody looking at me with a quizzical look on their face. After a while, they'll come up to me and ask, "Aren't you Harvey Pekar? I really liked that movie." That happens to me.

Landau: Does that bring people to the source material, your comic book?
Pekar: The sales of my comic book have improved quite a bit since the movie came out and I guess it's attributable to the movie. My comic, in the past, didn't sell very well at all.

Landau: Any plans for more acting or adaptations of your work?
Pekar: Yeah, I'd like to get my work adapted by movies again, just simply because there's so much money in it [laughs]. I'd be interested in working on a play or TV performance.

Landau: Have you been approached after the success of *American Splendor* to develop a television show?
Pekar: No. There was interest in making a movie before this movie was made. Back in 1980, Jonathan Demme was trying to make a movie on my life.

Landau: Sadly that's the normal timeframe to get a picture from development to the screen. Faster is the internet, and I noticed you have a blog at HarveyPekar.com, but it's not been updated in nearly three years. What happened?
Pekar: They stopped paying me.

Landau: Any chance of going live with that again?
Pekar: In view of the fact that I'm computer illiterate—what happened was my wife would get me on a computer and then I'd type my log out with two fingers and then she'd transmit it. That's how I do stuff. I mean, I write articles and reviews that way too.

Landau: Do you remember the first time you saw nudity in the movies?
Pekar: Gosh, I can't. It didn't seem to make a big impression on me, huh?

Landau: Are there any nude scenes that you particularly enjoyed?
Pekar: I like looking at good-looking women. That's something I've enjoyed.

Landau: Did you ever have any obsession over a screen sex siren?
Pekar: When I was a kid, I used to like Silvana Mangano, an Italian actress. The film that she was in that gained the most interest was *Riso amaro*. You know the Italian neo-realist films that were made after the Second World War? She was involved in that movement. You know, Gina Lollobrigida is real nice looking . . .

Landau: Coming from the underground comics scene, where people like your collaborator Robert Crumb have exorcized all manner of fetishistic fantasies, how come your autobiographical work is never overtly sexual?
Pekar: Because I'm so downtrodden . . . I don't know. If I could just get a girl out on a date it was a big deal. If you look through the book you'll find there are some sex scenes, but I didn't emphasize that. I didn't want to. That's what a lot of underground cartoonists were doing at the time. That was their stock in trade. I wanted to stay away from that stuff, doing what everybody else was doing.

Landau: I've read your comics for a long time, but the first time I actually saw you as opposed to a cartoon of you was when you made a series of guest appearances on *Late Night with David Letterman* back in the '80s. Do you have any plans to return to Letterman's show?
Pekar: Naw, he won't have me back.

Landau: Was there a true animosity there, it wasn't part of the shtick?
Pekar: No, it was definitely not. I had nothing to lose. I was very dissatisfied by being on that show. I wasn't getting much money, my books were not selling as a result of my being on the show, which is what I originally hoped would happen. I like kidding around and doing comedy. I'm not a professional, but I'm one of these guys who used to be a class clown or street-corner comedian. I like to joke around and do comedic work, but all he wanted me to do was a self-parody.

Landau: He was just making fun of you?
Pekar: Yeah, that's what it amounted to: Look at this slob from Cleveland—isn't it something, let's all laugh. I don't mind that for a couple of shows, but if that's what it's going to be all the time and I'm not getting anything out of it then why should I mess around. I said, "Screw it," I'm going to do what I want to do on the show, and I did. He's a control freak. He doesn't want to let go of control of his show. He knows damn well there's no way I'm going to let him do that with me. There was no point, from his standpoint, having me come back on the show because I would just make a shambles out of it.

Landau: But you're keeping busy.
Pekar: I'm doing everything I can do, man. My income is not sufficient from my pension and social security to live on, so I got to try and make it up some way. I'm not turning down much, I'll tell you.

Interview: Harvey Pekar

BRIAN HEATER / 2007

From the *The Daily Cross Hatch*
(July 9, 23, and 30, 2007).
Reprinted by permission
The Daily Cross Hatch.

Harvey Pekar feels a bit frustrated and under-appreciated—granted,
that's really nothing new for the artist we've come to know and love
over the past few decades, but in the wake of the 2003 film based on
the his longstanding autobiographical series, American Splendor, *things*
were unquestionably looking up for the Pekar. Sales of new issues and
anthologies of the series were selling briskly, and with the release of
Ego & Hubris, *his first non-autobiographical book in recent memory,*
even more praise was heaped upon the artist.

Macedonia *continues Pekar's recent streak of telling the stories of*
others. Co-written with Heather Roberson, the book recounts the author
and peace activist's journey to the titular republic, in attempts to explore

how opposing factions managed to avoid an all out war. As such, the book replaces the blood and guts we've come to expect from wartime projects with long stretches of text-heavy theorizing, which, suffice to say, hasn't gone over especially well with much of the action-craving comic audience.

We spoke to Pekar, from his Cleveland home about a lot of topics, but first and foremost, he made it clear that he had a few things to get off his chest.

Brian Heater: How many of these interviews are you doing, these days?
Harvey Pekar: I'm certainly not doing anything like seven a week—maybe two, three. I'm not really doing very many. I just did one for the *New York Metro*.

Heater: Is there less press around *Macedonia* than there has been with past books?
Pekar: There hasn't been much press. The thing is just coming out, but I'm not going to be doing any touring, or anything like that. It's kind of hard to say, but I'm somewhat concerned about this book. The language level I use in it is higher than usual. In other books I use a lot of street slang. But I'm really proud of this book. There's so little that's available about Macedonia. You have a big conflagration some place, everybody writes about it. You avoid a war, nobody gives a damn. There's just a lot of meat to this, and it seems like some people just aren't interested in politics, and can't deal with language on a somewhat higher level.

Heater: One of the things that struck me about the book is that not only is the language slightly higher, there's also a lot of text on the page, compared to a standard graphic novel.
Pekar: Yeah. People who read comic books like a lot of explosions and stuff like that. It's a book of ideas. I had 150 pages, and the best way that I thought to express the ideas was through discussions, which is the way Heather Roberson set it up. I was real happy with the book, and then I started to realize, "Jesus, I've gone too far."

Heater: What does that mean, "too far?"
Pekar: I've gotten some real nice reviews, but I think the language just confounds some people. They just don't want to read about stuff like that. To me, it's real important to be involved in this project, partly because it's gotten so little attention in the states—that, in itself makes it worth doing. *Spider-Man* fans just don't have a lot time for that stuff.

Heater: Why did you choose to tell the story through Heather?

Pekar: I had to—she's the one who went over there. When I was doing stuff, most of my career, I didn't have a hell of a lot of time to work on comics. I had a day job and I could only put out so much, and frankly, I didn't see anything changing, and then this movie got me some attention. And then, all of the sudden, there was some interest in my work. With that, I decided that I would expand into other areas that I was interested in.

A couple of people have noted that I've done some non-autobiographical things, and they're well received. *Ego & Hubris*—I don't have any idea how well it sold, but it got really good reviews, so I jacked it up another notch. Now I'm kind of concerned—I don't know how much slack publishers will cut me. If I do one book that doesn't sell well, it might really hurt me, because I don't have a history of selling a lot of books. It's just since the movie that I've been doing respectably, and I'm certainly not doing spectacular in the sales area. I'm really kind of tense about this book. It's funny, I come home and I read it, and I go, "Yeah, man, this is really good stuff," and then someone says, "The conversation's too academic." Too academic for who? A third grader? They talk like they're trying some new James Joyce text. You're talking to a worried man.

Heater: You obviously know the story through Heather, but was she also chosen as the protagonist so that people might have a more accessible reference point with which to enter the story?

Pekar: The thing was that on the one hand, I wanted to broaden the kind of things I was doing. I know Heather, and she told me about the Macedonia stuff. She told me that there was practically nothing in print about this stuff around here, and I check it out myself, and there's nothing. She was about to go over there, so I said, "Can you make some notes?" I always want to be the first person on the street to come up with something, and I thought this was important—I still think it's important! The questions she raises about the inevitability of war, and the stuff that's talked about with international agencies' involvement in the war, all of that's stuff's in there. So, that's the reason that I did it. The project excited me.

Heater: Was the medium of the graphic novel necessarily the best well to tell the story, or was it just the method you felt most comfortable using?

Pekar: Well, I think it's as good as any way to tell a story. If I had done it in a regular prose book, it might have been harder on them, because there wouldn't be any pictures. I really thought I had stumbled onto something fantastic—well, maybe not fantastic, but I really thought I had something here. Now I don't know. I think it's a real good book, regardless of how it sells or how good reviews it gets.

Heater: You were familiar with Joe Sacco's work, when you started work on *Macedonia*.

Pekar: Yeah—Joe Sacco used to work for me!

Heater: Was that an influence on the book, at all?

Pekar: Okay . . . I was interested in politics and whenever I got a chance, I used to write critical articles and tons of letters to editors, when I was younger. I can document my interest in politics, which goes back to way before I was even doing comics—in the '60s. I acknowledged Joe Sacco in the book, and I realized right off that people were thinking that I picked up stuff from Joe. I think Joe is really terrific—he's really outstanding. I have a great deal of admiration for his work, not only in the obvious things, but in the fact that he taught himself to draw so well. He was a journalism major in college—he didn't have an art background. He just worked on it, and came up with something really good.

But, first of all, when I talked to Joe about this project, he didn't know about what was going on in Macedonia, any more than anyone else did. I think he's described himself as a "war junkie." He's a really nice, mild-mannered guy, but he's really interested in writing about wars: fighting, strategy, the whole thing. I think you can see that in his work. He did a story about when the U.S. bombed Dresden, in the Second World War. With me, I'm into the social-economic stuff. I mean, it's possible that Joe pulled my coat to the Balkans, more than I would have been interested in them, otherwise. We were close. We're good friends, but we emphasize different things. In my books, there's not a whole lot of action, not a lot of guys jumping around. My stuff is real talky. I use a lot of text. I think the fairest thing to say is that Joe's work heightened my interest in the Balkans.

Heater: It's fitting, then, that you're writing about a war that never really was.

Pekar: Yeah. Heather went over there to see how they avoided a war. She found out that while they were avoiding a war, the Macedonians

Ed Piskor only drew Pekar on one page in *Macedonia*.

and the Albanians were not warming up to each other. There you can see the bad influence that nationalism has. Everyone thinks that they're the chosen people. And they're supposed to rule over everybody else. I wanted to get some of that stuff in there—that's going over people's heads.

Let's get one thing straight—Harvey Pekar talks about what Harvey Pekar wants to talk about. Should you ever have the fortune to interview the American Splendor *author, you'll likely find that, try as you might to steer the conversation in your own direction, Pekar is really the one at the reins.*

The good news is that the author generally takes the interview into interesting directions, and when he apologizes for dwelling on a note, you find yourself happily accepting—surely anything he wants to talk about is as interesting as the list you've concocted, in that old spiral notebook.

When I spoke with Pekar, he clearly had one burning subject on his mind: the perceived negative critical reception of his new non-autobiographical Macedonia, *and that, dear readers, is exactly what we discussed.*

Heater: Were you attempting to make *Macedonia* something pertinent to our own current political climate?
Pekar: I think the sections in there that talk about the build up to the disillusion of the Yugoslav state, I think that's important stuff. Because I don't think that people know a goddamned thing about that. I think it gives them a background and something to work with. And that doesn't take up that much space. The book is mainly devoted to [Heather Roberson] going around, questioning people in these different organizations, like when she goes to the university and talks to people. There's an international crowd of people that are trying to rebuild Macedonia, and she gets involved in that. This is really funny: along the way, there are a few incidents, where she gets hit on. She gets hit on, even on the airplane going over there. Some guy from Montenegro gets drunk and starts hitting on her, and that seems to be the favorite part of some people. They can relate to that, trying to pick up a girl—that's important. I probably shouldn't even be telling you this. You'll probably talk about what a complainer I am.

Heater: As much as this is a story about Macedonia, there are some larger lessons to be taken away, like the debate about whether or not war can be avoided.

Pekar: Sure. Like I say, it's the bad parts of nationalism. I was telling one guy about it, and he said, "these people, the Macedonians and the Albanians, would rather be hostile to each other than get along and create a bigger pie, and get bigger slices from it." People are so hung up on national identity. It's terrible. That's been one of the curses of humankind, going back into antiquity.

Heater: Would you have been less likely to have written the book were we not currently at war?

Pekar: This book that I talked to Heather about writing was just so attractive. There's other stuff that I've done that I didn't think would go over commercially. I did it because I thought I could do a good book, and let the chips fall where they may. Even the book, *Ego & Hubris*, with Michael Malice, I thought some people might just get mad, because he's just a difficult personality. But at least it got really good reviews. Like I said, maybe this is a step too far. I did any goddamned thing I wanted to, when I had my day job. Now I don't have the day job, and I don't have enough sources to support myself and my wife, so I got to make it on comics. Sales suddenly mean a lot more for me.

Heater: People have certain expectations from a Harvey Pekar book.

Pekar: Yeah, well, when I wrote *Ego & Hubris*, it went over all right. A lot of people told me that they liked it. There was nothing in the press about people having huge difficulties, though one reviewer called Michael Malice a "human cockroach." I thought, maybe I could get away with something else. The project seemed so important to me, but now I don't know. Regardless of what happens, I think it's a real good book. And I'm not just saying that about my contributions, I'm talking about Ed Piskor and Heather. I think Heather laid out stuff really nice. She wrote the epilogue of the book, and she talks about the couple of years that have passed, since the end of the book. She came back over, and went back there again, and wrote about her new experiences there. She's got a really good grasp of the situation.

Heater: How closely did the two of you collaborate? Did you actually co-write the bulk of the book?

Pekar: Oh yeah. She gave me this text, and I broke it down into panels. We talked about what to put in and what not to put in, and I asked her to write the epilogue. She's a bright woman.

Heater: Other than the books you've done with your wife, was this your first writing collaboration?
Pekar: Yeah, I think so.

Heater: But overall the process went fairly smoothly?
Pekar: Yeah. She took care of one end of it, and I broke it down and turned it over to the illustrator.

Heater: How closely do you collaborate with illustrators?
Pekar: I write little descriptions in the panels of what I'd like to see, and I call them up and go over the book with them, and tell them what I'd like to see. But here again, Heather was a great help. She took a million pictures, and gave them to Ed, and that resulted, if nothing else, in a really nice cover. I liked that, with the cross . . . The artists that I'm working with now, I have a lot of confidence in, so I don't try to spell everything out for them. And you really can't, because, if they're going to do something, they've got to figure it out for themselves. I do the panels and put them in the order that I want, and write instructions in there, and talk it over with the guys, and they'll send me stuff to look at. But I don't think I've ever asked anybody in the last few years to make any kind of major changes. Just maybe minor details, or catching some spelling mistakes, or something.

Heater: Did you used to attempt to assert more control over what artists did?
Pekar: Yeah, a little more. But I realized that they knew what they were doing, and I wasn't being very helpful. Also, I've got to say, when I started out, the illustrators that I worked with weren't as good as the people that I have now—although I don't have Robert Crumb to work with, but I have some real solid illustrators. Dean Haspiel has worked out real good for me.

Heater: Are these people you've hand-picked yourself?
Pekar: Different ways. Sometimes people would just come up and shove a bunch of work in my face. And once in a while it's good. Ed Piskor, he drove all the way down from Pittsburgh to meet me. And there's another woman that I'm doing some work with—you won't see it for a while, it's in the process of being done—her name is Summer McClinton. I found

out about her when I was working on a big project about the history of SDS (Students for a Democratic Society), and the guy who was overseeing it gave me her name. I contacted her and she sent me some stuff, and I thought, "god, this kid is really good." It happens in all sorts of different ways.

Heater: A couple of years ago, you put together the *Best American Comics* collection. Do you actively read new stuff as it comes out?
Pekar: To tell you the truth, no, I don't. I can't keep up with it. And a lot of it I'm not that crazy about. I try to check some of it out, though. I did learn something putting that book together, because I hadn't seen that much stuff around—nothing on the stands, or anything like that. I thought comics were in decline, and then I went to the Small Press Expo (SPX) in Bethesda, Maryland, and they had all of these people doing these small Xeroxed books, and I saw a whole hell of a lot of stuff that was good. There are a lot of really good people out there, but getting this stuff out there is a real problem. There's nobody interested in distributing alternative comics, for one thing. It used to be that there were several companies that specialized in distributing them, but that's gone.

Heater: There are still a handful of publishers, out there.
Pekar: Well, there are a few, but it's not like it was, when you had Capital City and Kitchen and a half-dozen of them.

By the last third of our interview, Harvey Pekar and I had essentially exhausted the subject of his new book, Macedonia. As he had made fairly clear in the first half-hour and change, the writer was rather unhappy with the way the book has thus far been received in critical circles. Let's face it, though, if he didn't complain so much, he'd hardly be the Harvey Pekar we've all come to know and love over the past few decades.

After a follow-up conversation with Pekar, it seems that things are looking up a bit for the author. According to Pekar, the new reviews that have begun cropping up "get" what he was going for, when he opted to tell the story of Macedonia's successful campaign to avoid war amongst its dissident factions.

In this final part, we discuss the future of American Splendor, the current state of jazz, and Pekar's long-abandoned artistic aspirations.

Heater: Are there any new *American Splendor* books on the horizon?

Pekar: Yeah. I'm going to do four comic books, like I did last year, for DC. This is the plan—and I've already done some of the work. They'll be coming out in September, October, November, and December, and then they'll collect them into a book, like they did last time, with *Another Day*.

Heater: So the first one must have sold pretty well, if they're going to collect a new one.

Pekar: Who knows? I sold so little, before the movie, that I don't want to think about it. I mean, I do think about it, and I freak myself out thinking about it, but I don't want to think about it, or I'll drive myself nuts, worrying about how, if this thing doesn't go over big, my career in comics is over.

Heater: Do you enjoy doing autobiographical work, as much as you used to?

Pekar: Yeah, I enjoy it, as much as I used to, but I've got to be careful not to be repetitive. Like I've done stories, a few times, about how inept I am with mechanical stuff. I'm going to give that a rest, for a while. When I was doing *American Splendor*, I would get out fifty pages a year, and now I'm doing more than twice than that, of just that autobiographical comic. And then I've got these other projects that I'm working on—a biography of Lenny Bruce.

Heater: Yeah—Nick Bertozzi said he was working with you on that.

Pekar: Yeah, I'm pretty happy with that, and I have these other things: a history of SDS and a history of the beat generation, that I made major contributions to, and I've adapted the original text of Studs Terkel's *Working*. I didn't mess with his writing—I didn't want to fool with that—I just took the writing and broke it down into panels.

Heater: Was he involved with the project, at all?

Pekar: No—I guess they asked to make sure that it was okay with him to do this project. And then when he said it was okay—he's about ninety-five now—they just went ahead and did it. I don't think he'd have a problem with what I'm doing, because I don't mess around with his stuff. I don't add or delete anything. I do it just the way he did it, and hopefully there will be some nice illustrations to go along with it. I've got a couple of other projects. For Random House, I'm going to do some long short stories—stuff with several stories, about twenty-five or thirty pages long. And then I'm going to do a biography about a woman that I've known for years and years, who went from being a welfare mother to being an MD. I think that's a pretty interesting story, and I want to get that down.

Heater: These are all comics?
Pekar: Yeah, yeah.

Heater: Do you feel like you're stuck with the comic medium, for life?
Pekar: Well, you know, I did a prose piece for a sociology magazine, not too long ago. I'm not writing off prose pieces.

Heater: You used to do a lot of music reviews, as well.
Pekar: I did, but I don't do them anymore. I'd spend all of this time listening to a record, and then writing a review. I'll spend hours on it, and what do I get? Twenty-five bucks. It's just not worth it for me, anymore. When that was all I had going for me, and I had this sluggy job, and I wanted to add some kind of self-respect, that was a big deal to me, to be any kind of a writer. I was the first guy in my group of guys to come out with stuff being published in a national magazine. I paid my dues, man. I was writing about jazz, from age of nineteen, up until a few years ago.

Heater: Is there still anything worthwhile happening in jazz?
Pekar: Yeah, there's stuff worthwhile happening, but the general public just can't comprehend it. I think, in several art forms, at one time—say, in the nineteenth century—you'd have these *avant-garde* artists, and the public didn't know what to make of them, for a while, but then they'd catch up to them. After twenty-five years, they'd start digging them. But in the twentieth century, people were coming out with stuff that hardly anybody caught up with. There's not too many people you see who are reading James Joyce's stuff, just for kicks. Non-objective painting, by Jackson Pollack and stuff—I realize that those paintings fetch a lot of money at auction, but you go to a museum and you see that kind of stuff, and then there's some old grandfather type, saying, "well, my grandson can paint better than that." There's just a disconnect.

People just can't handle it anymore. And the music just keeps getting farther and farther out, but it's just too hard for them to keep up with. And I don't blame them. If a guy's working a forty-hour-a-week job, and he goes home and is tired—to find out what's going on in *avant-garde*, you've got to really work on it, and train your ear. You've also got to find out how things are evolving, so it won't be a complete surprise for you. You see how this one guy developed his style from an earlier guy, and you have this sense of evolution. But if you don't listen to anything for ten years, and you go back and listen to the stuff of today, you just get shocked.

Heater: There's a scene in the *American Splendor* film—I'm not sure how true to life it is, but it's one of the more memorable in the movie. Before the concept of collaboration comes up, your character is attempting to draw the panels, himself. Did you ever have any artistic aspirations?

Pekar: That's the way I write scripts—they're a little more detailed than what they had: someone scribbling on a piece of paper. I divide the paper up into panels, and I use stick figures, thought and speech balloons, and captions. And I put a little description of what I want in the panel, for the artist. But I don't have any artistic talents. I can't do anything beyond that. I was just a total waste at that, when I was a kid.

Index